Advance Praise for *Free Time*

"As Jenny Blake says in *Free Time*, 'how we bake is as important as what we make.' Having run a multinational organization and now my own Delightfully Tiny Team, I know that Heart-Based Business *is* possible for organizations of any size, and we need it now more than ever."

—Howard Behar, author of *The Magic Cup* and
former president of Starbucks Coffee

"This book is a revelation—a detailed road map for building a business that fulfills you and serves the world, leaving anxiety and burnout behind. Jenny Blake's advice is both grounded and inspiring, and always connected to life as it is actually lived, at the human scale."

—Oliver Burkeman, author of *The Antidote* and *Four Thousand Weeks*

"With heart and smarts, Jenny teaches us how to think big, be strategic, and make time for what really matters. *Free Time* is an essential guide to running a business without running yourself into the ground."

—Ximena Vengoechea, author of *Listen Like You Mean It*

"Jenny Blake's phenomenal book *Free Time* taught me how to rethink my business, creating smart systems to focus on what matters most."

—Antonio Neves, author of *Stop Living on Autopilot*

"*The* go-to manual for running Heart-Based Businesses with ease, joy, and financial abundance."

—Farnoosh Torabi, host of the award-winning podcast *So Money*

"It is not about working harder, it is about working 'right-er.' Bigger results, better flow, less effort; welcome to *Free Time*."

—**Mike Michalowicz, author of** *Clockwork,* *Fix This Next,* **and** *Get Different*

"Wildly, wildly helpful. *Free Time* is a masterful blend of tools, tips, and frameworks to free your mind, time, and team—against a backdrop of pure delight. Imagine the most helpful entrepreneurial workshop you've ever attended, but held in an ice cream store with an infinite array of flavors. Grab a copy for yourself and your business-owning best friends."

—**Sarah Young, founder of Zing Collaborative and author of** *Expansive Impact*

"Hustle is dead. It never worked very well, and now it's burning us out. Jenny Blake is back with a generous, helpful, and more caring alternative."

—**Seth Godin, author of** *This Is Marketing*

"Leave it to Jenny to come up with an ultra-simple, seemingly innocent concept and turn it into a profundity with many mind-expanding insights! *Free Time* successfully balances our brain and heart, rocking between the mental *ah-ha!* and the deep intuitive *mmm-hmmm.*"

—**Penney Peirce, author of** *Frequency, Leap of Perception,* **and** *Transparency*

"'*Stress is a systems problem.*' This was one of the more arresting statements I've read in a business book in a long time. Jenny offers an important vision of entrepreneurship freed from burnout and overload."

—**Cal Newport,** *New York Times* **bestselling author of** *A World Without Email* **and** *Deep Work*

"After reading *Free Time*, I have gone from being semi-retired to relaunching my business. Jenny's wisdom shines through, especially as she presents the intersection of systems thinking and heart. I am truly inspired, but now, with a new path forward."

—**Denny O. Clark, disability workforce inclusion advocate and co-founder of Pinnacle Performance Consulting**

"A brilliant, insightful read that provides an actionable framework for reimagining the way we work. Jenny's depth of knowledge from her corporate and entrepreneurial career provide a fresh perspective on company culture and value-centric time management."

—**Mori Taheripour, author of *Bring Yourself* and faculty member at the University of Pennsylvania's Wharton School of Business**

"Jenny is openhearted, honest, and highly insightful. What makes her particularly unique is her willingness to pull back the curtain on her own business. *Free Time* is a delightful mix of grounding and spiritual strategies, plus uber-specific and systematic."

—**Lindsay Pedersen, author of *Forging an Ironclad Brand***

"A vision that knits together the aspirational, spiritual, and operational."

—**Herb Schaffner, president of Big Fish Media**

"For any entrepreneur who has felt stressed out or overwhelmed—and dare I say, that's most of us—*Free Time* will come as a revelation. Her crystal-clear thinking, smart advice, and rock-solid systems will give your business a powerful boost, while maintaining your joy and sanity."

—**Dorie Clark, author of *The Long Game* and executive education faculty at Duke University's Fuqua School of Business**

"A refreshing and informative outlook on how to create change in the world without sacrificing our soul."

—Petra Kolber, author of *The Perfection Detox*

"For anyone who wants to keep their team tiny, their business elegant, and their life delightful."

—Michael Bungay Stanier, author of *The Coaching Habit* and *How to Begin*

"Most entrepreneurs start their businesses in search of freedom; but to hold on to it, we have to protect our time. *Free Time* is a treasure trove of inexpensive, efficient ways to liberate ourselves from tasks that drain the life out of us—so we can reclaim our peace, freedom, and passion."

—Elaine Pofeldt, author of *The Million-Dollar, One-Person Business* and *Tiny Business, Big Money*

"You may think having more free time is a fantasy; not with this book. This is Jenny Blake at her best, architecting the unique path for you to achieve *Free Time*. Your business can be freeing *and* lucrative—Jenny will show you how."

—Laura Garnett, author of *The Genius Habit* and *Find Your Zone of Genius*

"This book will help you harness your innate strengths while recognizing how to work in a manner that leads directly to success. Jenny's frameworks are so practical and actionable that you will feel inspired by the work you want to do, while learning how to delegate and avoid busywork. All of us want to make certain our time is valued and not wasted. Free Time is your foolproof solution. I need more room on my bookshelf!"

—Allison Kluger, lecturer of Organizational Behavior at Stanford Graduate School of Business

free time

free time

Lose the Busywork, Love Your Business

JENNY BLAKE

Award-winning author of *Pivot*

IDEAPRESS
PUBLISHING

WASHINGTON, D.C.

IDEAPRESS
PUBLISHING

Printed in the United States

Ideapress Publishing | www.ideapresspublishing.com

SPECIAL SALES: Ideapress Books are available at a special discount for bulk purchases for sales promotions and premiums, or for use in corporate training programs. Special editions, including personalized covers, a custom foreword, corporate imprints, and bonus content, are also available. For more details, visit www.itsfreetime.com/special-sales.

Cover and diagrams by Together Agency: www.gotogether.agency

Interior design by Together Agency and Jessica Angerstein.
Set in Freight with headings in Circular.

Free Time, Heart-Based Business, Delightfully Tiny Team, and Free Time Framework, are pending trademarks of Jenny Blake Enterprises, LLC.
Pivot Method is an exclusive registered trademark. All rights reserved.

Some names and identifying characteristics have been changed to protect the privacy of the individuals involved.

Image credits: Alexandra Franzen (iPhone screen), Mafaz Mousoof (Nodes)

ISBN: 978-1-64687-066-0 (hardcover)
ISBN: 978-1-64687-079-0 (ebook)
ISBN: 978-1-64687-080-6 (audio)

Library of Congress Control Number: 2021915430

Subjects: BISAC: BUSINESS & ECONOMICS / Entrepreneurship.
BISAC: BUSINESS & ECONOMICS / Small Business. BISAC: BUSINESS & ECONOMICS / Operations Management.

10 9 8 7 6 5 4 3 2 1

To Jim Blake, aka Daddy-O: *Your brilliant insights, contrarian comments, and laser-sharp edits make every book better. You are the ultimate Free Timer, filling your hours with learning and creative expression, morning, noon, and night. Thank you for being you, and for all that you do. These are the great times!*

Work is love made visible.

—Khalil Gibran

Contents

PART **1**

ALIGN

2 DESIGN

PART

PART 3 ASSIGN

Introduction

My Journey from Full Time to Free Time

There is no way to happiness, happiness is the way.

—Thich Nhat Hanh

I t is one p.m. on a Tuesday, and I am glued to the couch, procrasti-eating so that I don't have to tackle the *one* thing I promised myself I would that day: Email Everest. As I polish off a pint of Ben & Jerry's Strawberry Cheesecake ice cream, a fellow business owner texts:

"Do you ever have the feeling of just wanting to burn it all down?" she asks with a laugh-cry emoji.

Why yes! Yes I do . . .

"Funny you mention it! I'm at Hooky Headquarters as we speak," I reply, "glued to the couch eating ice cream. I can't seem to move or motivate myself to do anything at all."

When invoked, *burn-it-all-down mode* (BIADM) means we have reached a point of weariness, burnout, frustration, or dread in our business, and we wonder (*fantasize!*) whether instead of pressing ahead in our chosen field we should just burn it all down and pivot into real estate.

1

Or fill in a vastly different fantasy alternative career of your choice, one that probably isn't any easier in actual reality.

I have had many burn-it-all-down moments in business: everything from complete exhaustion while launching my first book and leaving corporate life; to a petrifying plateau two years into self-employment where I didn't have enough to cover my rent; to overwhelmed exasperation watching the majority of my projected income vanish in March 2020 when the pandemic hit.

BIADM can be a passing fantasy during a crushing week, or a crucible you endure after years of veering slightly off course, until you realize you are completely lost. You might experience moments of BIADM in response to compare-and-despair while binge-listening to business podcasts, or during an exhausting social media infinity scroll. You might hear a fellow owner express wanting to burn it all down after losing their biggest client, or even landing their *dream* client that in actuality becomes a bureaucratic and logistical nightmare of paper pushing, hoop jumping, and people pleasing.

No matter when it strikes, the impulse to burn it all down is a signal flare. When you are stranded on burnout island, your body and your business start sending distress signals. These torching fantasies are a sign you are not working sustainably. Something is off, whether your schedule, your projects, your margins, your clients, your day-to-day work, your team, your delegation, or a mix of all of the above.

These moments are also ripe for our biggest business breakthroughs. I will share a few of mine in a moment—the ones that inspired this book—but first, the breaking points.

Business Stress Is a Systems Problem

Stress is a systems problem.

Not all stress, as there are terrible evils in the world and crooked societal systems wreaking havoc on people and planet. In the context of this book, however, many of the stresses of running a small business *can* be attributed to broken—or nonexistent—business systems.

It took me years to recognize this because stress often arrives mixed with success, and I had achieved successes that surpassed my wildest imagination. Still, they added complexity and raised the stakes higher. I knew the saying, "All business owners experience problems, just with more or fewer zeroes at the end," but I also knew there had to be a more systematic way to tackle these challenges so they would not reoccur.

I was accustomed to riding a rollercoaster of career highs and lows in high-pressure, fast-paced environments. Early in my career, that was my default way of working. Having built businesses throughout my childhood, I was used to being a time task-master and requiring *more, more, more* of myself. At fourteen years old, I developed a compulsive disorder called trichotillomania. Like nail-biting, when stressed I literally pull my hair out, something I still struggle with today.

I also developed a deep desire to serve others by reducing *their* anxiety, because mine was so overwhelming. Perhaps because I saw how hard my parents were working to pay the bills, I strove to do whatever I could to free them and others from what I perceived—at least, as a child—as burdens. If I could make others' lives easier, maybe I wouldn't be a burden either.

Partly as a coping mechanism and partly out of intrinsic joy, creating order out of chaos has always soothed me. I love tinkering behind the scenes of my business, teaching myself and others new software, voraciously gobbling up business books to smooth the path forward. I love open-sourcing my templates and solutions, from book marketing to rapid course design. One of my mugs says "I heart spreadsheets," and I color-coded my bookshelf long before it was a trend, with books stacked up to the ceiling in my New York City apartment. I procrastinate by tinkering in my business's operations, looking for new areas I can organize or automate.

Still, for years this mix of ambitions, combined with an unconscious effort to assuage insecurity through achievement, meant my career eyes were often bigger than my stomach. My boss at a political polling start-up, my first job out of college, often joked that I was "hiding five Jennys" in my office because of how much I juggled, a pattern that persisted in taking on too many roles in my own business years later.

While launching Google's global Career Guru coaching program in 2011, I was also putting the finishing touches on my first book, *while* taking two weeks off to attend a residential yoga teacher training. By the time *Life After College* launched six months later, I skidded into a sabbatical for a ten-city book tour. Days after the launch, when a friend asked how I was doing over burritos at Chipotle, I burst into tears. I was a frazzled mess. Clear that I could not juggle my side hustle and full-time job any longer, I gave my two weeks' notice to Google that summer.

In those first two years of self-employment, I was the only one working in my business. *Everything* hinged on me. When I needed to take a step back to rest, or to envision the next phase of my work, my income ground to a screeching halt. As an empath, introvert, and what psychologist Elaine Aron calls a "highly sensitive person," it was too much stress for my system. When running your own business, there is no reward for doing *all of the jobs*, other than burnout. I had to learn that the hard way, as so many of us do.

So I committed to building a better, more blissful business. One that would be heart based, systems focused, delightfully tiny, and fun. I strove to eliminate preventable stress—as much as I could, anyway.

I vowed to launch my second book, *Pivot*, with greater scale in mind. I sought the opposite life of that of an influencer. I resolutely *did not* want people to follow my work because of my looks, my lifestyle, or my ability to churn out ceaseless content, but for my bigger ideas. Soon, I stopped participating in social media altogether—a huge relief. No more keeping up with the infinite stream of content and comments, always feeling behind. By taking the focus off *me* at the center of my business, I could spotlight the programs and their value instead.

By the time *Pivot* launched in 2016, I was prepared with scalable streams of income. I trained a small group of people to meet the increased demand for one-on-one career coaching services, and eventually stopped doing one-on-one coaching myself. I built scalable corporate programs, launched a podcast that quickly became my favorite creative outlet, and streamlined my systems. I finally invested in "going pro" with software services to realize their full functionality, instead of squeezing everything I could out of their freemium editions.

Creating this space helped me land train-the-trainer (TTT) and intellectual property (IP) licensing deals with several dream corporate clients who implemented Pivot programs globally, helping me pull in nearly $700,000 in revenue the following year, a figure I barely believed when looking at my balance sheet. Freedom-lover that I am, I did this without any full-time employees—including me—as I was working ten- to twenty-hour weeks on average. This time, I was not the bottleneck to *Pivot* making its way into the world. So long as I released my grip on things being "perfect" without me, I could teach others how to deliver the material. Companies around the world could open-source it and teach in their own language, with their own context and internal examples.

When you run your own company, "hard" work no longer has a direct correlation to the profit you generate. In the entrepreneurial realm, time is decoupled from money. There is no guarantee that pouring more time into your business will yield positive results.

In a small business, there is no place to hide. Hard work itself is meaningless. The work must *work*—it must be strategic and revenue-generating, or you will quickly go out of business, like I almost did.

The Check Is in the Mail

Every one of my biggest business dips required imagining a new way forward, saying no to good opportunities, people, and pricing that no longer resonated. Each one sparked conversations with my team to clarify our priorities, increase our systems sophistication, and refocus on our strengths to serve the business best.

Even still, with all the progress I made on staying small while creating scalable programs, one of my biggest burn-it-all-down moments came three years after *Pivot* launched. Let's call it the seven-year business itch, a time where once again I was juggling too much, personally and professionally. I got married, bought a condo in New York City, and started attending Union Theological Seminary to "put myself in the path of pivot" of new people and ideas, studying the intersection of spirituality and work, and the growing "spiritual but not religious" population. I was squeezing intense academic reading and essay-writing into the nooks and crannies of my time and energy, jumping into empty classrooms to conduct work meetings in between lectures.

Amidst all this, I landed an exciting corporate client that booked me for workshops internationally, with the promise of licensing the material if those pilots went well. This engagement represented a hefty chunk of my income for the next six months, which I desperately needed to help pay for school, health insurance, and the new carrying costs of an entire household.

However, their "check in the mail" took its sweet time, notching up my anxiety with every passing month it was delayed. While we *had* agreed on up-front payment, I started the work long before the deposit arrived, in an effort to be friendly and accommodating. Clearly, these are *not* the best values to lean on when negotiating corporate contracts! Negotiating was my Achilles' heel as a recovering people-pleaser, but I hadn't yet figured out how to delegate this aspect of my business or improve enough to get comfortable. I always had more skin in the game than the multinational companies, therefore less leverage when negotiating. I wanted their business too badly. One check could make or break my business, while the expense of hiring me was barely a blip in their budget.

The frustration of waiting month after month for the money to pay my mortgage, racking up credit card balances to swing me like Tarzan from one branch of bills to the next, all while traveling internationally delivering trainings for this client, sent me over the edge. At the time, I had a director of communications who was wearing as many hats in the business as me, and a virtual assistant. Both were ready to make their own transitions, which meant I needed to rethink my entire tiny team and how the work would flow through it.

Despite years of striving to create more distance between my business's revenue and the time it would take me to earn it, I was back where I started in my first days as a solopreneur: stressed about money, overly reliant on one big client and one big check, and resentful at the boundaries I failed to set when negotiating the contract. Pressure weighed heavily. I still carried all the operational knowledge of how to run my business, juggling over ten streams of income that were legacies from years of experimenting.

No matter what I was delegating, the cognitive burden was still mine. It was the equivalent to one partner doing more household work than the other saying, "It's not just that I need you to help *do* the laundry, it's that I need you to help *notice* when the laundry needs to be done in the first place." In many cases, it wasn't that my team did not pull their weight on purpose, just that they didn't realize what needed to be done from a more strategic, forward-looking vantage point. I was stuck delegating tasks, when what I really needed was for team members to own their larger roles, including project outcomes and results.

Again I fantasized about winning the lottery or burning it all down, whichever came first. Alas, I still knew deep down that I never wanted to work for someone else, if I could help it.

So I gave myself permission to hit pause. I took leave from seminary school, stopped taking on new coaching clients, and I suspended publishing the podcast and my newsletter for six months. Once again, I vowed to rebuild, even better this time.

I started restructuring my business systems from the inside out, with clearly articulated operating principles so my team knew the logic of why and how I did things, a Manager Manual with full documentation on how to run every aspect of the business, and I expanded into what I call a *Delightfully Tiny Team* of three part-time people, four including me. Thank goodness I made those changes. What I dubbed "Jenny Blake Enterprises (JBE) 3.0," my business renaissance, occurred in the summer of 2019. In less than a year it would all be put to the test.

When the pandemic hit seven months later, I had unknowingly prepared by making these operational shifts. Six-figure contracts overdue to be signed were wiped off the table, and nearly every speaking engagement was cancelled or postponed two years into the future. Miraculously, I didn't want to burn it all down any longer. The pause in client work clarified my strengths, what income streams were no longer a fit, and how I wanted to simplify my business. It was the first time in fifteen years that I was not traveling every two weeks for work, so my creativity started to return. Because I had already restructured my team, our systems, and our offerings, I was able to keep the lights on with monthly recurring revenue from leading a private community for small business owners. We exchanged much-needed emotional support during those rocky months. I doubled-down on the podcast and published daily for three months, one way to serve my community during a crisis.

I revamped my sales process for corporate clients, and documented every step and talking point so someone else could help land new business, something I previously felt would be impossible. Now, I no longer hold sales calls, coordinate scheduling, or negotiate contracts. I leave those to specialists who can make it their focus and are willing to "be the bad guy," leaving me to do what I do best: using my voice in a *one-to-many* way. Specifically, to simplify complexity through what I call *ongoing public original thinking*, activities such as delivering keynotes, podcasting, sending my weekly(ish) newsletter, and writing this book.

This book would not exist if I had not found a way to reduce friction and return to creative flow again. Freedom, joy, ease, surrender, and serendipity became my new guiding success metrics. Now I know, deep within my bones, how non-negotiable it is to be present in my business and life. I know what *enough* looks like, what is worth pursuing and what isn't. I avoid chasing the hungry ghosts of money, fame, power, and control, what I call the Four Horsemen of the Business Ambition Apocalypse.

This anecdote, shared by Vanguard founder John C. Bogle in the opening to his book, *Enough*, captures my sentiments:

At a party given by a billionaire on Shelter Island, Kurt Vonnegut informs his pal, Joseph Heller, that their host, a hedge fund manager, had made more money in a single day than Heller had earned from his wildly popular novel Catch-22 *over its whole history. Heller responds, "Yes, but I have something that he will never have . . . enough."*

Heart-Based Business

"Are you ordering off yesterday's menu?"

This inquiry stayed with me for weeks after encountering it in a book called *Beyond the Known* by Paul Selig. It called attention to where I was stuck maintaining legacy programs in my business, instead of creating work based on *today's* menu of new options.

Where might you be ordering off of yesterday's business menu? Where are you making assumptions that are keeping you stuck, working on the wrong things or in the wrong way?

For Kajal Dhabalia, founder of Wholesome Soul, this question became her guiding light during a time of transition in life and work: moving, reorienting her business post-COVID, and supporting aging parents.

"Giving myself time to think about my menu—what was lingering out of habit and what was really calling me—made me realize how much I wanted to shift into well-being," she said, after unexpectedly closing her online art and gifts store business when the pandemic hit. A graphic designer by trade, Kajal took on design work to pay the bills, while researching wellness education programs.

"All along there was this resonant option there, but I just wasn't able to see it," she said. "But, now as I am in the middle of getting certified, I am excited to see how all my work is coming together even stronger than I could have imagined. I just had to let go of expectations around what I *should* be doing, and open myself up to the wisdom within that was there to guide me all along."

It is time to ditch yesterday's business menu. Instead of growth at the expense of your health and peace of mind, listen to the urges to simplify, streamline, and de-stress. Perhaps you, too, value small, agile teams that provide maximum freedom and optionality. On today's menu, you can seek just enough support to make things easier, but not so much that it becomes a burden itself, where you are struggling to earn ever-greater revenue just to feed the overhead beast. You can be thoughtful about who you seek to serve, and the impact you are making. You can work with integrity, honoring the health and humanity of all involved.

I call this operating mode *Heart-Based Business.* When I was leaving Google, I was so afraid of going broke, failing at business, making the wrong move. Every time those fears arose, I started countering with: but what if I earned twice as much in half the time? In later years, I added "with ease and joy" to include *how* I was working, and "while serving the highest good" to ensure I stayed focused on what was best for all involved.

Over the last decade this evolved to become a central guiding question for Heart-Based Business, one that I have shared with thousands of small business owners to stay focused on possibility instead of worst-case scenario outcomes. Heart-Based Business means engaging with an ongoing inquiry (feel free to create your own version with wording that resonates):

How can we earn twice as much in half the time, with ease and joy, while serving the highest good?

As Heart-Based Business owners, we know it is not about who can hustle, grind, and grit hardest to "beat" the competition. That type of business risks burning as an uncontrolled wildfire, destroying everything in its path. Compare that to a controlled fire, one that clears old underbrush, stimulating healthy growth in a contained, strategic, and systematic way.

Consider: does your business give you energy, or does it take energy?

If the latter, is it because of short-term efforts that are strengthening you for the long-term, or are you stuck in never-ending loops with no light at the end of the tunnel? Your business might have strong systems in place, but a few broken links that need fixing. Or, you may have the wrong systems set-up for what you are trying to achieve. Perhaps you have not yet created sustainable, repeatable systems in the first place, and are relying on fatigable human systems like willpower and memory.

You deserve to honor your life while you build your business.

Call it a "lifestyle business" if you want—a term I avoid for the pejorative tone many say it with—but what is the alternative? A *non*-lifestyle business where you are miserable by your own making, trading your precious present moments for a future vision that might not happen? What if you die before you mint those millions? Will you regret not investing more in the "lifestyle" ingredients of meaning, community, family, and vitality?

These ingredients are at the heart of *life-giving* businesses. *Free Time* is not about working as little as possible. Nor is it about creating a lifestyle business purely for one's own gain. *Life-giving* businesses energize everyone who participates in them, from the owner to team members to clients and community.

I don't work *full time*, I work *free time*: by repeatedly applying the principles and systems throughout this book to happily, and strategically, work less. When you run your own business, working less is often *harder* than working more. It requires building sophisticated systems and trusting a team to take care of smaller details.

In traditional corporate environments, "part time" conveys working only part of an expected whole (role). Let's redefine ten- to thirty-hour weeks as the *new* "full" time, as these hours, filled with engaged focus, allow us to have a fuller life outside of work. Of course, you will work more when needed during passionate sprints and for important deadlines, but you will also celebrate, guilt-free, weeks where you have achieved glorious spaciousness.

As much as I believe the typical, traditional corporate work-week needs restructuring, I would not dare prescribe what that looks like for you. I *do* want to give you a few permission slips. *There is also a blank template for these in the back of the book, ready to prescribe to yourself or a friend.* Many of us know, now, that what took us far in the early years—hard work fueled by adrenaline—is not what will carry us forward.

Forward, in this case, is not reaching a financial threshold or chasing vanity metrics while miserable. *Forward* is peace, harmony, progress toward a larger mission, abundant cash flow, healthy profit, and most of all—freedom. Freedom of choice around what to work on, when, and with whom. Free from the tyranny of your worst boss (*hint, look in the mirror!*) haranguing you day and night about your aptitude. Free from your secondary title, Chief Everything Officer, the roadblock to progress. Or perhaps you are far past these challenges, and you want to feel even freer to follow an exciting future that beckons.

Business-building is by nature a perpetual work-in-progress, but you *can* break down bottlenecks and bureaucracy by putting time-freeing systems in place. Even if you are a passionate entrepreneur for whom meaning is already deeply imbued in your mission, it can be hard not to get dragged under by the riptides of maintenance and minutiae.

What would be possible if you could follow a simple process today that would free your time far into the future?

Free Time Framework

Your mind is for having ideas, not holding them.

—David Allen

Free Time is a philosophy and a framework. In the context of running your business, Free Time has a double meaning:

- **As a verb:** The continual process of freeing your time to do your best work through smarter systems; and

- **As a philosophy:** Reimagining how we work, optimizing for freedom and Heart-Based Business values, instead of orienting toward money or growth at the expense of time and health.

In the concluding chapter of *Pivot*, I say: "We will all face many more pivots on the road ahead, big and small, planned and unplanned. My aim in this book is to teach you how to teach yourself to fish—to persevere and thrive—when navigating these changes."

When I mentioned this to my friend Charlie Gilkey, founder of Productive Flourishing and former logistics officer in the Army National Guard, he took it up a notch: "Design it so that *no one* has to think about catching the fish, because there's a system for that."

We can extend this metaphor further. Wallace Wright, author of *Learn Systems Thinking*, encourages an even more holistic analysis:

> *Systems thinking requires that we look at the bigger picture. What if there aren't enough fish left in the water source because of climate change? What if the water is polluted from the activities of corporations or individuals? Who controls access to the lake? How does the person who is obviously hungry afford to buy the materials necessary to catch the fish? What about the opportunities for expansion? Is there a local market for extra fish? Could this be a chance for a larger and longer-term investment?*

This is just one thought exercise illustrating systems principles that can improve how we think.

The Free Time Framework (FTF) is a process you can continually repeat as you move from friction to flow (more on that in the next section). Anywhere in your business that you experience friction, cycle through this process—Align, Design, Assign—to free-up time. The book is structured according to these three stages.

Free Time Framework

In **Part One: Align**, you will start with your mind, releasing yourself from invisible and outdated ways of working that are keeping your time unnecessarily and artificially constrained. You are your best asset, and systems are a skill. Before optimizing any project, ensure the work aligns with three key areas:

1. **Your values:** Operationalizing what makes you and company unique

2. **Your energy:** Discernment about what to work on (and how) to achieve results

3. **Your strengths:** Doubling-down on your talents, intuition, and imperfection

This stage is also an important gauge: If you discover the work or opportunity no longer aligns, you will phase it out. No need to systematize what should not be done in the first place.

In **Part Two: Design**, you will design smarter systems for your time, including streamlined processes for tackling work. You will become more discerning about what you work on and when, automating tasks before you have to think about delegating them. It will be impossible to truly free your time as a business owner if you work entirely alone. Your best bet is creating a lattice of support, one that complements your strengths and provides coverage for the rest.

The Design stage involves defining three key areas before delegating the work:

1. **Ideal outcomes:** How you will know when the work is complete

2. **Desired impact:** Results that these projects will achieve for your ideal audience

3. **Process:** Tackling the work in an intentional, streamlined manner

In **Part Three: Assign**, you will focus on working well with an agile Delightfully Tiny Team, even if no one works full-time. You will strengthen your delegation muscles to collaborate more effectively, without becoming a bottleneck for questions and approvals. You will ensure that every task is captured with a clear owner (ideally not you), that every question "lives three lives," and that each person in your business ecosystem is clear on three key things: **who** will do **what** by **when**, noting the "do not pass go" checkpoints along the way.

This Free Time Framework can help you navigate strategic projects as well as tactical day-to-day annoyances, starting with a simple diagnostic inquiry: **Are you in friction or in flow?** Wherever you encounter excessive friction, you will apply the **Align-Design-Assign** process.

Friction Versus Flow

The early days of any business are inherently scrappy, doing whatever it takes to create products and services that yield consistent cash flow. For many entrepreneurs, success can breed added stress.

When investigating the root causes among clients and colleagues, three common friction points arise:

1. **Pressure** to take on new clients to meet escalating overhead and payroll;

2. **Prices** that are too low, not reflecting the value delivered and increasing complexity of running the business, and

3. **Porous boundaries** with team and clients that consume crucial recharging time.

If you are currently experiencing any of these, with strategic shifts you can move your business's operating zone from friction to flow. By identifying where you are experiencing friction in your business, in areas large and small, you can apply the strategies throughout this book to simplify and streamline, freeing up time and energy. Let's look at both sides in more detail.

Friction ⟵〰〰〰⟶ Flow

- **Friction:** Disharmony, things are not clicking easily into place. You are experiencing resistance, procrastination, overwhelm, or even dread when contemplating next steps. Too many mistakes happen, work falls through cracks, and things start going haywire. You feel guilty, even embarrassed, by the state of your systems, and you might be questioning if your ambitions match your business strategy. Even prolonged confusion or boredom can be a form of friction: nothing is motivating you to get out of bed.

- **Flow:** You have eliminated most busywork and are focused on the vital few projects and clients. You spend the majority of your time working on tasks that you and only you can do, aligned with your greatest strengths, while delegating the rest. Mihaly Csikszentmihalyi, author of the seminal book *Flow*, describes this state as effortless achievement, a deeply immersive near-ecstatic bliss, where you barely notice time passing. According to a McKinsey study, executives report being five times as productive while working in a flow state. Synchronicities abound, and you are aware and engaged enough to create what *Good to Great* author Jim Collins calls "return on luck."

Where are you beset by the burdensome B's: getting bottlenecked, bored, or burned out? Running a business does not have to be so hard, or stressful, or overwhelming. We all go through dips along the way, sometimes on an hourly basis, sometimes daily, sometimes seasonally. Friction indicates an opportunity to transform your business into the next more sustainable operating phase. If you respond intelligently rather than react impulsively, you can elevate your awareness and actions from fire-fighting to systems thinking.

After all, you cannot continue to build a business or a team that is carried on your back. What if you experience an unforeseen life crisis that takes you out for months? Or a global pandemic renders your current systems (or entire business) inoperable, or you or members of your family become ill? Must everything grind to a halt? *No.* Remaining at the center of everything, with all the most important knowledge only in your mind, puts your business at risk.

This prompts the next question: Beyond reducing friction to find greater flow, how will you measure success once you are there? Will you keep yourself beholden to what you *should* measure, even obsess over, or intentionally redefine what matters?

The Missing Metric

Any friction-to-flow business transformation requires not only rethinking operations, but redefining what success looks like, shifting into a more holistic vantage point of time, health, spiritual, and financial abundance.

In the years after *Pivot* launched, I discovered the joys of operating this way. Instead of obsessing over goals and numbers, I was open to surprises. That's when I realized that in all the statistics available to help us better understand small businesses and the owners that run them, there is one vital metric missing.

More on that in a moment.

First, here is what we do know about how small businesses structure their time, team, and earnings. The U.S. Census Bureau defines a small business as one with fewer than 500 employees. *Side note: that does not sound very small to me!* Small businesses are an integral part of the economy, employing nearly half of the nation's workforce.

Out of the 31.7 million small businesses in the United States, twenty-five million have no employees; these are known as *non-employer businesses.* Just over five million small businesses have one to nineteen employees, and less than one million small businesses have twenty to 499 employees. That means that non-employer businesses make up the vast majority of small businesses, but it does not mean you have to work alone. It just means you may not employ anyone full time, other than you, the owner. According to VC firm SignalFire, more than fifty million people consider themselves content creators, the fastest growing small-business segment.

Let's take a look at how small businesses stack up to traditional metrics:

- Only 40 percent of small businesses are profitable. Of the remaining 60 percent, half break even, and half are losing money.

- 52 percent of small businesses are home-based.

- 86.3 percent of small business owners make less than $100,000 a year in take-home pay.

- 19 percent of small business owners work over 60 hours a week, with 89 percent working on weekends.

The business press celebrates companies with rapidly climbing earnings. One of the most common reports business owners rely on is the profit and loss statement (P&L) with three key figures: gross revenue, operating expenses to achieve that revenue, and net profit.

But there is a key metric missing from the P&L: *time*. Specifically, the time spent by the business owner, leadership team, and employees to reach these figures. Too many companies celebrated for their success lead burn-and-churn cultures where employees develop chronic illnesses they can't explain, too exhausted on weekends to enjoy what little "free time" they have.

In the remainder of this book, I am sharing an operating playbook that has worked for over a decade of running an agile tiny team that optimizes for free time, not just revenue. I track my time through an app called RescueTime running in the background of my computer and mobile devices. My intention is not bragging about earnings, but rather showing you one route to what is possible.

Analyzing combined data from the last five years, I work an average of twenty hours each week, with $505,000 in gross revenue. I earned an average of $257,250 in net profit; $330,250 if you include my salary, since I operate as an S-Corp. I am my sole employee. I spend an average of 832 hours per year at the computer—a traditional nine-to-five would be twice that at minimum—and I rarely check email or do work on my phone. Those extra thousand hours saved add up to 30,000 hours over thirty working years. I take two full months off each year, and do not schedule meetings on Mondays or Fridays, or before 11 a.m. or after 3 p.m., with rare exceptions. I consider four to five deeply focused computer hours each day full, sandwiched between two-hour wind-up and wind-down rituals that are as vital as the work time within.

My three ongoing team members average five hours each week to achieve these numbers, up to ten for brief windows during our biggest launches. When working on new projects, I often partner with specialists, such as a brand strategy firm (itself a Delightfully Tiny Team) every five years or so. I also work with professionals such as an attorney on monthly retainer, and an accountant that I meet with quarterly. I spend approximately $1,500 per month on software to achieve greater efficiency.

You can see a list of the nearly sixty recurring software services I use to run my business (with the monthly investment for each) in the online resources that accompany this book at ItsFreeTime.com/toolkit.

Contrast this with many executives and business owners who work long hours every day of the week, barely breaking even after accounting for team overhead, from the smallest shops to the most well-funded venture-backed start-ups. Franchising expert George Knauf said that throughout his decades of consulting, the owners of septic tank businesses were by far the happiest he encountered. Who was the most miserable? CEOs of Fortune 500 companies. The latter were stressed, constantly on the road, buried in emails and meetings, and pulled away from their families. One study found that Fortune 500 CEOs averaged only twenty-eight uninterrupted, productive minutes a day.

My friend Edward, a seasoned media executive, confirmed this. The happiest person he knows living in the Hamptons is Bob, the man who owns a gunite pool installation company there, not the well-to-do Manhattanites hiring him. Edward met Bob during a business offsite on Parrot Cay, a private island resort in Turks and Caicos. Meanwhile, Bob was there with his family on a lavish vacation. After striking up a conversation at the bar, Edward described Bob as radiant. He was tan, fit, and retired by his early fifties, with a beautiful family and kids he proudly put through prestigious Ivy League universities.

Allow me to introduce a new metric: the *time-to-revenue ratio* (TtRr), or if you prefer, the *time-to-profit ratio* (TtPr). These figures reflect the idea that we can optimize for revenue, ease, and joy at the same time; they are not mutually exclusive. Calculating your time-to-revenue (or profit) ratio means evaluating not just what you earn, but how much time it took you and your team to achieve those results. A larger TtPr percentage is good; it means you are achieving a higher return on investment (ROI) on the time spent to yield those profits.

To calculate your time-to-revenue ratio:

1. Divide your company's revenue* by 1,000
2. Divide that figure by the number of hours worked in that time period**
3. Multiply by 100 to yield a percentage

*Revenue can be substituted for profit and/or owner pay.

**You can run these calculations by owner's time only or by hours worked by the entire team.

To illustrate this with a personal example:

1. Owner **pay** of $330,000 / 1,000 = 330
2. Owner **time** to achieve that = 912 hours*
3. 330 / 912 = 0.3618
4. 0.3618 x 100 = **36% TtPr**

*For contrast, if I had worked 40-hour workweeks: (330,000/1,000) / 1,920 = 17% TtPr

The number of hours you consider abundant is however many you define that to be; there are no minimum or maximum hours, and you are not a better or worse business owner for working more or less. Some businesses—restaurants, farms, brick-and-mortar shops—often require more time by nature than those that are information-based or working remotely.

Not all time spent is equal, either; more on that in the Design stage (Part Two). As I sprinted to finish writing this book, I ended some days on deadline bouncing with enthusiasm. During other weeks, where my primary goal was catching up on email, I left long days feeling drained and dejected, despite my best efforts to shift into a more positive mindset.

Assess your ideal TtRr by how long you are energized by meaningful work, eliminating as much busywork as possible along the way. Think of it like weeding a garden. Busywork weeds will always resurface, but you will get better at spotting them by measuring your TtRr alongside other key business metrics.

There may be some "busy" work that others hate, but that you happen to love; I say keep it! There is no sense in delegating away everything you enjoy. Notice, though, when you procrastinate with smaller items in your comfort zone instead of tackling the twofold challenge of trusting someone else with those tasks, and stretching yourself to do the harder, more strategic work.

When I shared the TtTr concept with Michael J. Consuelos, a military veteran and pediatrician who pivoted to medical consulting just before the pandemic, he immediately put it into practice. One of his clients, a three-year-old healthcare services company with forty employees and ten million dollars in annual revenue, was growing at breakneck speed. Michael noticed that their "all in" approach was relying on increasingly long hours. "I could smell the early smoke of burnout," he said, as they struggled with prioritizing. "Everything needed to get done today."

So Michael posed the TtTr question to their founder and CEO: What's your time-to-revenue ratio? He explained that the ratio is improved by reducing time for the same revenue, or increasing revenue for the same amount of time spent. If you have too little time, or are making too little money, then there is room for improvement.

Michael also noted the time and opportunity costs of chasing initiatives that would not pay well, projects that distracted and detracted from work the company could perform better, faster, and with healthier margins. With this framework in mind, the CEO initiated conversations about his team's time investments, reprioritizing as a result.

For a segment of business owners with deliberately small teams, and no intention to grow them, time freedom is the ultimate aim, as measured by this time-to-revenue ratio. In many cases, they would not accept opportunities that would double their earnings if they also required quadrupling their time investment—unless the project was particularly meaningful, or they were at a stage in life where they needed a capital infusion.

Consider a hypothetical, if you were already earning enough to live on: Would you accept one million dollars if it meant working seventy to eighty hours per week, doing work you did not enjoy, for one year (no cancellation allowed), with a demanding and bureaucratic client?

High Net Freedom

I encourage you to pose this "million-dollar bureaucratic client" question to others; the answers may surprise you. As one person pointed out, it's a PG-rated version of the 1993 movie *Indecent Proposal* starring Demi Moore. Or for a twist, consider the premise of the History channel's reality TV series, *Alone*. Would you attempt to survive one hundred days in the Arctic, alone, for the chance to win one million dollars?

As a small business owner, you are in a privileged position if you know you can earn this much through your own efforts, or you are someone for whom no exchange of money is worth trading time doing work you hate. In truth, to work at all is a privilege: to breathe, to live, to have clean drinking water, to get a full night's sleep, to move comfortably in one's body.

I wrote *Pivot* for a group I consider *high net growth*, those who are asking not only "What am I earning?" in any job or income stream, but "What am I learning? How am I growing?" When those needs are being met, often in parallel, they aim for also making a broader positive impact. If you are reading this in your free time, you are certainly high net growth. You are likely *high net impact*, and it wouldn't hurt to be high net worth—inside and out, of course. But there is another core value that will supersede all of these: *high net freedom*.

High net freedom means you most likely do not want to become an operator of a huge business, with investors or shareholders to answer to, managing an org chart five layers deep. You want to be free to move, to do your best work. That said, emergencies happen. Sometimes *force mejeur* occurs, and you need to make sacrifices to survive.

The million-dollar bureaucratic client question sparked a fascinating discussion among my friends, family, and private podcast community.

Some *would* take the job, if they knew it was funding their bigger creative dreams. Others remarked that they had *already* worked this way earlier in their career at far lesser pay; at least this way they were ostensibly being recognized for their efforts. Some said if they knew their existing skills would never yield this much, an assignment like this could be game-changing.

For others, no amount of money was worth sacrificing their health and relationships. One person, citing the high opportunity costs of time away from his creative projects said, "No way. I would rather make thirty grand, with plenty of time to build my own million-dollar assets."

Uzma Iqbal was faced with this type of decision in the early aughts, when she was graduating medical school to become an oncologist. She had two job offers: one for a $120,000 starting salary, and the other for $500,000. The former would offer intangible rewards beyond financial gain, while she knew the latter would box her in. She took the lower paying gig.

"Boy, I was right," she said. "I never made much money in that first job, but I learned the skills to launch my own practice, perhaps now even making up for some of that money 'lost.'"

She asks herself a version of this question every day, reflecting on what her number *would* be. "One million dollars is an attractive number," she said, "But it's not the one that I would give up what I am doing now for, or how I am working." Uzma is content with how she is running her medical practice, with the flexibility to toggle her hours up or down.

Short of the hypothetical million-dollar client, the challenge for many business owners is ignoring the siren song of *money for money's sake*, despite survival fears for yourself, your family, and the business. Forgoing money as the main driver requires trust, because it is counter-cultural to imagine freeing up time and energy *first*, so that you can attract new and better opportunities next. After all, most business advice centers upon cash flow for a reason: without it, your business won't survive.

I challenge you to equally prioritize ease and joy on your path to profit. Not ease in the sense of laziness, though many successful entrepreneurs are known to tout "strategic laziness" as the secret to their success, but the ease of working in harmony with your strengths and your team. The intersection of revenue, ease, and joy is where you will find free time. Within your business, plot your current and potential revenue streams across these areas, looking for sweet spots that are abundant in all three.

I say and do this—aiming for the intersection of revenue, ease, and joy—as the breadwinner for my family. My husband, Michael, a contemporary artist, bootstrapped his way from Beirut to New York by running a graphic design business while doing voiceover work on the side, before completing his master of fine arts. My business is our main source of income. The principles I am sharing with you in this book support our household; my business is not a part-time supplement that requires a second full-time earner to be realized. As the primary earner, it would be tempting to take on the pressure of working around the clock, but I refuse to work this way, having hit burnout too many times before.

The Free Time Framework is a continual process to free your mind, time, and team. The specific software tools will change and evolve. By understanding the systems design process behind them, you can reduce friction and overwhelm. Following the Free Time Framework at a macro level for your business, and following it at a micro level within day-to-day work, will not eliminate burn-it-all-down mode forever. But it might just give you renewed hope for the future of your business, and your ability to steer your ship sanely and sustainably—dare I say—even *joyfully*.

Free Up Founder Time: Escape Velocity

Ideapreneurs require space and focus. You need time to wander, dream, reflect, and strategize. Every business owner is in the idea business: Your strongest asset is your mind, not your labor, at least once you move past the stage of solely delivering services. There is no scenario where a burned-out business owner does better than one who is energized, expansive, and engaged.

If your tires are spinning in mud, failing to gain traction, you need more of what I call Founder Time. You do not free your time by earning it, getting "enough" done, or waiting until no one is asking you for things. You free your time by freeing your time. Make your Founder Time windows unavailable to others starting *now*.

Yes, right now . . .

Start by creating a two-hour Founder Time block on your calendar that recurs weekly, during a time of day when you are most energetic. As they say in personal finance, "pay yourself first." Do not look for small segments sandwiched between others' requests; reserve windows that suit you best. During that window, you can tackle strategies from this book, along with the projects that will make the biggest impact on your business (more on this in Part Three).

Remind yourself that Founder Time is the most indispensable resource you have for building everything else in your business. It is the essential element to achieve *escape velocity*. In technical terms, this is "the minimum velocity that a moving body, such as a rocket, must have to escape from the gravitational field of a celestial body, such as the earth, to move outward into space." Constructing a Delightfully Tiny Team is an important vehicle toward free time, but freeing your mind comes first, by committing to building a business that runs smoothly without your constant presence.

Free Time Escape Velocity

One of my long-time *friendtors*, Michael Bungay Stanier, achieved Founder Time escape velocity, even if he sees his newest venture at an earlier stage. Michael exited the company he built for twenty years, Box of Crayons. He remains the owner and receives quarterly profit payouts, but he is no longer CEO, responsible for managing a growing team of over twenty people. Instead, he hired a president, training her over a three-year span of time, so he could transition out with confidence that she had the role covered.

Now Michael is focusing his energy and efforts on a new direction of creative expression by returning to a Delightfully Tiny Team of two to three core members (including himself), bolstered by a network of specialists for various projects ranging from a next book, a new podcast, a two-day literary festival, and yet-to-be-imagined projects that align with his best expression.

I had a fun Founder Time experience while working on the final edits for this book. I meet monthly with my business attorney, Francine Love, who had recently read an advance copy. When I moved our upcoming call to a Friday due to a conflict, she responded saying that day was newly unavailable.

"Sorry, I have started Founder Fridays for the summer (and hopefully beyond)," Francine wrote. "It was, in part, inspired by your book, so you can only blame yourself. :) Can we look at the next week?" I smiled. Although it meant waiting a few extra days, I was thrilled to know Francine was claiming *her* Founder Time!

Consider how you could free up Founder Time even more expansively. Graphic designer Stefan Sagmeister is famous for taking creative sabbaticals every seven years, closing his New York studio for one year. In a 2009 TED Talk on "The Power of Time Off," he said:

> *We spend about the first twenty-five years of our lives learning, then there are another forty years reserved for working. Tacked on at the end are about fifteen years for retirement. I thought it might be helpful to basically cut off five of those retirement years and intersperse them in between those working years. That's clearly enjoyable for myself. But even more important is that the work that comes out of these years flows back into the company and into society at large, rather than just benefiting a grandchild or two.*

Sagmeister has become renowned for the ideas he develops during these sabbaticals, and the work his team produces in the years that directly follow.

Achieving Founder Time escape velocity by following the Free Time Framework means your business and personal needs are abundantly met by recurring revenue and a well-oiled team machine. You are no longer conflicted about what to work on, how to find the time, or how to train new team members. Nothing is ever static, certainly in business, and nothing is guaranteed. However, there is a point of mastery and maturity—of the leader, the team, the operating systems, and the work itself—that becomes a virtuous cycle of sustainable systems and meaningful creativity.

Now, let's make sure you are building on solid ground.

Quiz:
What's Your Free Time Escape Velocity?

Go with your gut response as you answer the questions below. Take an online version or send this quiz to a friend at **ItsFreeTime.com/quiz**.

As a business owner, how often do you find yourself:

Feeling bad for not moving faster, or being farther along, in your business and/or creative projects	Rarely	Sometimes	Often
Down on yourself about the state of your systems, or your skills around tools and software automations	Rarely	Sometimes	Often
Tackling tiny, tedious, or time-sensitive tasks instead of your most important work	Rarely	Sometimes	Often
Looking ahead to a calendar stacked with meetings, with little time remaining for deeper thinking	Rarely	Sometimes	Often
Questioning whether your business model and structure is set up to match your cash flow goals	Rarely	Sometimes	Often
Wondering if your ambitions match your available resources and/or your team member's skills	Rarely	Sometimes	Often
Working on low ROI tasks, yet ones that still seem necessary	Rarely	Sometimes	Often
Worrying about "key person" risk because your business lives in the minds of the team, and if anyone were to step out, including you, problems would ensue	Rarely	Sometimes	Often

Feeling insecure because you don't really know how your business works, or how to strategically grow revenue	Rarely	Sometimes	Often
Feeling fuzzy, knowing team members do too, because you haven't clarified your path forward	Rarely	Sometimes	Often
Frequently answering questions from team members, when they could have done that critical thinking first	Rarely	Sometimes	Often
Taking less-than-ideal clients or projects to pay the bills	Rarely	Sometimes	Often
Saying yes to contracts at prices you know are too low	Rarely	Sometimes	Often
Skipping your own payroll or distributions so you can cover other business expenses	Rarely	Sometimes	Often
Frustrated by demanding clients, or lack of boundaries, feeling pressure to answer when you are off work	Rarely	Sometimes	Often
Apologizing for your delayed response or missed deadlines	Rarely	Sometimes	Often
Working nights or weekends when you do not want to be	Rarely	Sometimes	Often
Feeling exhausted and/or overwhelmed; pining for a simpler life or business	Rarely	Sometimes	Often

TOTAL FOR EACH COLUMN: R: _____   S: _____   O: _____

Scoring

Glance down the columns; if you answered mostly . . .

Rarely: Congratulations, You're a Free Timer!

Bravo! You are already soaring toward escape velocity. Give yourself kudos for systematizing your business and your role as well as you have; hopefully this book can spark a few new insights and refinements. Consider gifting copies to your team to get them up to speed, freeing up even more of your time in the process.

Sometimes: Bordering on Bottlenecked

Take your Free Time temperature: Your forehead is feeling warm. Have you stepped back from your business lately so you can approach it more strategically? If not, now is the perfect time to carve out Founder Time and reexamine areas with excessive friction, redesigning them for greater impact and time freedom.

Often: Chief Everything Officer

Free Time temperature check says you are burning up! And likely burning out. I am thrilled that you picked up this book. Give yourself credit for taking on the courageous challenge of running your own business in the first place. *Now have no fear, systems are here!* I will provide plenty of resources in this book and online toolkit to help you implement what you are learning in a snap.

Part 1

Ali

gn

Overview

When she was just twenty-one years old studying abroad in Buenos Aires, Wade Brill discovered a swollen lymph node on her neck. She had flashes of déjà vu from her sister's cancer diagnosis four years prior. When doctors confirmed she was indeed afflicted by the same disease, Hodgkin's lymphoma, she flew home to New York City to begin treatment.

Two months into her six-month chemotherapy process, her mother passed away from leukemia, just two floors down from Wade's infusion room.

Wade was beyond devastated. She describes that time as feeling like everything around her was crumbling. Her mom's passing shook the ground beneath her feet, never to be the same again. "Nausea slithered through my bones, swirling with the precariousness of my own health," she said. "The uncertainty of where I was going to live, how I was going to pay for my healthcare, and who was going to take care of me was overwhelming." At the same time, Wade vowed not to become hardened or resentful, but to take charge of her life.

The message that life is short took on new meaning. Wade committed to a life and business of purpose, emphasizing health and happiness. She founded an on-demand mindfulness and self-care platform and podcast, *Centered in the City*, to help others do the same. As she shares prominently on her website, Wade knows deep in her bones that, "We have one mind, one body, one life." Of her own health scare, and on mourning the loss of her mother, Wade writes:

Life was no longer about surviving. No, it was something bigger: it was about living. Each day became a precious gift that allowed me to prioritize and express my true self. During treatment, I spent my energy and time exploring who I was and what I valued. I steered myself through darkness and uncertainty so that I could find light and beauty again. I may not have been in control of everything that was happening inside my body, but I knew I could control my mindset, what I fed myself, activities I involved myself in, how I interacted with others, and with whom I spent my time. To this day, I work to own and love each breath, taste, smell, touch and sound I experience.

Running your own business presents powerful opportunities to rewrite outdated work rules. As Wade models for her community, you can build in a way that aligns with your health, your values, and your long-term success. No matter how smart your systems, if you build your business on quicksand, it will sink. Quicksand starts with your inner architecture: the values behind your business, how you operationalize those values, your mindset, and how you translate your unique vision and way of working to team members, contractors, and customers.

Once you identify a major point of friction, the first step is to **Align:** ensure that the projects and revenue streams in your business align with your values, your energy, and your strengths. There is no point in systematizing work you should not be doing. Aligning your business starts with considering three core elements:

- Values: What are your personal values? Are the core values of your business the same or different? How do your values inform tough decisions, when you or your team members must make a choice? For example, how do you make financial decisions? When a customer asks for a refund, do you default to giving back the amount they ask for, or to saving the company money? How are you *operationalizing* your values?

- Energy: Are the revenue streams in your business aligned with what energizes you? Does your day-to-day work energize you? Do your clients and prospective clients have "clean" light energy, or "dirty" heavy energy? Are you running your business in a way that is life giving or life draining? Where are you operating on the spectrum of friction to flow? Are you diluting your focus with distractions, or sharpening it by making clear choices about what is most important?

- **Strengths:** What are your biggest strengths as a business? What sets you apart? As the owner, are you doing work suited to your strengths, to make the biggest impact for the business? What about team members, if you have any? How "in the weeds" are you, doing work that you are not particularly skilled at? Where are you tackling tasks that someone else could easily handle, such as scheduling, paying bills, or placing orders?

As a result of her diagnosis and recovery, Wade aligns with her own values, energy, and strengths before taking on new clients. She gives herself permission to pay attention to what parts of her business and offerings light her up most. This improves clarity on what to delegate (for her, activities like accounting and editing) and what is fun and fulfilling enough to keep, such as social media and copywriting. Wade aligns next steps by first asking, "How can I serve?" This question helps her overcome nerves, particularly with sales and marketing.

"I remember I am here to help people close the gap of where they are now and where they want to be," she said. "When I approach my business from service, I am able to stay in my heart, connected to the person I am talking about instead of feeling overly salesy."

The chapters in this Align stage will walk you through realigning your business and projects so you can move from friction toward focus and flow. Agile operating principles, combined with a digital externalized mind that contains all context for your company, will create the necessary infrastructure to ensure everyone can work independently and effectively. That sense of ease and joy can then flow to your customers, creating a virtuous cycle of repeat business and referrals.

Align > Design > Assign >

Values

Operating principles stem from core values; they communicate the higher-level philosophy driving the processes required to operate your team's projects. Principles provide the logic of "why and how we do things here," the overall mindset and approach to work. Where *process* outlines exactly how you achieve desired outcomes within each area of the business, *principles* guide those process details at a higher level. What are your core values as a business, and how do you express those when you have to make hard choices? What is the visual voice of your brand that projects your core values outward? Clarifying your values is only a fraction of the work; the rest follows in operationalizing these core values through streamlined systems. How do you ensure vague-sounding bromides like "surprise and delight" or "underpromise, overdeliver" are honored throughout day-to-day interactions?

In this section, you will:

- Set agile operating principles
- Create an externalized mind
- Systematize the spirit of your business

1

Embrace Agile Operating Principles: What's Your Wi-Fi Password?

The path to managing complexity is, paradoxically, simplicity.

—Doug Kirkpatrick

Fresh off of a speaking engagement in Barcelona, I made my way to the airport and checked in with my friend Julie, who I featured in *Pivot*. I would be visiting her in London before returning to the states, but was set to arrive one day prior to her own return home from a hectic work trip.

"What's your Wi-Fi password?" I texted, already hesitant to bother her with minutiae in the middle of a work day. I knew Julie loved hosting, and I began anticipating how tiresome it must be to repeatedly give every visitor a complicated set of directions and arrival instructions. So I added, "And if you don't already have one, I'm happy to set-up a Google Doc for guests."

Julie thanked me for the idea, and I seized the moment in the minutes before takeoff to do one of my favorite things: save her time and energy. I set up a shell document for myself, figuring that I would add to it throughout my stay, collecting additional tidbits that could be helpful for future guests. I would leave it with Julie as a digital parting gift—certainly longer-lasting than a bottle of wine—a "Jenny" way to express gratitude for her hospitality by making her life easier for future hosting.

As I started working on the structure, I shared it with Julie, almost without thinking. To my surprise and delight, by the time I touched down in London two hours later we had nearly two pages outlined. She had been adding details as she thought of them, too. Once I arrived at her place I filled in a few blanks, along with photo documentation of what would be confusing to a newcomer in her modern tech-forward apartment. These were features she knew intimately, such as where the refrigerator and silverware were located, behind doors and drawers that blended in with the cabinets. By the time I left London, the document was nearly six pages, built out with links to nearby cafes and restaurants, and tips for finding one's way home through the labyrinth of cobblestone back streets, a path Julie had long-since memorized.

This is a small example of collaboration and efficiency in action. In asking one simple question, I kick-started a systems-thinking process, knowing I would not be her last guest. By reducing the *starting friction*, the friction that must be overcome to start motion, for Julie to set up an entire manual to her apartment (while she had far more important work tasks on her plate), I made it easier for her to hop in and add things as they sprung to mind. Within twelve hours, the doc had a table of contents, a short-link to easily recall where to find it, and elegant formatting with help from the template gallery.

Years later, while I was working on the first draft of this book and feeling fried from city life, our mutual friend Ann (my "New York City angel," who I met serendipitously in a shoe store ten years prior) invited me to stay at her house on the New Jersey shore while she was out of town. There I was again, texting her to ask that same starting question: "What's your Wi-Fi password?" Ann started peppering me with a series of texts off the top of her head containing instructions, directions to local restaurants, and detailed how-tos for quirky aspects of the house. I imagined how tiresome this would become the next time someone arrived. You know what happened next.

I stopped and asked her if she wanted me to set-up a Google Doc guide to her house for future visitors. "Oh! Like the one you did for Julie?" She asked.

"Yes, please!" I had no clue Ann had ever seen the document for the London pad, or if Julie had done anything with it after I left. Even the best systems efforts fall by the wayside if people forget to use them; however, they won't forget if the system is designed well, with intrinsic utility. It becomes harder *not* to use them! *That* is the mark of a successful system.

Sure enough, Ann's reply confirmed the value of the apartment doc. Julie had shared it with Ann in advance of a visit, saving both of them time and confusion. Now Ann would have one just like it. I smile at the thought of these small efficiency gains growing with every new guest, with no new effort required. That is leverage, no matter how light the tasks seem in the moment.

These docs are so simple, but they illustrate a way of thinking that makes life easier, over and over again. They reflect one of my core operating principles, borrowed from the world of agile development: "Each time you repeat a task, take one step toward automating it." (You will learn more about this in Part Two, the Design stage.) Your operating principles, whether you are explicitly aware of them or not, are already serving as a foundation for systems you do (or don't) have in your business. Articulating them is crucial, especially as you expand your team, as they set in motion a chain of reasoning based on underlying values.

Take a Stand: "Even Over" Versus Bland

What are the core values of your business? How do they inform the decisions you make, the people you hire, the work you produce? Once you are clear on your business values, you will bring them to life through operating principles that show your team how to put them into practice. Clothing company Beyond Yoga attaches a card to each item, reinforcing their values with every product they ship:

INTEGRITY   GRATITUDE   FLEXIBILITY   AUTHENTICITY

QUALITY   POSSIBILITY IN ACTION

As a customer I can see that my values align with theirs, so much that I am happy to prop this card up at the side of my desk as a reminder of things that I, too, believe in. Sarah Apgar, founder and CEO of FitFighter, a fitness company featured on Shark Tank that centers around her Steelhose free weight, spells her company values out in her email signature:

FitFighter Core Values

1. Service Is Our Compass
2. Team Is How We Win Lose & Play
3. Embrace Challenge & Be Curious
4. Exceed the Standard
5. Love Everyone & Act Human

One way to articulate your values, to more clearly see the tradeoffs you are willing to make, is by writing "even over" statements, as the originators of the Manifesto for Agile Software Development have inspired many businesses to do. As in, we value {important quality A} even over {important quality B}. The Agile Software Manifesto starts as follows (emphasis mine):

> *Individuals and interactions **over** processes and tools*
>
> *Working software **over** comprehensive documentation*
>
> *Customer collaboration **over** contract negotiation*
>
> *Responding to change **over** following a plan*
>
> *That is, while there is value in the items on the right, we value the items on the left more.*

What do you value more than other important qualities? How could you clarify your documentation to reflect these choices?

Embrace Agile Operating Principles: What's Your Wi-Fi Password?

Part 1: Align

Once you and your team are clear on your company's values and operating principles, you won't have to explain as much down the road. Feedback becomes tied back to both, empowering everybody with shortcuts for decision-making. They will increase your confidence when delegating, allowing your team to solve problems and serve customers in ways unique to you and your business.

You never know where articulating these principles might lead. This book started as a two-page outline that I drafted several years ago when preparing to bring on a new team member. I started free writing, capturing all of the previously hidden logic living only in my mind about how I work and why, and for two weeks I didn't stop. Ideas flashed morning, noon, and night—all related to elements of running my business that came automatically to me, but might not have to someone else.

Six months later, I turned that outline into an hour-long workshop for my private community with a series of templates to help them create their own operating principles. Two years later, I realized that perhaps these ideas—the chapters of this book—could be helpful to many more teams beyond just my own. Now you are holding the results of these efforts—my Heart-Based Business operating principles—in your hands.

As you read the chapters that follow, I encourage you to consider what you disagree with, and what is missing. What principles would you add? What is the essence of the underlying logic that has helped you get where you are, that will take you and your team where you want to go next?

CHAPTER 1 RECAP

Embrace Agile Operating Principles: What's Your Wi-Fi Password?

Two-Sentence Summary

Principles transcend process details. They provide the logic of "why and how we do things here."

Give Yourself Permission

Run your business your way, even if that's different from industry best practices.

Ask Yourself

What frustrates you and why? What "rules" are being broken in those moments?

Do (or Delegate) This Next

Set up a document called "Operating Principles," and start adding to it throughout the next few weeks, capturing how you approach work and business. In the Resources section at the back of the book you will find question prompts to guide your thinking.

2

Create an Externalized Mind

As the old joke goes: "Software, free. User manual, $10,000." But it's no joke . . . the lines of free code become valuable to you only through support and guidance.

—Kevin Kelly

Traversing Times Square at rush hour is always treacherous. Smashed between naked cowboys, confused tourists, and tip-hungry costumed characters, most New Yorkers avoid the area.

One day as I was leaving a speaking engagement, I saw a strange sight. Minnie Mouse was chasing after people, arms outstretched, aggressively trying to land hugs. Pedestrians were swerving left and right to avoid the onslaught of unwanted "affection." Nearby was another Minnie, with her costume head half lifted, perched atop her hair—a two-headed Minnie! It fractured the fantasy of Disney characters coming to life.

I call this incident "Off-brand Minnie Mouse." What would Walt Disney think, knowing his sweet Minnie was chasing people down, bordering on harassment, to garner tips? It certainly wouldn't fly at Disney World! The *New York Post* shared an article shortly before my experience titled, "Times Square 'Creepy' Costumed Characters Are Out of Control." The article cites a statistic: 47 percent of New Yorkers said they have had an unpleasant interaction with one of the "pushy plushies," with 22 percent noting unwanted physical contact. Now, it is certainly challenging to make a living as a costumed character, hustling for rent money. But I cannot imagine it getting any easier if you creep out the clientele!

Although your team is hopefully more graceful when representing your business and brand, you can never be sure. In addition to your operating principles, clearly outline processes that define how you work in a well-organized, easy-to-navigate Manager Manual: your externalized business mind. In doing so, you will be more confident and less stressed, better able to trust yourself and others to run operations smoothly, and communicate about your business clearly.

In an ideal world, no piece of information about the business (or your clients) lives only in someone's mind—yours or your team's. None. *Nothing.*

As you will learn through the Fiji Test (Chapter 22), if anyone were whisked away to an island vacation with no notice and devices left behind, the business could continue operating just as smoothly without them. That means every piece of data—process, passwords, rules-of-thumb—must live outside of any one person's mind.

Software will help you achieve this. Not tools like email or Slack relying heavily on search; look for something with more structure that is easily navigable, an internal intranet. In my business, we use Notion as our operations hub. Every bit of data has a home in our shared business dashboard: from task, project, and client tracking to the Manager Manual, with many sub-pages for each.

We store all files in Dropbox and Google Drive, making them shareable and cloud-based, accessible from any device. This has the added benefit of providing ongoing back-up in the event of hardware failure, or if anyone's computer were lost or stolen. I do not store any files on my computer's hard drive; they all live in Dropbox and Drive, with the same folder structure mirrored across all locations, including places like Notion and Evernote.

Centralizing our externalized mind with an organized Notion dashboard has the added benefit of bolstering the business's memory through easily searchable archives. No one needs to remember anything, except how to navigate our documentation. Notion is a comprehensive wiki-like tool with tremendous flexibility. It allows us to create a central location, or dashboard, for all information in the business. This includes our:

- Operating Principles
- Manager Manual with detailed processes on each area of the business, often referred to as *standard operating procedures* (SOPs)
- Monthly Metrics Dashboard
- Client and Member Trackers
- Podcast Production boards
- Meeting Notes for team meetings and one-on-ones
- and much more . . .

When we need to find information, it is all there. If it isn't, such as when I give feedback or a team member asks a question that has not yet been answered, we make sure to update the relevant places. With this central hub as our externalized business mind, everyone can continually improve our documentation. It means we are repeating ourselves less, making fewer mistakes, spending less time searching for missing data, and onboarding new people faster.

Note: Tools and software are ever-evolving, so that is not the focus of this book; visit ItsFreeTime.com/toolkit for a current list of all the software I use to run my business, with the monthly investment for each service.

One important subset of your Manager Manual, particularly once you have a team, are clear and specific brand guidelines about how your business expresses itself to the world. Brand strategy is no small feat, and I have always found it helpful to partner with specialists who help me articulate the visual voice for what I am creating.

Many business owners I speak with are hesitant to invest in brand identity, ending up instead with piecemeal clip-art-style logos that do not form a cohesive visual message. They fear "wasting" money, but I liken brand strategy to remodeling a house: The entire house is refreshed, functional, and able to generate greater impact and sales. It is not as if you are building a shed in the backyard, never to be used.

In our *Free Time* podcast conversation, Emily Heyward, co-founder of Red Antler, a Brooklyn-based agency renowned for working with many notable early-stage start-ups, encourages business owners to see brand strategy as an investment, not a cost.

"Brand is about having clarity around who you are from the beginning, and baking it into the foundation of your business," Emily said. "Your brand is not your logo. A logo is an important expression of your brand, and an unbelievable amount of work, thinking, and skill goes into creating a powerful logo—but it has to start with strategy, or it is meaningless. What is the idea this brand stands for, that you want to express across all different forms?"

When I hire specialists to create brand strategy for new projects, a huge part of their value is in the guidelines they deliver. This goes beyond straightforward items like fonts and colors, to address more nuanced do's and don'ts. For example, with *Pivot*, it was important to me that the arrow on the cover (and on worksheets) point up and to the right, a sign of progress and forward movement, not down or backward. How would my team know not to flip the arrow to fit a promotional image if I didn't mention it? Or, how would someone who doesn't have a natural eye for design know to line-up text elements on a grid if you don't teach them in your style guide?

In another example, a new team member asked about swearing and slang. I was happy she thought to ask, as it was missing from our guidelines. Podcast guests ask the same thing. I make a concerted effort not to swear in general, particularly on podcasts and in writing. After all, some shows and hosts pride themselves on being real; allowing, even welcoming, their guest's raw, unfiltered language. Others want to ensure shows are clean enough for parents to listen to while commuting even if kids are in the car, as I know is often the case for many of my listeners.

Define Your Brand

Consider hotel binders, or Airbnb digital guidebooks. They let guests know about local highlights to visit, features of the space, who to call for different services, and other helpful information for their stay. Similar to the Google Doc in the previous chapter that followed from the simple question, *What's your Wi-Fi password?*, your style guide is an important subset of your Manager Manual. Consistency is key to conveying a sophisticated, seamless, trustworthy brand. Style guidelines can include:

- **Intentions:** The tone you are setting overall, the "creative brand idea"

- **Vision:** What, how, and why this brand (and business) exists

- **Core values:** What differentiates you, and how to apply this to communications and creating new materials

- **Logo:** Wordmark with the company name

- **Icon:** Smaller graphic logo

- **Image guidelines:** Colors, size, placement, filters (or not)

- **Color palette:** Primary and secondary colors; hex codes for creating online graphics

- **Stationery set:** Digital and physical templates for business cards, envelopes, invoices

- **Font family:** Primary headline font, secondary fonts; what fonts should and should not be used for various use cases. For example, never use our logo font for something other than the name of our company.

- **Social media and ads:** Post templates, newsletter header, social or ad graphics for different formats and platforms

- **Photography:** Is stock photography acceptable? If so, what fits and what doesn't? What are the parameters for choosing images? Lighting, people (or not), clip art, inclusivity, size, cost, the platform you source from, etc.

- **Written communication:** What tone best represents the voice of your brand? Warm, chipper, serious? What is the personality of your brand? Playful, smart, curious, kind?

- **Where do you stand on using:** Emojis, animated GIFs, explicit language?

- **What's missing:** What feedback have you delivered recently to your team or specialists?

Remember, your Manager Manual and style guide are living documents. Even if the sections seem largely complete, each time you deliver feedback on work to improve it to your standards, that recipient should also automatically update those pointers in the related style guide section or process.

While I finished final edits for this chapter, Annie Murphy Paul released a book that had me squealing with glee, one that elucidates many scientific benefits behind the principles above.

In *The Extended Mind: The Power of Thinking Outside the Brain,* Annie outlines nine principles for expanding our intelligence: through our bodies, our surroundings, and our relationships. In a chapter on "Thinking with the Space of Ideas," she cites research on how visually mapping data increases intelligence.

That is *exactly* what externalizing your business mind will allow you to do. By seeing the details of your business, your operations, and your brand visually—in a cloud-based, neatly organized, easily navigable format—you and your team can become smarter and more strategic. Annie describes how the habit of *continuous offloading* clears space for making fresh observations and synthesizing ideas. She writes:

> *Whenever possible, we should* offload *information, externalize it, move it out of our heads and into the world. It relieves us of the burden of keeping a host of details "in the mind," thereby freeing up mental resources for more demanding tasks, like problem solving and idea generation. It also produces for us the "detachment gain," whereby we can inspect with our senses, and often perceive anew, an image or idea that once existed only in the imagination.*
>
> *. . . We should endeavor to transform information into an artifact, to make data into something* real—*and then proceed to interact with it, labeling it, mapping it, feeling it, tweaking it, showing it to others. Humans evolved to handle the concrete, not to contemplate the abstract. We extend our intelligence when we give our minds something to grab onto.*

With an externalized business mind, you too can delight in detachment from details. As Annie shares, studies show that individuals who can extend their minds solve problems more effectively in everyday life, even tapping into additional behavioral aspects of intelligence not currently measured by conventional IQ tests.

She remarks that "this nested set of principles, what we might call a 'curriculum of the extended mind,' is not currently taught in school or addressed in workplace training. That ought to change; learning to extend the mind should be an element of everyone's education."

I couldn't agree more. It is the driving impetus behind this book.

Create an Externalized Mind

Two-Sentence Summary

Create an external mind for your business by setting up a cloud-based, collaborative Manager Manual capturing every aspect of running your operations. Within it, create a style guide with parameters for expressing your brand values.

Give Yourself Permission

Let go of having to remember everything, trusting instead that what you need to know about your work, projects, and team has a home.

Ask Yourself

What stressors or small tasks could an externalized business mind free you from?

Do (or Delegate) This Next

Start a style guide if you don't have one, which will require setting aside time for deeper reflection. Ask team members to add to it every time you provide feedback.

3

Systematize the Spirit
of Your Business

The first thing you should always sell is joy.

—**Robert Herjavec**

Crickets. **Nada was the buzz emanating from my email inbox** shortly after I had committed to one of my biggest business investments several years ago. The lead of the project sent a welcome email and cc'd the team, and I replied to echo their sentiments with my excitement and availability for the kick-off call. Then, nothing happened. For days. I started to worry about whether my project was, in fact, in the right hands. I went from feeling like a distinguished guest to standing awkwardly by myself in the corner of a cocktail party. *Did I just make a huge mistake?* Only after I followed up a second time, already feeling like a bother in this new relationship, did anyone reply, and with a curt, perfunctory message. My first impression upon signing on the dotted line was not one that made me feel welcome, despite our email thread's subject line.

In sports, *unforced errors* are when the player makes a careless mistake because of nerves or lack of skill, not due to their opponent's skill or efforts. My onboarding experience with the team I described above—being met by silence during my first days as a client on their roster—is an example of an unforced error in business. The response time and message tone were simple mistakes that could be easily fixed through intentional systems design.

According to Joey Coleman, author of *Never Lose a Customer Again*, *buyer's remorse* is a common, even expected, stage along a new client's enrollment process. Design onboarding systems to preemptively address it by deciding in advance what you want their experience to be, designing a process to reflect those values, then doubling down to ensure new clients feel welcome. Ensure that every step clients take with your company is along a well-kept red carpet, rather than a discarded rug recently freed from the garage.

You can reduce unforced errors by systematizing the spirit of your business, operationalizing core values so they go beyond words into repeatable actions.

For example, the business value of "surprise and delight" has become a customer service cliché. To use it as an example, if it is a value you share, this necessitates further reflection: Have you put effort into your onboarding systems lately? Are they *good enough,* doing what is expected, or intentional and joyful? Just because you are aware of the cliché, or share a value of "surprise and delight," does not mean that you have your process dialed in: consistent and efficient, yet still personal and warm.

I know the team I described above cared about me and my project. Rather, it flags a customer experience systems gap, one that could be easily closed. I ended up grateful to have worked with them, *despite* my onboarding experience. Imagine, if on the day of the welcome message, flowers or a creative gift also arrived at my house. Or members of the team sent personalized welcome videos right away via email, through a service like BombBomb, about why they were excited to work on *this* particular project. Or, at a minimum, if they replied same-day to get our kick-off call on the books! That alone would send an impression of a buttoned-up team who is "on it." You choose how intricate you want this to be, but no matter what, be deliberate.

Operationalizing a value like "surprise and delight" can also be as straightforward as a helpful and candid customer service reply, as happened when I sent constructive feedback to one of my favorite gifting services, Greetabl. When Paige, their Customer Happiness Manager, said she would share it at the next team meeting, I felt heard. I was grateful that she would roll-up my feedback and they would take it into consideration.

When I replied to thank her, Paige responded with, "We get the best insight from Greetabl fanatics because you all tend to have our best interest at heart :)" That was true. Rather than sending me a run-of-the-mill reply, she had enough autonomy in her role to craft a warm, personalized response. I felt like I was corresponding with a real person (*imagine!*), not a customer-service robot. One year later, Greetabl's co-founder and CEO, Joe Fischer, offered his scheduling link in their weekly email blast so he could get direct feedback from customers on areas for improvement. A chance to chat with the founder of a favorite company? *Delightful!*

These special touches come from intentional process design for the values that embody the spirit of your business. Before I set-up my own systems for "surprise and delight," my team and I were only meeting this value intermittently. For example, after speaking engagements, I always liked to thank the host with a small gift or handwritten note. But as my day-to-day life got more complex, many of these gifting opportunities fell through the cracks. At one point, I was so delayed (*ahem*, bottlenecked) that we sent thank you gifts from November out in April, with micro-guilt compounding for every week that I knew they were delayed.

Our gifting process was muddy and confused. Although gifting was aligned with my value of generosity, we didn't have the workflow in place to make it happen smoothly—until we created a system for what John Ruhlin, author of *Giftology*, calls "strategic gifting."

I asked my team to take the first crack at writing a new gifting strategy. First by conducting research with industry experts like John, then drafting Manager Manual guidelines based on section prompts for purpose, philosophy, and process (there is a template for this in the Resources section at the back of the book). Together we considered questions such as: What is our philosophy on gifting? How can we empower team members to surprise and delight people randomly, without approval from me? What is our quarterly budget for this, and how can we track it as we go, encouraging team members to use the budget in full? How can we systematize the "life of a gift" as it travels from idea to delivery?

Next, we set-up a quarterly recurring task and a Kanban-style board in Notion called "Gifting Database" where any team member can add a new task, or card, for someone we would like to send a gift to. The card, with the recipient's name as the title, travels across this board with the following headings, representing six stages in the process:

1. **Idea:** Add a card as soon as we think of someone, so we don't forget.

2. **Missing information:** What details we need to find, such as a mailing address.

3. **Select gift and write message:** This allows me to personalize the note, even if team members place the order. We indicate what type of gift to send across five levels of investment, starting with a small surprise to something more substantial, with preferred vendors for each. A field for maximum spend gives the team room to make their own choices within each tier, without asking for added permission.

4. **Place order:** Once we personalize the message, we assign it to the next team member with a due date. Tagging cards with the gift category also allows for batch processing (i.e., ordering all gifts from a certain vendor at the same time).

5. **Track and confirm:** We check a "done" box once we know the gift has arrived.

6. **Archive:** This is the last step, once all above steps are complete.

Oh the sweet relief! Finally, we had operationalized values that were so important to me—generosity, surprise, and delight—but that I had been embarrassingly slow at creating systems to manage. Instead of continuing to drop the ball, or backing up dozens of gifts as I struggled to write notes or make decisions in a timely manner, my team and I were thrilled with how smooth the new process was, a feeling that telegraphed to our community with each subsequent gift delivered. Now our gifting process is as automatic and joyful as playing with a coin sorting machine as a child (*coins, what a throwback!*). I can drop a digital name card in the queue with a quick note, and I know that my team will take it from there. The output will be a well-organized deliverable that I do not have to revisit.

As Deborah Lahti, director of Pivot programs on my team, recounts, "When I was explaining our process to a friend, I highlighted the words *warmth* and *generosity*. If one thing has been cemented in my experience so far it is that warmth in communications is very important to JBE and that a spirit of generosity flows through everything we do, whether communicating with each other internally or with clients and community members externally." Deborah had been working with us for just two months when she shared this.

How quickly can you reinforce your most important values with your newest team members, not just giving permission to go above and beyond, but implementing a clearly outlined process, budget, and workflow?

CHAPTER 3 RECAP

Systematize the Spirit of Your Business

Two-Sentence Summary

You can take the guesswork out of expressing the spirit of your business values, even ones that don't seem at first brush to lend themselves to systematization. Avoid unforced errors by creating a clear process for things you do not want to slip through the cracks.

Give Yourself Permission

Create systems that bring your values to life, while still leaving room for personalization and special touches.

Ask Yourself

Where is there friction between what you say you value and how you are expressing this value to clients?

Do (or Delegate) This Next

Choose one value where you are experiencing friction with implementation. Take the first steps toward outlining your philosophy and systems for this value: What problems can you solve? How can your business more actively express this value?

Align > Design > Assign >

Energy

How you bake is as important as what you make. If you and your team tackle projects with resentment, that work is less likely to gain traction: stress will be embedded into its DNA. When you work with ease and joy, projects are far more likely to find their ideal audience and achieve lasting impact. Notice your energy as you work. Pay attention to interactions with your team and clients: When and with whom do you feel most in the zone? When do you feel most disconnected or drained? What are the most energizing aspects of your business, and how can you double-down on them? What interactions, relationships, or practices have bright, aligned energy and which ones create unwanted friction?

In this section, you will:

- Set purposeful intentions
- Let it be easy, let it be fun
- Give yourself golden hour

4

Set Purposeful Intentions

The life of one day is enough to rejoice . . . if you can be awakened,
that one day is vastly superior to one endless life of sleep.

—Zen Master Dōgen

Sarah Devereaux remembers the moment she redefined her relationship to work. A superstar in a fast-paced technology company rising rapidly up the ranks, she recalls looking even further up the proverbial ladder and asking herself, "Who cares if I make it to executive leadership if I am forty pounds overweight and perpetually exhausted with no time for my kids?"

She committed then and there to three overarching intentions for any new project or line of work: that it be joyful, contribute to her learning and growth, and create good in the world. Setting this intention allowed her to filter opportunities, especially ones that seemed good on the surface, but that were not energetically aligned with her new aims.

Not long after that, she went on maternity leave. She geared up to return to work, only to find that the company was reorging her out of her position. She was faced with two choices: take severance and move on, or find another role within the company. Sarah's clarity of intention allowed her to make the tough decision of leaving the secure choice behind after over a decade at the company, to take new risks in the form of a leadership role at a nascent start-up, while in parallel building out her own practice, Third Coast Coaching.

Purposeful intentions steer you through tough decisions toward your highest contribution. In her preface to the 25th Anniversary Edition of *Seat of the Soul* by Gary Zukav, Oprah Winfrey recounts the impact that setting intentions had as a seed of her career success. "It caused a profound shift in the way I conduct all my relationships, business and personal," she writes. "Using [the] personality to serve my soul—and making sure the two were aligned—changed the way I did everything."

Zukav's book sparked a shift in Oprah from "the disease to please" toward holding herself responsible for every action, thought, and feeling— her new "living creed." Oprah cites this passage from Zukav as the one that changed her life:

> *Every action, thought, and feeling is motivated by an intention, and that intention is a cause that exists as one with an effect. If we participate in the cause, it is not possible for us not to participate in the effect. In this most profound way we are held responsible for our every action, thought, and feeling, which is to say, for our every intention.*

As a result, Oprah created a new policy for her show producers: to state a clear intention for every show topic and interview over her storied thirty-year career as a talk-show host. She wouldn't interview a celebrity just because they were famous or had a movie coming out, unless it aligned with a larger intention to bring value to her audience. Before launching anything new Oprah checks in with herself by asking, "How do I use this in the service of something greater than myself?"

Sometimes you will be tested on how committed you are to intentions you set, and to remaining aligned with your highest work and strengths. These moments are tests asking, "How committed are you, *really*?" I see them with clients on the cusp of a courageous decision. These tempting-opportunity tests remind me of the candid camera "dollar on an invisible string" prank: you wind up chasing something seemingly attractive but not meant for you.

Weeks after Sarah launched her coaching services, a former colleague asked her to return as a pinch hitter to do some facilitation. It was tempting: The contract paid well, she had the time, and it could lead to significantly more work if the team decided to scale the workshop. On paper it seemed like a great opportunity, so she said yes.

"Then, I realized how much anxiety it was causing me," Sarah said. "I wasn't ready to jump back into that environment so soon after leaving, even as a contractor. I had to tell the person who hired me that I changed my mind. I wasn't going to do it." Once you are clear on your intentions, even great opportunities that are a wrong fit become sandpaper to the soul.

Part of intention-setting involves examining underlying, unconscious intentions muddying the waters of desired business outcomes. Business coach Jerry Colonna asks the powerful question, "How are you complicit in creating the conditions you say you don't want?"

As I shared in the introduction, I would often approach negotiations with potential corporate clients from a place of people-pleasing, wanting to be *liked*. I wanted them to see me as warm, accommodating, easy to work with. This intention directly interfered with my desire to generate strong licensing deals that honored my intellectual property (IP) and what I knew were market rates, ones I had benchmarked with industry colleagues. Time after time, my unspoken desire to be liked got in the way of my equally strong desire to negotiate a great deal.

Turns out I was not alone in this particular challenge. Only years later did an advisor, Stephan Mardyks, tell me how difficult it is for an IP creator to negotiate their own deals for this very reason; their primary role is to show up as the friendly expert, while someone else can come in and be tougher when talking with procurement or legal, without as much reputational impact.

Intention-setting can be powerful at a more granular level: *within* everything you create, and even when you are sensing what steps to take next. For Penney Peirce, author of *The Intuitive Way*, *Frequency*, and others, the focus starts with imagination and self-entertainment. She stopped using the word *intention* altogether because it "futurizes" things, replacing it with *focus* instead. During a podcast conversation for our Penney & Jenny series, she explained it this way: *Thinking* happens in our left-brain, whereas *imagination* happens in our right brain, where unlimited possibilities exist.

"If you would like to entertain certain opportunities, put your attention on that idea or reality in your imagination first," Penney said. "That's a higher frequency. Focus your attention into the imaginal idea and enjoy it, really experience it in a tactile way, and have fun with it. Soon you may have synchronicities or sudden changes, but it's not like you are working so hard to go through all these steps and pay your dues to get it. It just shows up."

With this perspective of play instead of willpower, you are better able to tap into the flow of collective consciousness that helps everyone do what Penney calls "the next just-right thing." She calls it "stop and drop," a process of getting quiet enough to allow *the next just-right thing* to bubble up from within your field.

"You don't attract ideas and opportunities from the outside because there is no outside," she said. "Everything is already within you, and whatever you need emerges in the moment with you when you need it." When you no longer need the information or experience, it goes back on the shelf, a "pantry with millions of ideas."

> **CHAPTER 4 RECAP**

Set Purposeful Intentions

Two-Sentence Summary

Set clear intentions for the work you do. Align your energy and the project plan by starting with your desired impact.

Give Yourself Permission

Say no—*no excuses needed*—to people or opportunities that drain or diminish you.

Ask Yourself

What one word or theme would you like your business to help you achieve this year? What word or theme captures the impact you want to have on others?

Do (or Delegate) This Next

Set an intention for work you plan to tackle next, before you begin.

5

Let It Be Easy, Let It Be Fun

All our sweetest hours fly fastest.

—Virgil

So many business owners start with The Statistic in mind. You know the one I'm talking about: *that* one, the one that offers some variation on the sobering perils of taking an entrepreneurial risk, that nine out of ten businesses fail within their first five years. Or that of one hundred start-ups, only twenty will remain after five years, and after fifteen years, only *one* will remain.

If the majority of small businesses are doomed to failure before they even start, The Statistic goads us to buckle down and get ready to work. *Hard.* Build sweat equity the grueling way, with your blood, sweat, and tears.

Before you affirm that all great accomplishments inevitably involve hard work, and that the qualities of grit and tenacity are what separate those who make it from those who don't, consider that there are two types of challenging work: hard work and Hard Work.

Lowercase *hard work* is rewarding. It's challenging, and it pushes us to the edge of our stretch zone, where we discover flow. Uppercase *Hard Work* is worn as a badge of suffering, one that mostly leads to burnout. There is a better way, and this better way begins with us.

How you build is as important as whatever you create. *Easeful work* means aligning with your natural talents and holding a positive attitude; it does not mean that the work itself is easy or without challenge, especially for others who do not share your particular gifts and interests.

To illustrate this, pretend you are traveling to see a friend, and they baked you a cake in celebration of your visit. Imagine a split-screen that shows two outcomes unfolding side-by-side.

Cake Baking: Scenario One

With sweat dripping down his brow, and batter splashed on his cheek and across his now-soiled favorite shirt, your friend dons an oven mitt and pulls a yummy-smelling cake out of the oven. Fatigue and frustration building in his voice, he hands you a fresh piece.

"Here," he sighs with exhaustion. "I made this for you."

No sooner have you taken a bite, he collapses onto the couch, complaining about how hard baking is, and how concerned he is about what you will think of his cooking skills, and how it tastes. He is desperate for praise.

How does this hypothetical cake taste? How do you feel eating it, knowing that your friend has completely exhausted himself attempting this "gift"? Perhaps you would feel equal parts grateful and guilty, and become a bit distracted by the consequences of this well-intended confectionary gesture on your friend's mood. It is hard to enjoy the fruits of his labor, given that the process itself seemed so stressful.

Cake Baking: Scenario Two

Now imagine returning to your friend's house for a second baking experiment, one year later.

As soon as you walk in, his favorite holiday music is playing even though it is only June. He's dancing, singing, and having a blast! With delight in his eyes and glee in his voice, he pours you a glass of bubbly as you sit and converse. He is immersed in baking, yet exudes warmth and focus as you tell him what's new with you. He's listening deeply, and investing care into you as he tends to his latest creation. You can tell he's improvising, sprinkling all manner of random pantry sweets into this one-of-a-kind cake, tasting joyfully along the way.

He doesn't set an oven timer. As he relaxes with you in the living room, he's leaning on his sense of smell to know when the cake is done. At last, when the kitchen smells irresistibly delicious, he gets up to turn the oven light on. Sure enough, the cake has risen perfectly in the middle, with a golden brown crust forming along the sides. Your friend pulls out the cake, sets it on the counter, and pours you a glass of almond milk, his curated beverage to match the taste and experience he's creating for *this* particular cake.

"Here you go!" He says, eyes sparkling. "I made this for you!" It is clear that he can't wait for you to try it, as he is staring with eager anticipation as you try your first bite. "So, how is it?!?"

"Incredible!" You respond, taking another bite. "What *is* that, a blueberry?" you ask of the secret ingredients that ended up creating a cake you have never tasted before. "Yep! And there's coconut oil, almond butter, chocolate chips, and banana—and, wait for it—*popcorn!*"

How does this cake taste? Are you enjoying imagining eating it?

In the two scenarios above, which cake tastes better? Surely the second, and not just because of the ingredients—because it was made with care, joy, and creativity. Because you know that it was made with love, just for you, and that eating a slice not only energizes you, but your friend who made it as well.

The DNA of a business, relationship, creative project, or any living organism is set at the outset; how it starts, and how it develops. Those energetic fingerprints are embedded into every fiber of the final product. Two final products may look the same, but how they were created matters, even if imperceptible to the recipient. Perhaps not all recipients, or customers, or readers, or listeners will notice, but many will—even if they can't quite put their finger on it.

I have been the cake baker in both of these scenarios, and not just in the kitchen. *Who are we kidding?* My cooking skills more often mirror scenario one. My husband, Michael, is the one who models inventive, joyful cooking with scenario two. As a *synesthete*, someone who perceives information through multiple senses, Michael cooks like he paints, "tasting" colors to create unique flavor combinations. He feeds our dog with the same reverence, producing each and every bowl as a product for his fictional restaurant, Ryder's Plate. Lebanese culture celebrates food as love, as generosity, and as self-expression. I come from the land of food as function. I admire seeing others cook with in-the-moment abandon, as Michael learned from his mother, Aida, and from his grandmother Archalouis before that.

I have also been both cake bakers with my two previous books. As I mentioned in the introduction, my first book, *Life After College*, launched in 2011. As a first-time author moonlighting while working at Google, by the time I started my sabbatical and launched the book, I was already in desperate need of a break. I remember talking about how *hard* it all was. While that book did well, I was determined not to make it feel so heavy next time.

When *Pivot* launched five years later, I made a point to enjoy and be grateful for every part of the process. In my podcast and newsletter where I shared behind-the-scenes updates on my process, I made sure never to complain or call it hard. Writing a book, after all, is a privilege, as is launching it. Sure, it is complex, but I started to appreciate and embrace the creative problem solving involved. Nobody wants to attend a launch party—*or read a book!*—where the author seems haggard, overworked, and overwhelmed. Nor will that book have a "special sauce" quality if the author dragged themselves through writing it.

With this third book, *Free Time*, I had so much fun during the writing process that I was *sad* just before the final edits were turned in! Over a span of ten years, by repeatedly reminding myself of these cake-baking principles and putting them into practice, my relationship to book writing transformed. It evolved from a pressured, anxiety-ridden, inner-critic-fueled burden into an immersive creative playground that I didn't want to leave.

Close The Loop: Indecision *Is* Your Decision

Don't trade time for money, as the saying goes. Don't trade time for open loops either. Open loops are like record skips; niggling glitches, thought-itches that aren't scratched yet. They represent unresolved questions requiring an answer that lead to rumination when left unsolved.

Sometimes no amount of spinning will yield fruitful results; the indecision itself is a signal. It consumes energy that could be put to better use. Decision fatigue is real. We only have so many creative-thinking cycles each day.

At a major inflection point in my business, I spent six months trying to figure out how to move a private community off of a certain social media platform whose growth-at-all-costs practices grated against my values. At first, I thought it was a simple question of which new software to use.

Only after months of churning, indecision, and even taking a community design class, did I realize that my tech indecision— this open loop—was not actually about software. Software was only the surface-level issue. It reflected qualms about my time and next direction. I spent six months burning energy debating which tool to select, before realizing that the indecision was its own decision. The best course of action was downshifting the program to focus my energy on fewer projects, reducing the need for new software altogether. My indecision helped me see that I could not juggle everything I was responsible for in business and family, while also pouring energy into something new, at least without being mediocre at all of it. The new projects would be getting leftovers, fragments of frenzied attention. If I had not made that tough choice, this book would not exist. As I say in *Pivot*, "Decisions are data." Sometimes *indecisions* are data too.

If something is too hard, take it as a signal to pause, regroup, and revise your approach. If the process of what you are doing, building, or creating is no longer fun, *stop*.

One of my mantras is "Let it be easy, let it be fun." Every time I have paused a project to remind myself of this, I have come up with something even better. Those upgraded solutions are more innovative, creative, and authentic than the original direction beset by friction.

Remember: Don't do *us* any favors! Nobody wants to eat a cake that you hated making.

CHAPTER 5 RECAP

Let It Be Easy, Let It Be Fun

Two-Sentence Summary

How you bake is as important as what you make. Enjoying the process imprints positive energetic fingerprints into the final product.

Give Yourself Permission
Pause when a project feels hard; regroup to find an even more resonant approach.

Ask Yourself
How can you transform or release what is burdensome in your business? For a problem area: What new, next approach would be easy and fun?

Do (or Delegate) This Next
Identify the project that is draining you most. Do something delightful as a next step, no matter how tiny.

6

Give Yourself Golden Hour: What's Your Job Today?

Sleep is a time machine to breakfast.

—**Meme**, author unknown

In photography, *golden hour* **refers to the exquisite quality of light** just after sunrise and just before sunset. Cinematographers call it "magic hour" and arrange shoots during this time. Subjects appear perfectly lit in soft reddish hues, glowing and radiant, in contrast to the harsher light with unfavorable shadows or glare on their faces when the sun is fully up.

Consider that you, too, have *golden hours*, one or two times per day that are optimal for your peak energy and creativity, given your unique circadian rhythms. Make sure you allocate your golden hours for your best work. In the morning, I can get five to ten times more done than during the afternoon witching hours before dinner, when as one of my clients put it, "I don't even know my own name."

Another strategy you may find helpful for knowing *what* to slot into your precious golden hours is to ask yourself: What is my job today?

It might not be what you think.

When I ask the question, *"What's your job today?"* what comes to mind? You might think about the work that you do to get paid, whether you work for somebody else or you work for yourself. Oftentimes when you are self-employed, a significant chunk goes toward working for your clients. In addition to whoever is paying your bills, you also have a slew of inboxes. Sometimes you spend the day or week working for notifications, responding to other people.

What do you *want* your job to be today?

There may be periods of life where you say, "My job today is helping my kids with school," or "making sure our puppy is sufficiently exhausted and engaged so as not to chew up the entire house."

This question does involve trade-offs. There are only one or two jobs that you can unfailingly commit to every day during that ideal golden-hour window with your best-available energy, which is why it is so important to be discerning about what that job is. This dovetails with what we know about neuroscience, and the brain's use of energy. The brain uses significant energy for intense thinking, so it is important to slot that time into our schedule intentionally.

Setting-up daily streaks can play a powerful role in reducing decision-fatigue about what to work on, and will help make what is most important to you—your job today—a priority. Once you are on a streak, you don't want to disappoint yourself by breaking it. With things like meditating, working out, and doing your creative work or strategic thinking about your business, those streaks compound. Each day is not equally powerful. It is day one that is powerful in itself, but by day ten, you get compound benefits of accumulating many days in a row.

I experienced this when I shifted to daily podcasting, formerly weekly, for three months after the pandemic hit in 2020. My mind became faster and more creative at generating topic ideas. By day ten, my podcast was better than it was on day one. With streak momentum growing, my interviewing skills improved, and my focus was sharper. Every podcast episode is a project unto itself; in our case, containing over fifty steps across seven stages.

I became faster at taking episodes from recorded to published; what was taking weeks now only took several hours.

My streak then came to a screeching halt that summer, when restless quarantiners in our neighborhood started lighting illegal fireworks every night, all night, for two months. Then, in a cruel twist of irony as our local fireworks abated, a port explosion in Beirut—one of the biggest non-nuclear explosions in history—wreaked havoc on Michael's home city. Miraculously, his family was okay even though they live just one mile away, with shattered glass and twisted metal scattered throughout their home. His city was in ruin; entire neighborhoods equivalent to Manhattan's West Village—filled with commerce, restaurants, residential buildings, and so many memories—crumbled. The country plunged deeper into crisis.

None of us could sleep more than a few consecutive hours in a row during this time. Nearly two months into what felt like psychological torture, my physical health cratered. We weren't getting sleep. We were cranky and grieving for Michael's country. I couldn't think, or work, or conduct interviews anymore; my words were gone. Meeting basic responsibilities became taxing, not to mention lost hope of doing any actual work. Exercising fell by the wayside.

What's your job today?

This question, combined with a new streak, saved me from spiraling out.

For the foreseeable future, my job would be working out. That was my most important goal each day, and I would do "work" work as a bonus. I put up an autoresponder, and gave myself guilt-free permission to exercise during my best energy window in the late morning, then stretch, shower, and only think about what to work on after that.

I knew that some of my lack of life force, drive, and motivation had to do with not applying myself physically in the way that all of us have evolved to do. "Sitting has become the new smoking of our generation," as Nilofer Merchant shared in her viral TED Talk on the subject. True to the trend, I pandemic-purchased a Peloton, and it was one of the best financial choices I made that year. My friend and I remarked how this applied to our businesses.

We were *happy* to each fork over nearly $3,000 because of how much joy these stationary bikes brought into our lives. To set a proper tone upon its arrival, I committed to a daily streak, one that lasted unbroken for fourteen weeks, primarily by deciding "my job today," first and foremost, was working out.

"My job is working out" was a deeply beneficial mindset when I needed it. My exercise streak propelled me to a point where I looked forward to the daily endorphin delivery.

Later, I shifted to "my job is my podcast," or writing this book. That means that the first thing I do before I do anything else, the one and only most important task each day is to move my "job" forward. Record a podcast episode, write five hundred words for this book, be present with my family.

Or, as my friend Ann says, "My job is cooking a healthy meal," despite having at least two other official jobs. Ann works a full-time job as senior counsel for a large pharmaceutical company and has a side hustle running estate sales on weekends. She prides herself on taking care of her college-aged sons who pop in and out when they are home from school.

I have been a fortuitous taste-tester with a front-row countertop seat to her time-saving kitchen strategies. She had practice finding smart systems that work: Ann started cooking meals for her family every day when she was nine years old. For starters, she does not bother asking what anyone wants to eat for dinner, which immediately reduces decision fatigue. She grew up spending summers at her family's mozzarella farm in Italy, so every vegetable dish starts with olive oil, smashed (not chopped) garlic, and salt. *Everything* is delicious.

When I asked how Ann has the energy to cook healthy meals every night after a long day of work, she exclaimed in her signature New Jersey accent, "*Nobody has time for that!*" Instead, she spends fifteen minutes in the morning cooking in a single pot (less mess) before her first meeting, while everyone in the house is still asleep. No one hovering in the kitchen means they can't weigh in on her dinner menu. In the time it takes for the coffee to brew, Ann has prepared a sumptuous, healthy meal that will last for at least two days; only one if guests are around, because none of us can help going back for seconds and thirds.

Free Up Even More Founder Time

Building on the first Founder Time block you set aside in the Free Time Framework chapter, it is time now to create more containers, within your golden hour windows, for strategic thinking. This is a "do not pass go" moment! You will never free your time if you leave it to chance; you must claim it intentionally and systematically. If you can, take the next fifteen minutes for the items below:

1. Block off the ***next possible*** Monday or Friday you can, ideally both, by adding an all-day Do Not Schedule (DNS) block on your calendar. If you prefer to block off a different day of the week, that works too. Some people appreciate a mid-week break for running errands on Wednesdays, for example. Some meetings may be impossible to move within the next week or two, so this might happen three to six weeks out. If you operate a brick-and-mortar business, this may also take more creative finagling to find coverage.

2. Optional, if it resonates: Set-up a weekly ***recurring*** all-day DNS on your calendar for the day/s of the week you selected. Super bonus: Create a ***daily*** DNS that recurs during the week when you are most energized, your golden hour/s.

3. Audit the ***already-scheduled*** meetings on your calendar that fall into these DNS blocks in the next two months. They will fall into two categories: easily movable (just ask, it is not the end of the world) or must-keep. Move the ones you can, and know that soon, as long as you don't schedule over your DNS blocks (aside from rare high-priority

exceptions) you will be well on your way to Founder Time Freedom.

4. If you have team members, particularly someone who helps with scheduling, let them know not to add anything to these blocks unless it is urgent and they check with you first.

5. Tell your inner board of directors the same thing! Boundaries are necessary for freeing up time to work *on* your business. If you do not set them, clients and everyone else will happily (even if unknowingly) request, schedule over, and steamroll your golden hours—the ones you *need* to envision, design, and build a thriving business. Now is the time to address this, as it only gets exacerbated by success.

6. **Bonus:** Add something just for you in one of your newly created Founder Time blocks, even if the first one occurs a few weeks out. Maybe it is a fitness class, lunch with a friend, or even a staycation. My friend Lindsay considers these part of her "People Operations culture budget," similar to the perks a company like Google might dish out, even though she is her only full-time employee.

Take the inquiry, "What is my job today?" one step further by expanding your job titles beyond the traditional scope. One of my coaching clients appointed an imaginary Chief Wholeness Officer to counterbalance the demanding inner voice of her VP of Productivity. Recruit a fictional VP of Wellness, VP of Fascinating Projects, or VP of Curiosity.

Every day until further notice, orient around making your job today happen, ideally within your golden hours. You will wake up with a clear, guilt-free focus. Remind yourself that doing this *one* thing means it has been a successful day.

CHAPTER 6 RECAP

Give Yourself Golden Hour: What's Your Job Today?

Two-Sentence Summary

For your most energetic window of the day, decide: What is your job today? Schedule Founder Time blocks to work on your business during your golden hours.

Give Yourself Permission

Define success based on the linchpin activity that you want to slot into your best energy windows this week, no matter how urgent other deadlines seem.

Ask Yourself

What is your job *today?* (Remember, it might not be what you think.) How ambitious do you want to be right now, and in what areas? What trade-offs are you okay with making?

Do (or Delegate) This Next

What would give you the biggest boost and sense of accomplishment this week? Identify your golden hours and block that time in your calendar for your most important job this week, perhaps even starting a tiny seven-day streak.

Align > Design > Assign >

.

Strengths

Surely you have heard the phrase, "How you do one thing is how you do everything." How can that be true when the work that you most enjoy lights you up so much that you could immerse yourself for hours, forgetting to eat and reluctantly peeling yourself away only for bio breaks? Contrast that with the work you dislike most: you drag yourself to your desk, muster your limited willpower only to apply yourself to a task you dread, most likely yielding only passable results. How you do that one thing you love is *not* how you do everything. It is a pocket of blissful work that yields greater results than working on what you are mediocre at. The good news about being a business owner is that you have full autonomy over your time and strategic projects. The bad news? The responsibility is yours to fill or reduce the many roles that aren't aligned with your unique strengths. Aligning with your strengths requires ongoing reflection: Are you doing the work that you and only you can do? How can you remove barriers to create more space for your strengths?

In this section, you will:
- Build your business intuition
- Continuously bust bottlenecks
- Embrace imperfection

7

Build Your Business Intuition

As long as we settle for thinking inside the brain, we'll remain bound by the limits of that organ. But when we reach outside it with intention and skill, our thinking can be transformed. It can become as dynamic as our bodies, as airy as our spaces, as rich as our relationships—as capacious as the whole wide world.

—Annie Murphy Paul

I t was a quiet pre-dawn morning, and I was happily reading in candlelight. Until I almost burned the house down.

More on that in a moment.

Some people do not believe in coincidences or synchronicity. But some signs are so on-the-nose it would be impossible *not* to interpret them as divine redirects delivered on a silver platter. What I love about coincidences—signs, symbols, sign-posts—is that they are often delivered with a wink, a smile, and sometimes a loving smack upside the forehead. Even for the biggest skeptics, who say that what we notice and how we interpret signs is simply based on our own biases, we are still the ones noticing *something* catchy in our environment and deriving meaning from it.

Books seem to fall off the shelf in perfect timing. Penney Peirce's classic *The Intuitive Way* did just that for me in 2014. After picking it up, a pathway opened to a new way of operating in my business and my life. I stopped stressing and striving, and instead listened to the steady stream of clues always surrounding me, but previously unacknowledged. Penney has since become a dear friend, and we have had over a dozen podcast conversations on her book topics, such as frequency, soul groups, dreams, perception, and transparency. Her books, and these conversations, sparked one of my most cherished *friendtorships* and a powerful, delightful way of doing business.

Intuition can be one of your greatest strengths in business, but it must be based on a mix of education and practice, developing your "book" and "street" smarts. Pay attention to what happens when you listen to your intuition. Penney recommends keeping a record of those moments and evaluating how they shake out.

As she cautions in *The Intuitive Way*, a pessimistic attitude can impede the flow of information. "Beware of unnecessary negativity," she writes. "On the other hand, *needing* things to be positive can lead to gullibility. Without common sense, intuition can turn to delusion. Yet without optimism, it's difficult for intuition to occur at all."

How do you know if your intuition is leading you in the right direction? Return to the Free Time gauge: *friction* versus *flow*. Pay attention to abrupt signals, surprises, or alarming occurrences, such as the morning I almost burned the house down. These moments can indicate when you are no longer in flow, despite what your heart wants, or what your mind thinks you *should* be doing. These signs are speaking to you, letting you know that it is time to lean on your intuition as a strength signaling what to do next.

On this particular morning, it was 3 a.m. and I could not fall back asleep. I often fantasize about springing out of bed and stealing a few quiet hours to myself before the world and my household wakes up. At 4 a.m. I caved and got out of bed. I had one chapter left on a roarin' good read, so I made a cup of coffee, lit a candle, and dug in.

Except that candle happened to be underneath a stack of papers that I hadn't noticed in the pitch black of the living room, a particular stack representing a big decision I was pondering.

Next thing I knew, while reading happily in candlelight, our protective German shepherd, Ryder, quickly stood up, ears at attention. *That's unusual*, I thought, before noticing the papers—perfect kindling—were aflame.

I started blowing (*duh, wrong move*) and the flame size doubled.

I grabbed the flaming pile of papers and quickly took them to the sink, thankfully avoiding hand burns in the process. I ran them under water, looking at the newly charred pile atop dirty dishes, and I started laughing.

This stack of papers contained over a dozen real estate listings for properties with restored barns in the country. I owned a rental property in California that had just become vacant, and it was not in good enough shape to be competitive on the rental market any longer. The stack of papers that were now aflame contained options for a 1031 exchange of the California property for an equivalently priced house in rural Connecticut, offsetting capital gains taxes from the sale.

Although New York had always felt like my soul city, it was late October of 2020, and I was exhausted. I was experiencing what Dr. Ann Masten calls *surge capacity*, fried from nearly a decade of city life, and from keeping my business marginally afloat while raising a puppy and navigating a pandemic. So you can understand the magical thinking that had me fantasizing about parlaying a property I owned into one that would provide more spaciousness, quiet, and nature.

Except the pile of options literally caught on fire. "Burn it all down" was no longer just a tongue-in-cheek catch phrase (I had written that part of this book just one week prior!), it was the *actual* outcome of my property search.

Whether you believe in an active cosmic intelligence at work or not, coincidences activate our own intuitive clues through the process of interpreting them. At that moment I knew one thing for sure: I should *not* travel to go see a single one of these properties. In fact, this most likely meant to stop the search altogether. We had one property visit set up for the following day, and that clue remained unaddressed. Did the burning pile of papers mean that the red barn would not work out? Or did it mean that was the *only* one we should consider?

Upon visiting the property, I knew. *Burn the search down*, the entire search, and do not go further down this road of barn-in-the-country options. *Save yourself the time and trouble.* My mind might have taken me on several more two-hour train rides each way to visit those places, but my intuition, in the form of reading the burned-listing tea leaves, saved me the hassle.

That awareness does not make decisions any easier in the moment. When we got home from the visit, one day after the papers burned up, I crashed. I burst into tears. I was dejected and regretful for the time I had spent chasing this new set of rabbits. The search appeared to be for no reason, and now it provided no new relief at the end of such a trying year. As the saying goes, unanswered prayers are a form of "no, not yet, or not good enough for you." I would have to sit with the discomfort and uncertainty, and wait to be shown the next step.

Sure enough, six months later, I sold the California property and decided to double-down on myself and my new direction. After a decade of self-employment, I was ready to go all-in on a new book and podcast. You are holding the results of that decision in your hands, as I decided to work with an independent publisher, Ideapress, for greater freedom and flexibility. I invested much of the property sale proceeds into pursuing this new direction, and I am grateful you are here reading as a result!

Start to develop your own systems intuition, a strength that can be further refined over time. Ask yourself: What am I noticing? Where am I experiencing friction in my business? What is that friction trying to tell me? What signals or serendipities are occurring, and how can I sense clues about the one best next step?

Then, trust that an answer will emerge when it is time. As Penney says, "I may not know the answer right now, but some part of me already knows, and this part will get through to me at just the right moment. I know what I need to know just when I need to know it."

Most of all, practice applying your intuition, noticing when it speaks to you in your day-to-day business activities and larger moves. When Howard Behar, former president of Starbucks Coffee Company, went to interview with the CEO, Howard Shultz, he recalled intuitively sensing that taking the job would be the right move.

"This will probably sound strange to you," he said during our *Pivot* podcast conversation, "but I believe the walls talk, that walls absorb negative and positive energy. I could just feel it. As I walked through, I knew that it just felt right. The walls were talking to me, saying that this was a good place."

Howard accepted the job in 1989. For twenty-one years, he led Starbucks' domestic business as president of North America. He became the founding president of Starbucks International, opening the very first store outside of North America and Japan. During his tenure, he participated in the growth of the company from twenty eight stores to over fifteen thousand stores spanning five continents, then served on the board of directors for twelve years before retiring. All that started from feeling into the energy within Starbucks headquarters' walls on the day of his interview.

"I was never let down once," Howard said. "From the very beginning it fit me perfectly like a glove."

CHAPTER 7 RECAP

Build Your Business Intuition

Two-Sentence Summary

Intuition is a skill that you can develop, one that provides essential information for strategic direction and decisions. Strengthen your business intuition through active listening, learning from others, observation, and subtle messages from synchronicities.

Give Yourself Permission

Trust your intuitive hits, even if you do not have a verbal or rational explanation (*yet!*) to validate the "memos" or make sense of your insights.

Ask Yourself

Oprah says, "Your life is always speaking to you. It speaks in whispers guiding you to your next right step." Are you listening? What is your life whispering to you right now?

Do (or Delegate) This Next

Try this exercise: Stand up and close your eyes. Frame a question that results in yes or no by starting with: "Is it in the highest good for . . . ?" Notice if your body naturally leans forward or recoils back. That's your intuition speaking to you: forward means *yes*, backward means *no*.

8

Continuously Bust Bottlenecks

*Those who flow as life flows know they need no other force.**

—Lao Tzu

**But one must do some flowing where there is an income stream.*

—My Dad

I n early 2021, the *Ever Given*, an enormous ship longer than the Empire State Building carrying 220,000 tons of containers, got stuck between the banks of the Suez Canal, a central trade route off the coast of Egypt, due to heavy winds as it traveled from Asia to Europe.

For six days, four hundred ships backed up for miles, creating a domino effect of delays stalling as much as $10 billion of cargo for each day that the behemoth *Ever Given* blocked the waterway, creating a backlog in global shipping that would take months to clear up.

Perhaps you have heard the phrase, "A rising tide lifts all boats." Well, that is exactly what the world was waiting for to free global commerce again.

If the (up-for-debate) *butterfly effect* refers to tiny movements that can have massive impact across the world, the *bottleneck effect* means one broken link can prevent or delay all manner of progress, months and years into the future. When two business's bottlenecks collide? *Watch out.* You will end up as I did, getting dropped by your accountant two weeks before taxes were due, in an emotional explosion of overwhelm on all sides.

Finding yourself embarrassed, missing important deadlines, or profusely apologizing to others on a regular basis can be signals that you are blocking the Suez Canal in your business. I once had the opportunity to submit an excerpt of *Pivot* to a magazine whose audience I was excited to reach. Due to a failure of delegation—neglecting to assign an owner other than myself— this fell into the email abyss as we waited for permissions from the publisher before sending my submission to the magazine editor. By the time I realized no *one* person owned this, I had missed the deadline and the opportunity. I was embarrassed to not have followed my own teachings on a relatively straightforward set of next steps.

Cliché it may be, the adage "you are only as strong as your weakest link" is true in business. Your weakest link is a bottleneck preventing the smooth flow of work from an operations perspective, or the one preventing you from taking on new work or clients. You might be the best in the world at what you do, but if your systems are broken or outdated, your clients will quickly become frustrated and go elsewhere. The fancy term for this is *theory of constraints*: an ongoing process of identifying and then solving for the greatest limiting factor (*limfac*, for short) in the way of progress toward a goal.

Sure, some businesses create bottlenecks by design. Consider any hot new restaurant in a big city. The entire point is that you *can't* get a reservation. Sometimes they are easy to spot: At DŌ, a small shop in the West Village selling edible raw cookie dough, or Prince Street Pizza in my former Nolita neighborhood, the lines snaking around the block signal scarcity and irresistible goods. As a result, the perceived value of their products goes *up*, not down. The service bottlenecks in proportion to demand are illustrated by these daily lines, letting passers-by know that whatever is inside *must* be worth waiting for.

Consider a different type of bottleneck: the business owner who doesn't delegate, therefore letting important client emails fall through the cracks, like a client I'll call Maria. She was decades into her career, with a glowing reputation as an executive coach. However, due to her resistance to technology and setting up business systems, she still handled scheduling, sales calls, onboarding, invoicing, contracts, *and* service delivery—and that was on top of the marketing and ongoing public original thinking she was putting out into the world! The line out the door for her services put her at risk for seeming (and becoming) scattered and overwhelmed.

Instead of raising her prices to reduce demand or communicating her capacity by saying, "I would love to work with you, but I currently have a waitlist. I can let you know when my next opening is," she continued to accept every client interested in working with her, at whatever times worked best for *them*. As a result, she worked around the clock and on weekends, coaching during the day and handling all the related admin at night. Her bottleneck stemmed from an underlying scarcity-related belief: that demand would go away if she did not meet it all right now. *Feast or famine,* she figured. *I'd better take it all on, since I don't know how things will go in the future.*

Contrast this with Lindsay Pedersen, owner of consulting firm Ironclad Brand Strategy, and author of *Forging an Ironclad Brand*. After years of trial-and-error, Lindsay, a former Clorox brand manager, now sets her prices purposefully high. She prices services based on the *value* she delivers (not her time), so that she does not need to take on every client. In fact, a successful quarter often means working with just a handful of clients. Lindsay offers prospective clients the same three packages with non-negotiable prices, listed on her website, so that she does not need to send customized proposals. The rate card is the same no matter who is interested, with three price tiers (and sets of deliverables) that reflect "good, better, best" versions of her offerings.

Even though Lindsay prefers to still lead the culmination of each project—a two-day in-person strategy retreat with the CEO and executive team—she also subcontracts some of the work leading up to these retreats to people she has trained in her brand strategy methodology, including a project manager who handles client communications. Lindsay does not feel the need to step back from delivering services entirely, because that is her unique genius and the work she loves. But she is working on building a train-the-trainer (TTT) version of her programs, which provides a dual win for busting bottlenecks: creating the materials necessary to onboard a team member for serving her clients, and allowing organizations to roll out her teachings internally, in a more scalable way.

Bottlenecks are a systems or delegation issue: Either someone is not letting go or not deciding quickly enough, or there is not a smooth enough system in place yet to meet the demand.

When I first read *The E-Myth Revisited*, a bestselling business classic by Michael Gerber, during my first years of self-employment, it did not sink in. Gerber lost me at setting up my business with the efficiency and scale of McDonald's, and I could not envision how my location-independent, knowledge-worker business related to the central story of the woman who owned the bakery, juggling her three hats of entrepreneur, manager, and technician. Gerber emphasized building one's business operations (and documentation surrounding it) as if you were going to expand to five thousand locations, saying, "The true product of a business is the business itself."

I put the book down midway through and kept moving, wondering what all the fuss was about in entrepreneurial circles. It wasn't until I picked it back up, *eight* years later, that I realized just how much work I was unnecessarily holding onto, and how that was holding me back. Gerber reinforces the importance of getting out of the way of the day-to-day with zingers like, "If your business depends on you, you don't own a business—you have a job," and "Most companies don't work, the people who own them do."

Dave Crenshaw started running his own business at twenty-three years old, and for two decades now he has counseled entrepreneurs on achieving greater focus and getting out of their own way. He helps them pare down from "ten to twenty different job descriptions" to one or two focused roles in line with what he calls their *most valuable activities* (MVAs). The more time business owners spend on their MVAs, the more valuable their business becomes. Spending too much time on the rest, the LVAs or *less valuable activities*, prevents the business from growing and keeps the owner stuck.

When he onboards new team members, Dave communicates his own MVAs: creating valuable training and delivering that training. To hold himself accountable to delegating as much as possible, he tells his team: "If I am doing *anything* other than those two things, I am not leading properly." Twenty years into his own business, by practicing this skill, Dave is proud to say that he now spends 80 to 90 percent of his time working on his MVAs.

To identify your MVAs, Dave suggests estimating what it would cost hourly to replace you, the owner, across various tasks in the business. How much would you have to pay to delegate different elements of what you do on a marketplace like Upwork? Some tasks will be $12 an hour, some $50, some $500, and others still that are so unique to you they may be worth thousands of dollars or more. Hold onto the most valuable MVAs; everything else is an LVA, so work to delegate those over time.

Dave challenges you not to *assume* a task is impossible to delegate. If you were selling your business, what *would* the next owner do? These thought exercises will increase the value of your business, reducing *key person risk* since it won't be as dependent on you.

You might be bottlenecking your business in the following ways:

- **Your to-do list:** How many items have been hovering in the low-priority pile, and for how long?

- **Your services:** Are you serving your clients in a way that provides an ideal experience? Or are things falling through the cracks because you have too much on your plate?

- **If you have a team:** How many tasks are your team members waiting on you for, unable to proceed without input? How many of your client-related tasks are dependent on you?

- **Maybe you feel the lack of "efficiency oxygen" in your day-to-day work:** Are you furiously treading water just to get the minimum required done?

Do not use this as a chance to beat yourself up for all the systems you do not yet have! Systems add up over time; it is hard to create them all at once. As with many habit changes, awareness is the first step. I created a Bottleneck Buster tracker, available in the toolkit online, that helped me stop complaining and start strategizing, by observing for two weeks where work was blocked.

If the flow of work in your business is a river, consider:

- Where are the *eddies*? Eddies form downstream of an obstruction, such as after a boulder, resulting in water that flows in the opposite direction from the rest of the river, sometimes violently so, in swirls of water.

- Where is the water *stagnant* in your business? Where are things slow, stalled, or inefficient?

- Where are the *rapids*? Are they happening now, or can you see them up ahead? On a scale of one to six, what category are they? In river rafting, Class I rapids are easy, Class IV are difficult, and Class VI are "extraordinarily difficult."

Many business owners find themselves in a frustrating chicken-and-egg conundrum. What comes first, the cash flow or the hiring and delegating? Does hiring help free the owner's time to generate sales, or will it stress the system while risking what little surplus exists? For example, can you hire someone to help with sales, who works entirely off of a success fee, so your interests are aligned? Or if you feel too strapped for time to work on systems at all, which *one* system or bottleneck, if you were to address it, would free up the most time? What would be possible if energy were flowing smoothly through that area of the business again?

In *Fix This Next*, author Mike Michalowicz outlines a Business Hierarchy of Needs to ensure you focus on freeing up the most important energy in your business. For example, if you try to fix back-end systems before cash flow issues, you might find yourself out of business. Only once you have solved for sales (creating cash), should you move on to profit (creating stability), order (creating efficiency), impact (creating transformation), and finally, legacy (creating permanence). As with most systems, the process is not linear or "one and done." You will cycle through and spiral upward as your business grows in sophistication. But without solving for cash flow first, it will be impractical to address higher-order business needs.

Looking for the most important next step toward releasing clogged energy can become part of your regular check-ins. Every week or month you can look for, and solve for, the biggest bottleneck—so long as it connects to a vital part of the business.

Techtuition: Stop the "Bad at Technology" Story

If you currently hold the belief that you are bad with technology, it is likely you won't even try to learn new systems and software. Younger generations, while they do have the advantage of learning how to navigate newer technology at an earlier age, are still not preprogrammed with an exact user manual for every device, app, or user interface they encounter.

They are skilled in several things: a willingness to try, to make mistakes, and to "just Google it." There's a website for this purpose I remember fellow Googlers sending to friends and family who emailed with straightforward one-search-away questions: lmgtfy.com. If you don't yet know this acronym, LMGTFY.

I remember my boss at the start-up, a Stanford economics professor, handing me his brand new Blackberry, fresh from the box. These phones had just hit the market; no one knew how to use them. Within five minutes, I had answered all of his questions about how to complete various tasks. I didn't know the device any better than he did, but I had the willingness to try.

Techtuition means you are willing to fumble, feel stupid, and get frustrated. You comb help centers, search engines, and community forums for answers, and then hire help when needed.

After all, when technological change is more gradual, you *are* able to adapt. You adjust to your phone's operating system after updates, right? There is more that you can figure out on your own than you might think. Those who develop a strong techtuition follow the same steps, just at a faster, more automatic clip, as they also take pleasure in traversing learning curves.

After turning fifty years old, my friend Petra Kolber, a former Reebok ambassador and fitness instruction star turned author and keynote speaker, decided to launch in a new direction. First she took up deejaying, reconnecting to her love of music and movement, by hiring a tutor to teach her the ropes of mixing strategies, equipment, and software. Then, she pivoted toward a new project, "Women of a Certain Age," to help other women build confidence even as society practically throws them under an invisibility cloak in their second half of life.

As part of this project, Petra put her belongings in storage and committed to traveling the world for at least one year, booking one-month Airbnb stays along the way. She bought herself a new camera, and last I spoke with her she was networking with younger YouTubers in Los Angeles who counseled her on equipment to buy and new software to learn. As she offhandedly told me, probably not thinking anything of it, "Next I need to teach myself Final Cut Pro." Petra offers a shining example of embracing *techtuition.*

There is no question the specific tools I mention in this book may change, or become out of date. That is why my emphasis is not specific software recommendations or how-tos, but rather the *logic* to apply when assessing and integrating any new system.

Get excited about new software, but only as it helps you make meaningful improvements, otherwise you risk stacking up switching costs from chasing "shiny new objects." Having a *strategy* for software is crucial; with it, you will know what tools to introduce as a means to a desired end. Systems, software, and automation allow you to scale, bust bottlenecks, save time through shortcuts, build institutional smarts and memory through documentation, and ultimately make projects easier to collaborate on and accomplish.

Instead of stacking endless apps together, you and your team will be strategic about what goes where to create the most leverage. As tools free your time from more mindless, repetitive, or confusing tasks, you can apply your mind where it belongs: to ever more strategic and meaningful work.

CHAPTER 8 RECAP

Continuously Bust Bottlenecks

Two-Sentence Summary

Make a habit of continuously identifying and busting bottlenecks. Instead of Frankenstringing apps together, be strategic about key software to create leverage and ease.

Give Yourself Permission

Look anywhere in your business that you are procrastinating and consider: Can you cut it altogether? If you were to restart this project today, would you invest the same resources? If not, give yourself permission to consider shutting it down, even if slowly to prevent unnecessary disruption. Sometimes you have to say no to the *good* and the *shoulds* to make room for what's next.

Ask Yourself

If the flow of work in your business is a river, where are obstructions causing eddies, and where is the water stagnant? Where is it flowing freely, and where are the rapids ahead?

Do (or Delegate) This Next

Visit the Free Time Toolkit online to set up the Bottleneck Buster template. Week one: Observe what is piling up or falling through the cracks; do not start troubleshooting yet! Week two: For each item, brainstorm one next step, system, or small refinement that would improve workflow. Week three: Review; did you notice improvement? Continue refining and repeat this process.

9

***

Embrace Imperfection:
Cookie Dough and Tiny Streaks

Flaws are awesome—so, "flawsome"!

—Tyra Banks

One of my favorite after-school snacks when I was in elementary school was just-add-water cookie dough from Costco, a warehouse retailer. *Oh, how glorious those big boxes were!* Our house always had at least one industrial-sized container of this yummy magic powder in the pantry.

As soon as my brother and I got home from school—*babysitter's wishes be damned!*—we grabbed a cup, sprinkled some mix in, then added water to ensure the consistency was to our liking. His was runny, almost drinkable; mine was thick and gooey. Something about the ease, taste, and DIY assembly was so joyful to us! The cookie dough never made it into the oven, and I have a feeling that for the manufacturers, the oven was never the point.

Now, in my adulting wisdom, I gravitate toward "no cooking needed" chickpea-based dough, of course designed to be eaten straight out of the package. What's the point of actually baking the cookies when the dough tastes so good, and eating it safely raw expedites the cookie-to-mouth process? There is no replacing warm, gooey, perfectly baked versions, either. In New York City, Levain Bakery takes the cookie cake with their inch-thick creations, as does By The Way Bakery for going gluten-free.

What is the *cookie dough* in your business? In what areas can you skip the baking process, or go back to basics on what you consider a finished product or aspect of your routine? As the saying goes, "Done is better than perfect." How brilliant the person who discovered they could ship cookie dough itself as *done*; every bit as delicious for the customer, and with a certain mischievousness baked in.

I wrote the first draft of *Pivot* in fifteen-minute increments, as that is all I could muster while running my (at the time) service-based business. If I didn't serve the clients or land new ones, I didn't eat. The book would have to wait. When I tried creating larger, full-immersion windows for *Free Time* in the earliest days of conceptualizing it, they eluded me. *Who are we kidding*, I preferred to procrasti-tinker with software instead. So I reminded myself that ten or twenty minutes—of anything—is *better than nothing* (BTN).

BTN is the cookie dough in my business. When I create workshops or online courses, I purposefully ship them "half-baked" so that I can gather feedback, survey my incoming audience and answer their specific questions in the moment, and not procrastinate via perfectionism by trying to create the most beautiful course that ever lived. If I waited for that moment, given my skills, energy, and interests, I would not have a course at all.

You *can* get better at getting out of your own way. Design pilots, or small experiments, that are safe to start with limited downside but potential to invest more energy, effort, and resources into if successful. Stick to deadlines if for no other reason than to get over the perfection hump. Aim to get an initial imperfect draft that others can bounce off of and provide feedback on, sooner than later; give yourself one week for each major component if it's a complex project.

Can you find fifteen or twenty minutes each day to:

- Stretch? Go for a run? Ride a bike?

- Tidy the kitchen, or process a stack of mail?

- Respond to messages?

- Read a few pages of an inspiring book?

- Listen to a podcast at one and a half or double the speed?

- Make one decision about something preventing you from moving forward?

There are certain aspects of my day, work, and time that are less negotiable, where less is less, not better than nothing. Strike a balance between delivering excellent work, but also not waiting for that work to be perfect before releasing it.

Where are you waiting for perfection—the fully baked batch of cookies—when you could just as happily, and more easily, aim for a few quick bites of cookie dough instead?

Nearly every time I finish interviewing someone for one of my podcasts—I have conducted over 300 interviews over six years—I shake my head at all the awkward moments, filler words, and stumbling for the right thing to say or the next question to ask. But nine times out of ten, I hit publish anyway, with only light editing. I do not have time to be perfect; this is the only way for me to release work regularly into the world. I embrace *the awkward*. I sometimes joke that my podcast could be alternatively titled *The Awkward Show*; I am most nervous interviewing my author heroes, and if I am not nervous I'm probably making my guest blush by fangirling out on them before we dive in. If I weren't crazy about them, they would not be a guest in the first place!

Perfectionism is exhausting, and on a more practical level it leads to diminishing returns. The extra 90 percent of effort to achieve marginal 10 percent improvement is not worth it. Trust that with the right blend of just-enough quality, originality, and personality, your creative dough will be delicious *as is*—no further baking needed, not so overcooked that your cookies burn.

Refocus: Eyes on Your Own Paper

Taking on a new, meaningful project brings out all of one's gremlins, mental blocks, and existential crises. *Who am I, what are my strengths, what is my unique contribution, and how can I best express it? Is this whole effort futile and worthless, or is there something here? Is the market for this already too saturated?* When I start spinning out about these questions, I return to one of my favorite Rumi passages:

> *You say you can't create something original?*
> *Don't worry about it.*
> *Make a cup of clay so your brother can drink.*

I phrase this as *eyes on your own paper,* as a teacher might say when administering an exam. That means putting your community first when designing anything. Do not waste time worrying about competitors. Stay focused on what makes you unique. When you ask yourself, *Why me?*, do as my friend Claude Silver advised, and ask instead, *Why not me?* Comparing yourself to others is not fruitful, unless you are learning with curiosity from another person's strengths.

When you find yourself feeling pangs of compare-and-despair, getting overwhelmed by *shoulds* when looking at how another business operates, blaming another person, or even resenting them for something, refocus. Eyes on your own paper: Re-examine your own projects and sphere of influence. What can *you* do differently? What can you ignore?

You have permission to stop checking up on *the industry.* Unsubscribe from newsletters that you are receiving just to stay in the know. Stop following your competitors on social media if following them does not bring you joy. Take one whole day (or week, or month!) without any of these *newsish* inputs.

Capture the imaginary characters in the boardroom of your brain. Who is sitting around the table, challenging your decisions, making noise, offering critiques? Personify them. For each, write down their personality traits—down to what they are wearing and their facial expressions—their primary motivation, and their biggest fear. Note what you would like to say to each board member, acknowledging their concerns and asking for their cooperation.

As Oliver Burkeman reminds us in *Four Thousand Weeks*, "Peace of mind, an exhilarating sense of freedom, comes not from achieving validation but from yielding to the reality that it wouldn't bring security if you got it." For more on this, I also recommend Ichiro Kishimi and Fumitake Koga's bestselling book, *The Courage to Be Disliked*.

My friend Michael Bungay Stanier, who you met in the section on escape velocity, and I happened to start working on new books at the same time. We committed to writing at least a hundred words every day for thirty days, reporting our "check mark" each day via Marco Polo, an asynchronous messaging app. On day six, I noticed many interesting shifts:

1. **I started looking forward to writing in the morning.** This had not been the case for years, ever since *Pivot* launched, given how much energy I poured into that project. I started enjoying pondering what to write about each day. My imposter fears dissolved, as our thirty-day commitment ensured that I would write every day no matter what.

2. **Idea "downloads" started pouring in:** They came while I was showering, commuting, and walking. We used to have to run hot water in our sink for at least five minutes before showering, if we wanted it to be a hot one. This tiny streak operated the same way. The first five days were uneventful, my heart was not in it yet; but ideas accelerated starting in week two.

3. **Hitting 100 words was joyful, easy, and fun.** I enjoyed reporting back to my accountability buddy, and my word counts often surpassed the minimum. Contrast that to when my stated minimum goal was higher at 1,500 words twice a week: I wasn't writing at all.

4. **I piggybacked the tiny writing streak with another important practice:** movement. I paired my daily writing minimum with at least ten minutes of exercise: yoga, Pilates, cycling, or stretching. On some days I did more, but this required me to do *no less than* ten minutes. Along with my hundred words, ten minutes was easy enough to fit in—no excuses—and I always felt better for having done it.

5. **Others started to join in, even without a formal invitation.** Close friends who knew about this streak started to say, "Hey, I did my 100 words today!" It was as if the tinyness of the task gave them, too, permission to do something creative for themselves.

After Michael and I completed first drafts of our respective books, even both preparing to launch new podcasts in similar timing, he forwarded a newsletter from songwriter Nick Cave, who captured in more poetic language how the two of us had been helping each other make progress.

Nick traded song lyrics for a painting with his friend Thomas, whose spirits were also down, at a time when both were feeling creatively blocked. He said it was easier to create something for his friend than for himself, and vice versa. Their commitment—starting with trading just one piece of art each—was reinvigorating, igniting prolific creativity for both:

We are, Thomas and I, indebted to one another, like friends often are. Occasionally he FaceTimes me, standing, roaring and laughing, in front of his enormous sun-blasted canvases, created on his patio in Malibu, overlooking the sea. They are mighty, defiant and subversive works, a testament to one man's struggle with his own destructive energies and the miraculous healing power of art.

CHAPTER 9 RECAP

Embrace Imperfection:
Cookie Dough and Tiny Streaks

Two-Sentence Summary

Embrace "cookie dough" in your business—work that is awkward, imperfect, and incomplete—by building and launching anyway, while gathering real-time feedback. Perfectionism is a losing game with diminishing returns.

Give Yourself Permission

Publish work that isn't perfect. Publish something every week, even if it seems small or "uncooked."

Ask Yourself

What is a pilot version of one of your in-progress projects that your community can benefit from? How could that early feedback help you shape the product in more meaningful ways, rather than keeping it private until it is perfect?

Do (or Delegate) This Next

Identify an important project you are stuck on. With a friend, set-up a tiny two-week sprint for the pieces you must complete. Check out the book toolkit for a template to help run two-day strategy sprints with your team.

Align Resources

For free tools and templates to help implement strategies from the **Align** stage, visit **ItsFreeTime.com/toolkit**.

A sampling of resources for this stage include:

- Business Tech Toolkit: An ongoing list of the software I use to run my operations

- Manager Manual template: Copy and paste these questions for every area of your business as you build out principles and processes

- Bottleneck Buster tracker: Observe for two weeks where you are getting stuck

- Two-Day Strategy Sprint template: Run these with your team for dedicated focus

- Rapid Prototyping: How to create and launch a course with real-time feedback

Part 2

Des

sign

Overview

"Time is money," Benjamin Franklin wrote in 1748. This is now a shared cultural assumption, at least in the United States. Time, in Franklin's context, is framed in terms of money, earning potential, and trade. Both time and money are man made, shared mythologies, so it makes sense that we have woven these ideas together in our industrious capitalist society.

"Stop trading time for money" is one of the first maxims business owners learn when scaling beyond service provider or freelancer. Trading time for money is not altogether bad; but it is risky as a long-term strategy when you need to take a break. Additionally, you cannot meet business demand that goes beyond your available time and energy. If you have twenty hours per week available to deliver services, the only way to grow your business is by increasing prices, and there may be a natural ceiling on what your ideal customers can or want to pay.

By reconsidering long-held notions of the relationship between time and money, we can design a fresh take on the correlation between the two. One of the best ways to free your time is raising your prices if they match the value you provide. You can also increase your profit margin by cutting expenses and improving operational efficiency, the focus of this book. Healthy, abundant pricing is imperative to your success and to your free time. Beyond the earliest days of product testing and iterating to fit your market, and your own skill- and confidence-building, if you are charging too little, it will be difficult to ever feel *truly* free.

During our *Free Time* podcast conversation on the psychology of pricing, Jacquette M. Timmons, financial behaviorist and author of *Financial Intimacy*, encouraged listeners to look beyond the numbers. "If success with money were purely a mathematical problem to be solved, then everybody would have more than they wanted or needed. And yet that's not the case."

Jacquette suggests investigating deeper motivations and underlying emotions, drawing parallels between our business and key relationships. If the business were personified by someone in your life, who would it be? What are the patterns and connections? For example, does it mirror a dynamic with one of your parents? If so, in what ways?

She also looks at pricing in a binary way: you either get it right, or you get it wrong. You know when you get it wrong because sales are not flowing and you are not cash flow positive. You might even be running a profitable business, yet you, the owner, are still broke.

"People sometimes dismiss the fact that their business is not there just to be successful on its own," Jacquette said. "One of the best business decisions a small business owner can make is leading with personal finances—not just what you need right now, but also in the future."

When people don't price their services well, they risk entering martyr mode. "You end up giving your business everything, including your future," Jacquette said. "Give yourself permission to put yourself first. Don't sabotage your health by being available to people that may not be able to afford you. Think of another way to be of service to this group."

Many business owners I speak with still charge too little for their services, and cram their calendars full of client work as a result. When pricing, they are overly preoccupied with potential clients' budgets, even negotiating against themselves. To adapt a phrase from Byron Katie, author of *Loving What Is* and founder of The Work: If you are thinking about their business (and budget), and *they* are thinking about *their* business (and budget), who is thinking about yours? She writes, "We're both over there. Being mentally in your business keeps me from being present in my own."

I counsel business owners who are still serving as service providers to multiply their rates by at least three to account for three T's: taxes, team overhead, and their time. The third T is particularly important, given that they are incurring switching costs *and* opportunity costs generated by working *in* the business during those sessions as service providers rather than *on* the business as CEO. As one self-employed friend described this upcharge when signing lucrative clients that would take him away from bigger creative projects in progress, "They need to pay for the way back. I call it the *where-was-I?* tax."

A few years into running her leadership development company, Zing Collaborative, Sarah Young came to a stark realization. While she was doing work that she loved with people who she enjoyed working with, her calendar was crowded with "tiny boxes": appointments and meetings with little white space in between.

"When I got quiet, I was forced to face an uncomfortable truth," Sarah writes in her book, *Expansive Impact*. "I filled my calendar with obligations not always from a place of love, but sometimes from a place of fear." She said "yes" to too many things, out of fear of not having *enough*: "enough income, enough clients, enough work to justify the idea that I was running a successful business."

It took Sarah several more years of "unraveling, followed by a global pandemic, to wipe out the hundreds of tiny boxes," on her calendar allowing her to start anew. Today, her continuous practice is to say "yes" only to the most resonant opportunities, which still requires mindful effort.

This second stage of the Free Time Framework, **Design**, will help you create space for your most important work, ignoring distractions along the way. Once you know a project is aligned with your values, energy, and strengths, *then* you and your team can design how to approach it; otherwise the design stage may lead to wasted effort on work you should not be doing at all. Before starting any new project, you will clearly define three areas:

1. Ideal Outcomes: What are the ideal outcomes, large and small? How will you measure success? How will the finished product look? How will you know when it is complete?

2. Impact: What impact will this project have in the world? Who is it for? What problems are you solving? What will someone say

when they share it with a friend? What do they write when they send you a thank-you note for creating it?

3. **Process:** This is where you design how you and your team will work toward your ideal outcomes and impact. You will create a project plan with key milestones, and decide how to communicate along the way, noting what to do when problems arise.

Time is money is only part of the equation.

Try this instead: *Time is life force.*

When I am mired in work sapping my energy, I remind myself of this. As a business owner, I know money can be replenished and creatively earned, a next challenge to solve. I made the decision many years ago to have fun playing the money game, to experiment with how I could stretch boundaries of possibility and time, inviting nonlinear breakthroughs along the way, something you will learn more about in the first section of this Design stage. You will also learn how to time-block and bake in batches.

Your time is far more precious than money. It is your life, your energy, your presence, your memories, your dreams, the quality of any given moment. As spiritual teacher Nisargadatta Maharaj, author of *I Am That*, says, "To work in the world is hard, to refrain from all unnecessary work is even harder."

Align > **Design** > Assign >

Outcomes

Design the process and ideal outcomes before starting work on a new project. Notice when you are stuck thinking something will be long, arduous, or exhausting, requiring "hard work" or intense willpower. Invite nonlinear breakthroughs by opening up to the possibility that results could happen quickly, spontaneously, serendipitously, joyfully, easefully. "Don't push the river," as the Zen saying goes. Listen to others' needs, then create with confidence. Stop mopping with already soaked time sponges: doing repetitive, reactive work without cleaning up the actual mess. Instead of reacting and responding in the moment, create systems to free up time in the future. Notice micro-guilt and its cousins: people-pleasing, worrying, and saying yes to lukewarm opportunities just to avoid saying no. Design your time to help you thrive. As author Cal Newport puts it, in a world increasingly ruled by the Hyperactive Hive Mind way of working, you must "commit to concentration."

In this section, you will:
- Invite nonlinear breakthroughs
- Apply serendipity as a business strategy
- Solve for Sisyphean systems

10

Invite Nonlinear Breakthroughs

Planning rests on the idea that time is not instantaneous, but continuous.

—Bahar Noorizadeh

❝ **Please welcome to the stage . . . *Leanne Hughes!* Host of *First Time Facilitator*.**" Leanne's palms started sweating as she made her way to the front of an auditorium packed with hundreds of people attending the We Are Podcast conference in Brisbane, Australia. Between breakout sessions, she entered her show name into a contest for one lucky host to gain exposure.

Except for one small catch: her podcast did not exist yet.

By throwing her hat into the ring via blue post-it note, even while it was only a figment of her imagination, Leanne opened herself up to what I describe as a *nonlinear breakthrough* (NLB): an unexpected sharp turn of clarity or success, rather than a linear, long, or otherwise time-consuming analysis or slog.

Notice when you are stuck thinking something will be arduous or exhausting in your business, perhaps assuming that the only way to achieve progress is "up and to the right," through hard work and intense willpower.

Invite an NLB instead: Open yourself up to the possibility that results can happen quickly, spontaneously, serendipitously, joyfully, even easefully. Look for examples of people or situations related to the one you are in to find proof that NLBs are possible, even if they don't seem likely according to how *everyone else* is doing it.

That shift in strategy, envisioning a path that might just be easier than expected, is exactly how Leanne achieved liftoff. At the time, Leanne had been running workshops while working in her corporate learning and development role. Entrepreneurship was still a risky-seeming dream. She loved listening to podcasts as a refreshing way to start the day while walking her two dogs. Leanne flirted with starting her own show, but had not yet committed. She bought a conference ticket anyway to hear some of her favorite podcasters speak.

If she *were* to start a podcast, she knew it would be centered on something she was excited to learn more about, so on her little blue scrap of paper she wrote "First Time Facilitator," mirroring her own path. Leanne made a commitment: "If this gets chosen, I am going to start this podcast," she told herself.

And then . . . almost as if in slow motion, as the emcee reached into the hat, Leanne says, "I just knew. I knew it would be my piece of paper." It was. In the thirty seconds it took to walk onstage, she created the podcast's elevator pitch. Her moment in the spotlight sealed the deal.

Three months later she released the show, giving her the courage to quit her job one year later. Leanne has published over two hundred episodes, with another NLB quick to follow. With her value of "constructive delusion" around taking bold risks, Leanne pitched the organizer and ended up *emceeing* the We Are Podcast conference the following year. Now the tables were turned, and Leanne welcomed her heroes to the stage. She had opportunities throughout the weekend to hang out in the green room, attend dinners leading up to the event, and connect during a speakers retreat following the conference.

Inspired by her podcast, Leanne now leans heavily on voice and video to communicate with current and potential clients, even landing a big project from a three-minute Loom video that she made in one take.

"As a facilitator, clients hire me based on my ability to communicate," she said. "Voice connects so powerfully with my audience, too. Thank you podcasting!"

Nonlinear breakthroughs invite us to be surprised not only by the outcomes of any business effort, but by the path to get there.

Transcend Tug-of-War with Sacred Third Solutions

My friend Christine Arylo, author of *Overwhelmed and Over It*, teaches an NLB-related concept that she calls the "sacred third solution."

The *sacred third* is not about merely considering a third *option*, as that further activates the intellect. In contrast, "The sacred third is about moving toward wholeness," Christine says. "By framing the conundrum as an inquiry, you activate intuition, imagination, and contemplation."

The difference between *asking* and *inquiring* is that with the latter, you may not get an answer right away. "You are putting it into the larger field of collective consciousness," Christine says, noting the importance of allowing solutions to emerge.

During a big transition in her life, she realized that the way she had been asking, "Where should I live?" was making her anxious. Her mind was running in circles through yes/no, either/or scenarios such as, *Should we stay in Seattle? Or should we move to North Carolina? Or go somewhere else?*

So Christine shifted toward a more expansive inquiry instead: "Show me where [my partner] Noah and I can root so we can both thrive. Where will we prosper?"

In the first version, her mind was tirelessly searching for answers. With her updated inquiry, Christine was able to get quiet, allowing her curiosity and intuition to lead her toward more resonant solutions, still unfolding day by day.

You can spot opportunities to invite nonlinear breakthroughs by returning to the friction-versus-flow gauge, or by applying a related lens: drained versus delighted. For example, one morning, I was flipping through the final pages of a business book to prepare for an interview with the author later that day. Although I found their path interesting, I was left with a nagging emotional residue upon finishing it, one that occurs sometimes after I finish business books: *exhaustion.*

I was tired just *thinking* about implementing their strategies! The pages were filled with exhortations to work harder, more consistently, and more persistently than anyone else. The author reminded readers—how could the Personal Development Police ever let us forget?—that we are the average of the five people we surround ourselves with. The path to success was a long, hard climb fueled by discipline, habits, daily actions, and of course, *hustle.* I put the book down, already drained.

Do not get me wrong, these are all beneficial qualities in proper doses. But that is also why I am passionate about building smarter systems. Systems can help take things off your plate, your mind, and your languishing projects pile. Most of all, smarter systems can ease the micro-guilt of not getting "enough" done. What if the more easefully you worked, the more you would enter a flow state, and the more creative work you would complete? Remember: how you bake is as important as what you make.

Linear relationships, in systems thinking, are those with constant proportions between two elements. They can be drawn as a straight line. According to Donella Meadows, author of *Thinking in Systems, nonlinear relationships* are ones where the cause does not produce a proportional effect.

"The world often surprises our linear-thinking minds. If we've learned that a small push produces a small response, we think that twice as big a push will produce twice as big a response," Meadows writes. "But in a *nonlinear* system, twice the push could produce one-sixth the response, or the response squared, or no response at all."

Inviting nonlinear breakthroughs opens up possibilities, beyond "only when, then" traps. Consider ways you are unknowingly adhering to an outdated factory-like system, whether setting an alarm, what you wear to work, when you work, what you work on, what you accept from clients, or how you manage your calendar. Who do these "best" practices actually work for?

You can invite nonlinear:

- Breakthroughs
- Solutions
- Revenue
- Marketing
- Goal-setting
- Word-of-mouth growth

I remember taking a breathwork class at a small yoga studio in Brooklyn, during a particularly vexing time in my (non)dating life, trying to break a lifelong pattern of choosing emotionally unavailable men, then feeling unworthy of even crumbs of their attention.

I couldn't stand dating apps. Well-meaning friends and family reminded me that "it's a numbers game," and told me to aim for quantity instead. But how could I justify even one more miserable hour on yet another bad date, when I knew I could be home reading a good book?! I always replied saying, "Serendipity is my dating strategy."

Before we started the breathwork course, the instructor had us sit in a circle and set intentions. During my turn I said, "I'm here to change the way I approach relationships forever. I am looking for a nonlinear breakthrough." She scoffed. The whole room laughed! With a patronizing tone, the instructor said, "*Hah*, well personal development is a lifelong journey. It's hard work."

Lo and behold, I *did* have a nonlinear breakthrough that night. And this NLB did, in fact, transform everything. As cheesy as it may sound here in writing, my heart said to me, "As long as I am beating, I am not broken." And my lungs said, "As long as we are breathing, we are not broken." It was revolutionary to be reminded that I was whole, every day, supported by the miracles of a beating heart, breathing lungs, and an intelligent, resilient body. No one could take that away from me, therefore I had so much less to fear. I could be abundant in my whole life, including relationships. That would be NLB enough. In the weeks that followed, haikus landed fully formed into my mind. One that stayed with me:

Mind like water, drop
down into that place where all
is quiet, serene.

As it turns out, I am now married to the person I was nervously dating at that time. We met walking in opposite directions down a New York City street. *Serendipity, baby.*

How can you generate nonlinear breakthroughs in business? First, start by opening yourself up to the possibility. Ask for one. Say, "If this is in the highest good, I invite a nonlinear breakthrough. Show me the first next step."

My income over the last decade has typically grown steadily, with some bigger jumps and a plateau or two in-between. I am always open to the nonlinear hockey stick *and* I am always grateful for an abundant plateau. Plateaus are not a problem if you are happy with your take-home pay.

As I write this, podcaster John Lee Dumas (JLD for short) is celebrating over one hundred consecutive months of earning six-figure monthly profit from his podcast, *Entrepreneurs On Fire*, as he shares in detailed monthly revenue reports on his website. When peers pressure him to grow because he is at a plateau, JLD celebrates their comments. His plateau, one he and his Delightfully Tiny Team are incredibly proud of, allows him to honor his value of freedom. JLD has no interest in scaling up his team or adding complexity with new products just to keep his revenue chart pointing "up and to the right."

Expand your beliefs about business-building to include the possibility of easeful growth *and* positive plateaus.

Part 2: Design

Invite Nonlinear Breakthroughs

Two-Sentence Summary

Open yourself up to the possibility that results can happen quickly and joyfully. Invite nonlinear breakthroughs (NLBs) and stay attuned to signs giving you clues about what one next meaningful step to take.

Give Yourself Permission

To be surprised! Drop the idea that progress is going to be a long, hard slog. *Let it be easy, let it be fun.*

Ask Yourself

What would be possible if you invited (and received) a nonlinear breakthrough in your most challenging business area?

Do (or Delegate) This Next

Identify an area where you feel stuck. Notice if thinking about progress linearly is adding pressure. Reframe the problem as an open-ended inquiry.

11

Serendipity as Business Strategy

Let me release what wants to leave, and welcome what wants to come, trusting that my needs are always met.

—Tosha Silver

POP!

Pause.

Pause.

Pause.

Wait.

Wait longer.

Pop!

Pause.

Pause.

Wait more.

Pop!

Pop!

Wait.

Pop! Pop! Pop! Pop! Pop! Pop! PopPopPopPop!

If my popcorn poem does not immediately spark business metaphor brainstorming, let me serve it up for you lightly salted with melted butter and coconut oil: You never have full control over how the work you do lands in the world. But hitting publish on big projects anyway, ideally ones expressing your unique gifts, plants important *serendipity popcorn* kernels. I could write an entire book on the sweet relief of surrendering obsession over outcomes; thankfully Tosha Silver already did in one of my favorite books to recommend to friends, *Outrageous Openness*. For now, let's focus on how to apply these principles in business.

Serendipity popcorn happens when you release your small experiments, or pilots, out into the world, without knowing what will result. Sure enough with luck, effort, and persistence to turn up the proverbial heat, *pop!* Someone's interest will spark. Another will be impacted by your work and recommend you to a friend. Another still will find you from a random search, then reach out for an interview. Someone else will read or listen to that interview, and *pop!* The chain reaction becomes unstoppable.

The pops start slowly at first, but if you stick with steadily launching your ideas, they accelerate. By putting yourself out there, you never know what exactly will pop or when. You toss idea kernels out into the world, and they transform into opportunity popcorn in their own perfect timing.

For a powerful illustration of these *tipping points*, in Malcom Gladwell parlance, search for Buzzfeed's video, "Ultimate Chain Reaction created by 2014 mousetraps and 2015 Ping pong balls." The set-up: over two thousand mousetraps each contain a single idle ping pong ball sitting atop the trap. As you can infer from the title, there is just *one* more ping pong ball than mousetrap. Once it is set free into the scene, this spark sets off a sweet symphony of activity.

Tasha McCaskiel remembers starting Black Girls in Media, a member-based networking organization supporting minority women in the media industry. In the early days, people in her network thought she was wasting her time with the business, but she knew it had potential to impact many others through events, master classes, and digital resources.

"I was close to giving up on it, because I was broke and needing a job," Tasha recalls. But in surrendering the outcome, even as she was down and crying, she started seeing her first new members enroll. "I took that as a sign that I was on the right path," she said. "I have been growing and succeeding ever since."

For Tasha, moving forward with faith that things will work out as they should keeps her calm and focused, not spiraling into overthinking. "I create, release, then hope for the best," she says. "Not every idea works, but not every idea fails either. I would rather release than sit and wait for things to be perfect, which is impossible."

Another example of noticing friction, making efforts to resolve it, then surrendering the final outcome: my team and I needed to get 250 books to Barcelona for a speaking engagement. The Penguin U.S. team was twenty five books short, so we placed an order with Penguin U.K. They failed to tell us they also did not have stock; we only discovered this days later when following up. As a final attempt, we placed an order through Amazon Spain that showed same-day delivery. After the order was confirmed, shipping got extended to a date past the event. Two days later, Amazon Spain cancelled the order because it was set for delivery in "a suspicious country not normally associated with this account."

At that point my team member and I read the writing on the wall: this order was not meant to be. We cancelled it and didn't force these extra books, trusting that we would have the perfect amount on the day of the event, easily able to send copies later for anyone who ended up without one. Sure enough, we had enough.

On a related note, there are many business gurus that will insist you set specific goals, going so far as to say you cannot run your business effectively without them. I disagree. Sometimes I set goals because they are fun to aim for, and at other times I surrender completely to whatever wants to come my way, holding the belief that what I currently have is plenty, and that I can creatively generate more when needed. These coaches will have you capture annual revenue goals, set a precise desired number of product sales, and identify clear platform-building follower targets, then work toward them by mapping month-by-month progress, then checking in weekly on exactly how you are going to hit these goals.

While I do see the benefits of these practices, they can lead to overly obsessing about achieving particular milestones and specific metrics. For example, I would often feel deflated if I set a launch goal and I did not reach it, whether in terms of sales or enrollment numbers. It left me focused on all the people who *didn't* sign up, rather than the participants who excitedly had and were now entrusting me with their hard-earned money. Of course, falling short of goals that are important to you provides learning opportunities. You can continue adjusting and experimenting until you hit them. With this mindset, it is not a question of *if* you will hit the goal, but *when* and *how*.

Basecamp co-founders Jason Fried and David Heinemeier Hansson share their philosophy on avoiding imposing arbitrary targets in their book *It Doesn't Have to Be Crazy At Work*, in a chapter called "Our Goal: No Goals." They write:

> *Do we want to make things better? All the time. But do we want to maximize "better" through constantly chasing goals? No thanks.*
>
> *That's why we don't have goals at Basecamp. We didn't when we started, and now, nearly 20 years later, we still don't. We simply do the best work we can on a daily basis.*

When I was launching *Pivot*, I decided that I would market the book with magic and serendipity as the primary grease for my launch wheels. I did not want to stress over implementing myriad marketing techniques by working twelve hours a day. I trusted that the book would find the right readers at the right time. Instead of dragging myself through draining work that I tend to procrastinate terribly on, such as writing articles for publications, I leaned on marketing strategies that I have the most fun with, such as being interviewed on other people's podcasts and recording episodes for my own.

Marketing with magic and serendipity didn't replace strategy, diligence, and hard work, but I was so much more relaxed with the launch of *Pivot* compared to *Life After College* five years prior. With *Pivot* I did not care if I made bestseller lists. Overexerting myself to attempt the feat would have been a misuse of my time and energy, given that I had so little control over that particular result. I did not check my sales statistics for at least three months. Other authors thought I was crazy not to do so, if not entirely negligent as a business owner. They would refresh their Amazon rank hour by hour, day after day, and I was unmoved. I was not attached to the results of the launch because I knew that this project was a part of my business for the long haul. This mindset enabled me to enjoy the process and talk about my work with grace and ease, rather than stressing and sweating over sales numbers I wasn't hitting.

Josh Kaufman, author of *The Personal MBA*, also found peace with his version of measuring his book's success. Even though it is an international bestseller, with nearly one million copies sold, it never "made any of the lists," author parlance for being listed in *The New York Times Book Review's* list of bestsellers, or another prestigious ranking.

"Those higher status signals can feel good in the moment," Josh said, but they don't meet his calculus for impact. Instead of pursuing status markers, he decided to spend the same amount of time and energy creating more effective *systems* to sell copies of his books for the next fifty years. "When it comes to long-term results, there's no contest."

Now, when he is faced with tempting choices of what to pursue, he asks: "Does this sound interesting? Enjoyable? Will it stretch me in an important direction? Or is this the kind of thing that sounds promising, novel, or high status, but doesn't have long-term implications? Will it pay long-term dividends beyond exploring what's 'cool' right now?"

In his book *Start Finishing*, author Charlie Gilkey, who you met in the introduction, talks about three levels of success. Depending on your available time and energy at any given moment, you may want to purposefully aim for different levels of success for a project, knowing your capacity to work to make it happen:

- Small success
- Moderate success
- Epic success

Another important consideration, one Charlie places within the small category, is *intrinsic* success. That means identifying what benefits are in it for you within a given project, even if the results or revenue figures do not appear successful by outside standards. For example, even if I had zero podcast listeners, hosting it would still be worth pursuing because I get to hone my interview skills, develop ideas out loud, make new friends, and connect with authors I admire.

With serendipity as a business strategy, you do not have to design precise outcomes, have all the answers right away, or a detailed plan mapped out from the start. As Carl Jung wrote to one of his correspondents in 1933, just "quietly do the next and most necessary thing."

CHAPTER 11 RECAP

Serendipity as Business Strategy

Two-Sentence Summary

Create the conditions for serendipity popcorn. Release work that invites pops of opportunity and inbound interest, looking for joyful ways to turn up the heat.

Give Yourself Permission

Stop *striving*. Embrace surrender and serendipity as parts of your business strategy.

Ask Yourself

What would happen if you surrendered any outcomes you are obsessing over? How would it affect how you work as you continue pointing in that direction?

Do (or Delegate) This Next

Spend the next few days playing Serendipity Signage. What words jump out from trucks, busses, storefronts, song lyrics? What animals cross your path that are different from most other days? What are these messages highlighting for you?

12

Solve for Sisyphean Systems

I have configured servers, written code, built web pages, helped design products used by millions of people. I am firmly in the camp that believes technology is generally bending the world in a positive direction. Yet, for me, Twitter foments neurosis, Facebook sadness, Google News a sense of foreboding. Instagram turns me covetous. All of them make me want to do it—whatever "it" may be—for the likes, the comments. I can't help but feel that I am the worst version of myself, being performative on a very short, very depressing timeline. A timeline of seconds.

—Craig Mod

Sisyphus, a Greek mythological king, was a trickster punished for cheating death. Zeus sentenced him to an eternity of futility, rolling a giant boulder uphill only to have it roll back down once he neared the top. In today's world, these giant boulders come in the form of never-ending inboxes and notifications.

Many of these Sisyphean systems surrounding notifications are, by definition and *by design*, "hard to contain or eradicate," the definition of cancer. Staying caught up with social media is impossible, given that it purposefully captures attention through features like the never-ending infinity scroll home feed. I call it the *crush of the inbound*. With so much incoming, it takes Herculean willpower—or a shift in systems and mindset—to resist the urge to respond all day, every day, into eternity. If we get caught in these addictive systems, we miss the chance to do our best work, in our best timing.

In her book on *Life Admin*, author Elizabeth Emens recounts a story about the late Supreme Court Justice Ruth Bader Ginsburg, nicknamed "Notorious RBG" by admirers. Early in her career as a leading civil-rights lawyer and professor, Ginsberg described her young son James as "lively." Teachers called him "hyperactive," and the school would call often as a result. As Emens recounts:

> *One such call came after Ginsburg had been up all night writing a legal brief. She picked up the phone in her office and said, "This child has two parents. Please alternate calls. It's his father's turn." After that, the calls came barely once a semester because [Ginsberg said] "they had to think long and hard before asking a man to take time out of his work day to come to the school."*

The gender-based assumptions in this story are frustrating; that the school had no qualms about interrupting Justice Ginsburg's work, yet called less frequently so as not to bother her husband. RBG was "notorious" for a reason, always pushing boundaries and breaking barriers, through her personal life as much as the legal precedents she methodically pressed for to increase women's rights. In this example, by making one seemingly simple request, RBG shifted out of a Sisyphean system.

By requesting that the school alternate their calls, she established a different protocol, reducing her subsequent burden. What she *didn't* do was grin-and-bear it, telling herself "just this once," without implementing any material change to prevent these time-consuming interruptions. Making shifts like these require awareness, stepping back to see a bigger picture and possibilities, then implementing a pattern-interrupt or new process for repeating situations that are not serving our best work.

Part 2: Design

You have three options when solving for Sisyphean systems:

1. **Time:** Stop underestimating the time required to complete this task if you frequently feel behind. If it is important to you and your business, strategically plan to invest more time in the activity, treating it as a discrete task at recurring intervals. Block time on your calendar, rather than responding ad hoc throughout the day in micro-moments. Set-up co-working sessions with friends so you hold yourself accountable for the time you need to complete this work.

2. **Team:** Delegate or automate the task, or as much of the subtasks within it, as you can. Create groupings of like tasks and address them as a whole. For example, reduce email volume by setting up a request form that feeds into a spreadsheet instead of processing requests individually, or use an automated scheduling tool to reduce coordination back-and-forth. Release your grip and give greater responsibility to your team, including problem solving along the way.

3. **Transcend:** If you are stuck playing a game you can't possibly win, you may need to transcend it, completely shifting your mindset or parameters. Consider public figures who put up autoresponders that say, "Due to the overwhelming number of emails I receive, I am no longer able to read or respond to these messages." Alternatively, depending on volume, the autoresponder might indicate that the person reads every single response, but does not set any expectation of providing a response in return, noting who to contact for different business streams.

When I find myself stuck in Sisyphean systems, I remind myself to focus my attention back on four central business aims:

1. Robust, recurring revenue

2. Streamlined systems

3. Regularly publishing ideas and podcast conversations

4. Serving my community by being as helpful as possible to as many people as possible

In the opening to this book, I encouraged you to think about your most meaningful metrics, the vital levers in your business. Now let's reverse-engineer what *actually* moves the needle on them, so you can determine what work to ramp up or scale back.

To begin, divide your current marketing practices into *direct* revenue-generating activities versus *indirect* revenue-generating activities. Direct activities can lead to a sale right then and there, whereas indirect requires hoping that something ignites in due course, so a potential sale *might* happen a few steps down the road.

Direct income-generating activities include:	Indirect income-generating activities include:
• Making sales calls	• *Many shiny things!*
• Asking for referrals	• Posting social media updates
• Adding a "Buy Now" Button to a product or service on your website	• Sprucing up your bio
• Launching a new product by inviting your community to enroll	• Creating quote cards in Canva
• Pitching an upgraded service to previous customers	• Taking an online course
• Advertising a product	• Procrasti-branding to ensure everything looks perfect
	• Reading a book (even this one, unless you take action and put into practice what you are learning)

Notice where, in your business, you are falling into the trap of keeping up with time-consuming *indirect* income-generating activities. Be ruthless: Should it stay or should it go? If it stays, do *you* need to be the one responsible? What opportunities are you missing on the more profitable *direct* income-generating list because you are tied up with lower value distractions?

Stop Sailing the Sea of Shiny Shoulds

Who benefits from getting you addicted to your phone, to your inboxes, to your notifications, to your social media accounts? Unless you are someone who is energized by the aforementioned activities, you are a pawn in somebody else's growth-at-all-costs game. Frittering your attention away does not benefit you, but it very well may benefit the platforms you are spending it on. As the saying goes, "If you aren't paying for the product, you *are* the product."

With all the noise online, it is easy to get lost sailing the *sea of shiny shoulds*. Some *shoulds* are an obvious yes or no. *Shiny shoulds* tempt you. Deep down, you know you do not want to pursue them, but you feel lingering pressure and obligation. They are shiny because "everyone else is doing it," even succeeding with them.

Social media is just one example of a business should. Do you enjoy posting for the sake of posting, interacting, and replying? If yes, post away. If not, you have two choices:

1. **Quit completely (no regrets).** Why post, why do anything at all, if you do not enjoy it? How could the ends justify the means in terms of fractured attention and diminished energy? Why participate in a system that doesn't support you?

2. **Design this as another business system with a regular, process-based cadence.** No, you don't *love* it, and you know you don't love it, but you cultivate it all the same, just as you would keep up with monthly bookkeeping or quarterly tax preparation.

I tried outsourcing the task of social media to software and to team members, and it ultimately didn't resonate. It grated against my value of integrity to have other people posting for me, or scheduling tweet-bots. I was also contributing to a *tragedy of the commons*, in that I had stopped reading the main feeds of what others were up to. Therefore, all my posts became about "me me me," and if I didn't have the desire or bandwidth to reply to messages, I was just another person on a soapbox shouting into the ether.

Alexandra Franzen, co-founder of Get It Done, shuttered her social media accounts in 2015, and her business has only grown since. Before deleting her accounts, she enjoyed being active on Twitter. But the time-effort-energy calculus just didn't add up.

"As the years rolled along, I started to become very aware of how much of my time and creative and mental energy was getting tied up," she told me in one of our podcast conversations. She estimated that every thoughtful tweet took about ten minutes to craft, not including replying to the resulting comments. When she multiplied that by forty years, she realized she would have spent years of her life on Twitter alone.

"When I saw that number, three years, I felt sad," she said. "It is not that social media is bad. It's amazing. But for me, that didn't sit right. I realized that I don't know how long I am going to be alive in this world. All of our lives are so precious."

What started as a three-month hiatus became six years and counting of a more simplified business approach. When she examined how clients found her, she realized her greatest strength was word-of-mouth, as is happening in this moment as I share her story with you. There was no negative business impact from closing her social media accounts; her newsletter continues to grow steadily year-over-year.

One of her weekly newsletters had the enticing subject line, "This is what my iPhone screen looks like. . . "

"It is a calm place," Alexandra wrote. She has all notifications turned off, with just eight apps on her phone hidden on a secondary screen. "Out of sight," she said. "They're not the first thing I see."

Alex has an inner circle of friends and family who can reach her easily, and sends text messages from her computer because "it's faster and feels way better than hunching over a tiny phone screen." Alexandra now lives in Hawaii, and has hired her own Delightfully Tiny Team to help do the work that is most meaningful to her: writing, coaching, leading retreats, and teaching courses.

I have not missed social media either. If anything, more people come to me now, asking how my business functions without participating in it. Instead of spreading myself thin, I focus on writing books (every five years or so), speaking, developing a strong newsletter community, and podcasting, which I love. These two main ongoing channels—newsletter and podcast— work well for me, and align with my strengths and energy. Although I might miss reaching some new people by writing articles or posting snippets on social media, I would miss my deep creative focus more.

Quick! The floor is lava! Hop to nearest furniture for safety!

Do you remember playing this game as a kid? Perhaps the Netflix TV series, *Floor Is Lava*, jogged your memory: adults lurching across oversized furniture props while bubbling "lava" threatens them from below. The team that reaches the opposite side of the room fastest wins.

When it comes to particularly vexing areas like email, remember: *The floor is lava.*

Email is a never-ending nesting doll of tasks and decisions. Treating email like a task is the equivalent of saying "run business" as a task. Neither one works. You need systems.

Back to the hot lava bubbling below. The best way to clear your mind and free up time is to treat the infinitely repeating areas of your business like that lava floor. As the owner or team leader, your job is *not* to simply react and respond. *The floor is lava!* You are the observer, the conductor, the one *creating* that next piece of furniture (a process) that you and your team can jump to. Even better? Ask your team to help create the furniture with you.

I have wasted so much precious energy worrying about my inbox. When I *wasn't* worried, I was buried in it. In 2020, my second highest activity after Zoom meetings (141 hours) was email, clocking in at 138 hours, even with team members helping. In 2019, email was my most frequent computer activity, representing 20 percent of my time for a total of 200 hours.

Cal Newport, author and associate professor of computer science at Georgetown, shifted my perspective during our *Free Time* podcast conversation about his book *A World Without Email*. "Your job is not email responder," he said in reply to me sharing my decade-long inbox overwhelm woes. "Your email-responding is serving an *underlying job*, and there are other ways you could service that same job."

Similar to *the floor is lava* mindset, Cal says getting stuck in never-ending systems means we are ignoring the root problem. "You are taking Advil for the hurt knee instead of getting the knee healed," he said. "That's when it becomes Sisyphean and never-ending, because you are only responding at the surface level."

For each email he receives, at least until his systems are in place, Cal asks himself: *What is the right way to do this process? How do I want information flow to work for this job, and what trade-offs am I willing to make? What are the jobs I want to keep?* He considers opportunities by asking what footprint it will have on his cognitive resources.

Cal has at least four different email addresses, named after different roles in his work life. Some for his work as an author, some for his work as a professor, and one to ensure he doesn't miss out on delightful surprises and randomness: interesting@, an address that he notes on his contact page as one he reads, but doesn't respond to. "Clarity trumps responsiveness," he told me. Correspondents email knowing he most likely won't respond, rather than being left to guess.

Cal is supported by a Delightfully Tiny Team of specialists, none of whom work full-time for him: a speaking agent who works on commission from successful bookings, a publicist from Penguin Random House who helps coordinate media opportunities, and skilled technicians for things like podcast engineering and website updates.

I was dancing in lava for years, never *truly* stepping back to see the entire picture. Due to my own overwhelm, I had not applied disciplined observation to note every single type of email that arrived and what processes I needed to develop as a result. When I finally did this exercise, in a *floor-is-lava* observation mode that I dubbed "RETIRE THE WALL," of 200 languishing emails, I came up with over 15 categories that I share in this book's toolkit online. The next time you sit down to tackle email, check out that list and take on the role of observer in your inbox: What related processes are you missing that you can create?

Reduce decision fatigue by mirroring the founder of modern management, Peter Drucker, who noted that we rarely face truly unique, one-off choices: "Don't make a hundred decisions when one will do."

Part 2: Design

CHAPTER 12 RECAP

Solve for Sisyphean Systems

Two-Sentence Summary

Remove yourself from Sisyphean systems by creating higher-level processes for them (or opting out altogether). Remember: the floor is lava!

Give Yourself Permission

Stop apologizing for the delay. Trust that you will answer at the perfect time, and that it may even be perfect timing for your recipient.

Ask Yourself

What feels like a never-ending task? Are you treating symptoms instead of the root causes?

Do (or Delegate) This Next

Identify the top stress-inducing reactive "lava" in your business. Look for a way to make a single decision one time to eliminate dozens of day-to-day decisions that follow. This could be implementing a web form or survey for inquiries of a certain type, or deciding once and for all not to accept certain requests.

Align > Design > Assign >

Impact

Design with your desired impact top of mind, creating solutions that serve the highest good for all involved, including your team, clients, and broader community. Always be listening to what your customers need through smart systems that are built into the background of all that you do. This allows you to continually collect feedback, roll it up into meaningful themes on a regular basis, and improve your products for greater resonance. Part of designing for impact is to build your business to be ready (with ease!) if you get a lucky break, or viral moment of visibility. This is less about magical thinking or waiting for a lottery-ticket success shortcut, but rather encouraging an ongoing systems audit. Your words carry energy; be mindful of the impact of how you describe your community and customer journey. Consider the myth of meritocracy, that hard work is all it takes, despite one's starting circumstances. Or touting earnings, or a bootstrapped business as a primary marker of validation, given that this language fails to account for the invisible privileges that success can be tied to, in addition to persistent effort. Acknowledge: What brand of boots were you born in?

In this section, you will:
- Always be listening
- Scale by getting ready for a big break
- Use life-giving language

13

Always Be Listening

Through empathic listening, we can create a space in which others feel safe to be themselves. This virtuous circle of connection is a listening loop. It feels good to go deeper in conversation and to see and hear people as they truly are, rather than as we wish them to be.

—Ximena Vengoechea

Every month, one of my favorite packages arrives in the mail: a surprise blend of coffee from a subscription service, Trade, that knows my preferences:

- Experience Level: Intermediate
- Brew Method: Coffee maker
- Additions: Nope, I take it black
- Roast Level: Medium
- Taste: Surprising and unconventional

I light up when I see the red plastic packaging in the mailbox. Dopamine and caffeine, *yippee!* I tear the bag open to see which producer and flavor I will be savoring this month, examining the creative name and label, the way one would when selecting wine. I pry open the top for the best part of the new bag ritual: inhaling that gorgeous smell of flavorful, freshly ground coffee. Each bag arrives with a note about the blend, and "why we picked it for you." This month it is "Balanced & Fruity: Caramel sweetness stars in this tremendously drinkable blend, brightened by a Meyer lemon acidity and a nutty-sweet finish." *Yum!*

What follows on the card is as important: a message that says "tell us how you like this coffee," asking me to log-in and leave comments. This is an example of *built-in listening*, a systematic way of ensuring there are feedback mechanisms built into the business. On Trade's website, there is a clear "Take the Quiz" call-to-action for new visitors, walking them through a quick set of questions.

In the classic movie *Glengarry Glen Ross* (1992) Alec Baldwin's demanding character, Blake, exhorts his sales team to "always be closing." Shift this to *always be listening* (ABL), by making a practice out of continuous open listening, setting up a variety of systems to do this.

For example, throughout my business I have set up the following:

- An open, ongoing podcast listener survey at ItsFreeTime.com/survey

- Podcast listeners can submit voice memos, questions to air on the show, via /ask.

- Every month, subscribers who support the show submit questions for a live Q&A call.

- When newsletter subscribers join, the first message asks them to click on which of four profiles fits their journey best.

- At the end of every course, there is a generalized "Quick Course Survey" for feedback. Participants choose their course from a drop-down menu; eliminating the need to create a new post-course feedback survey for each new program.

- When I launch new programs, the enrollment process includes a pre-course survey asking about participants' biggest questions and challenges for each module. I can then build the course with their specific questions in mind.

- When I set-up a waitlist for a new program, those who are interested fill out a brief form asking for their name, email, and biggest business challenge that I can help solve.

Listening can become an embedded, ongoing practice in your business too. As with so many things, you can strengthen the *always be listening* principle through systems. Set up ongoing listening mechanisms—with all proper consent of course, not tracking people around the internet without their permission. In addition, ensure that a monthly recurring task rolls the feedback up for review, to improve products for greater resonance with community and clients.

Look for ways to build listening moments into all that you do. Team members can get creative; beyond rolling up one-off feedback that comes from customer emails, you can build an entire world with ABL in mind, embedding listening moments throughout your business to inform every new project.

Tools like Answer The Public and SparkToro can help you search for, and listen to, what *future* customers might be looking for, based on what they are already asking and consuming as it relates to your business. In botany, a rhizome is an underground stem growing continuously and horizontally, forming lateral shoots and adventitious roots to grow upward or outward. Possibilities occur at every nodal intersection, like the networked maps of plane routes at the back of airline magazines. On its homepage, Answer The Public describes the value of its rhizomic listening research as follows:

> There are 3 billion Google searches every day, and 20 percent of those have never been seen before. They're like a direct line to your customers' thoughts. Sometimes that's "How do I remove paper jam?" Other times it's the wrenching fears and secret hankerings they'd only ever dare share with Google.

One major advantage of subscription-based businesses or revenue streams, in addition to the beautiful predictability of *monthly recurring revenue* (MRR), is the ability to listen to a core set of customers in an ongoing way.

Rather than seeing a purchase as the end of a marketing process, subscription-based operations must ABL by catering to their most valuable resource: *current* subscribers. From a systems perspective, this creates a *positive feedback loop*, or *virtuous cycle*: The more you listen, the more you can improve, the longer your subscribers' stay, the stronger the word of mouth, and the more you can attract new subscribers.

Mentioning Trade at the start of this chapter is an example of this. Not only did they conduct an intake survey upon enrollment to understand my preferences, but they delivered something valuable to me each month: exposure to new delightful coffee blends. And now, here I am telling you about their service.

In his book, *Subscribed*, author Tien Tzuo extols the benefits of this approach. Gone are the *Mad Men* days of focus groups, phone surveys, and user interviews, he says. "No more hoping and praying you get a hit product. Why? Because the market research is already baked into the service."

Volvo Cars certainly seemed to be listening to the millennial segment of their market when they launched a subscription service, Care By Volvo, with a four-month minimum lease, a far lower initial commitment than typical two- to three-year vehicle lease programs.

I piloted this program at a time when I did not know if I could or wanted to commit to owning a car in New York City, yet renting something for the summer would have been four times pricier. The program tagline on their website was pitch-perfect for a family like ours: "The all-inclusive car subscription from Volvo: Subscribe online. No long-term commitment. The modern way to lease a car." Of course, once customers who are new to their elegant cars can try before they buy, they will be far more likely to want to stick with the service even after meeting the minimum commitment.

Subscription services are, by definition, well-positioned to "immediately start listening, learning, and optimizing," Tzuo writes. "When you design your service in conjunction with your subscribers, and inform that service with usage and behavioral data, you can make something that they really love and that evolves with their needs."

Returning to Trade, when I log in to give feedback, there is an enormous "above the fold" question that takes up the entire screen: "How was your last coffee?" with a button that says "Rate it," followed by a simple thumbs up or thumbs down icon next to each of my past blends.

If I click thumbs up, a pop-up appears: "Tell us what you liked," and the suggested text says "If you want, tell us more." After I hit submit, the thank you screen says, "Thanks! Your rating has been saved. Share Trade with friends, and they'll get a free bag when they sign up," with a button to refer a friend—smart, since I just told them I loved my last blend. They can also see which brands are most popular by "listening" to the data about how many separate reorders are placed for certain blends, based on initial exposure through the subscription.

If I click thumbs down, the message offers a personal-sounding mea culpa: "We're sorry you didn't like the coffee: tell us what went wrong." A simple set of buttons allows me to indicate why. Taste: Too Traditional or Too Unexpected, and Roast Level: Too Light, Too Dark; with an open comment box for any additional feedback. This time, the final screen does not ask for a referral, but smartly states, "We're sorry you didn't like the coffee. We've improved your recommendations based on your feedback."

Another example of ongoing built-in listening comes from Peloton, the at-home fitness powerhouse. (I ride in a closet under a stairwell; don't judge, it's a New York City apartment!). Beyond tracking top-line metrics such as equipment sold and number of monthly subscribers, Peloton can build in listening through a variety of methods, such as total number of classes taken:

- Across categories (biking versus yoga)
- Within categories (climb ride versus recovery ride)
- From each instructor
- From a collection, such as core strength, endurance, or beginner
- From a style of music (80s, 90s, classic rock) or featured artist

They can also infer data from:

- Class ratings after each session: thumbs up or down; difficulty on a scale of one to ten

- Number of people who bookmark certain classes

- and probably more that are not privy to me as an outsider

All of this happens seamlessly within the experience, whether people are using the fitness equipment or the app itself, without members having to go to the trouble of submitting feedback through a contact form on their website.

Finally, deep listening can be baked into your client onboarding experience. Together Agency, a branding company based in Brooklyn that I worked with for *Pivot* and *Free Time*, differentiates themselves by their unique listening process. The first thing they do upon engaging with a new client is to send an exploratory survey called a brand questionnaire. It includes provocative questions ranging from "If your brand were a texture what would it be?" to "What are your three non-negotiable rules of life?" and "What topics could you talk about endlessly?"

After clients complete the survey, the Together team conducts an in-depth, live question-and-answer session with the client, with everyone on their team—from co-founders to lead designers—asking thoughtful follow-up questions to close gaps in their understanding. These steps reflect Together's unique process for active listening, one that gives clients confidence that their important goals are thoughtfully taken into consideration, often sparking new insights for the client during this creative excavation process.

Listening is an active verb for your business, not a one-off event. Create recurring listening systems that allow you to continually improve what Tzuo calls the "never-ending product."

Always Be Listening

Two-Sentence Summary

Systematize listening to your community by building listening moments into all that you do. Regularly review that feedback to help determine product improvements and what to build next.

Give Yourself Permission
Not to have *all* the answers or best ideas; tune into your community instead.

Ask Yourself
How can you embed ongoing listening loops throughout your business?

Do (or Delegate) This Next
Create at least one general feedback survey that you could send customers, community members, newsletter subscribers, or even friends and family. It can be something as simple as, "If I could solve your biggest challenge around {your business focus}, what would it be?" or "What would you be thrilled to achieve in {focus area} in the year ahead?" Visit the Free Time Toolkit online for an example of a general course evaluation survey.

14

Scale: Be Ready for a Big Break

Overwhelm is the abundance you asked for.

—**Unknown**, via Jasmine Star

Sarah Apgar burst into Shark Tank and rode out on a tidal wave, earning nearly a million dollars in revenue during the months following her successful pitch.

You met Sarah in the section on values; she is the founder of FitFighter, a fitness company and "a way of life that makes you Mission Ready." She originally designed her signature Steelhose strength training tool to train firefighters better for the rigors of the job. In addition to founding and leading FitFighter, she is an Iraq military veteran with degrees from Princeton and Dartmouth, a volunteer firefighter, and mom of two, among many other accolades.

I was awed watching her on TV, gracefully throwing her Steelhose into the air while seamlessly delivering her two-minute opening pitch. Robert Herjavec captured my sentiments, calling her "one of the most impressive human beings we have ever seen." Although it may seem like a lucky break, in our *Free Time* podcast conversation months later, Sarah shared the fuller picture of her journey. She poured years into organic product development.

Leading up to her time in the tank, Sarah put in thirty days of diligent practice and run-through conversations with friends to capture this "lightning in a bottle" moment, setting her on the path to become the billion-dollar brand that matches her biggest vision.

How about you: Are you ready for your big break? Or would your business break? Would you gleefully ride the wave you have been preparing for, or would your business systems collapse under the crush of surging interest?

One thought exercise I encourage my team to ask regularly is, "Are we Oprah or Tim (Ferriss) ready?" This is less about magical thinking, waiting for a lottery ticket success shortcut, but rather encouraging an ongoing systems audit by imagining interviews with hosts I admire. Would my team and I be ready to catch the wave of interest and incoming leads that either of their two podcasts would generate, without our systems crashing?

If you scale with sloppy systems, your problems will only multiply. Hence, the adage from Bill Hewlett, co-founder of Hewlett Packard, that "More companies die of indigestion than starvation." One of Tim Ferriss's readers labeled this the "hug of death" resulting from outsize traffic due to products he recommends. If the small companies don't see it coming, they sometimes run out of inventory, servers crash, or they experience other flubs. These are the last problems a company wants to face when meeting outsize incoming demand.

Make it easy and inviting for big (*the biggest!*) opportunities to come to you. Be ready before the wave, not scrambling or fumbling after the fact. In systems-thinking terminology, this is known as expanding *service capacity* and addressing *limits to success*. Service capacity refers to your team's abilities to meet demand, the maximum level of service production; the latter can occur when achieving market saturation due to your success.

This "big break" thought exercise precipitates at least five categories of questions:

1. **Do you have scalable streams of income that can capture the incoming interest heading your way, without you or anyone involved being the bottleneck?** Can customers purchase courses and

services without being limited by your time-for-money capacity? What if 1,000 people were eager to purchase something from you—could you handle that? In terms of revenue streams, are you selling products to support that? What if it were 10,000 or 100,000 people clamoring for your offerings?

Tattoo artist Scott Campbell started minting his designs as *non-fungible tokens (NFTs)* based on blockchain technology. With his online marketplace, All Our Best, he experiments with transcending the typical time-for-money exchange, as many tattoo artists are paid by the hour for sittings. In contrast to artists who produce physical assets like paintings, tattoos are more ephemeral; they fade, and can't be passed on from one recipient to the next.

"Musicians don't get paid by how long it takes them to create a song," Scott said in a *New York Times* interview. "You'd never go to a gallery and think, *How long did it take the artist to paint it? I'll pay him for his time.*" NFTs allow Scott and other artists to receive royalties each time their digital tattoo design changes hands, giving the work life beyond its application onto a human canvas. When someone purchases one of his NFTs, they also get scheduling priority for a tattoo sitting.

2. **Are your team and systems prepared to handle this inflow of traffic and interest?** Could your systems for customer service and fulfillment handle ten or one hundred times the load? How can you simplify so that team members with less skill and experience can complete related tasks?

My brother, Tom Blake, is the co-founder of Flexible, a real estate investment company that makes it easy for property owners to sell, partner, or lease on their terms. His vision is to create a successful company that runs on its own, through sophisticated repeatable systems. A question he asks himself when upgrading his operations with scale in mind: "How can we design roles and responsibilities so a virtual assistant can have the same output as a rockstar?"

Prior to documenting his marketing systems for handling leads, it seemed necessary to have experts handle these tasks, ones he paid nearly

$150 per hour. With detailed systems and documentation in place, he is now able to work with virtual assistants to fulfill many steps in the process at $15 per hour, ten times less than his initial expenditure. This has a dramatic impact on his bottom line for a central business area, while ensuring Flexible is ready for interest surges.

3. **Would you be proud of what people are seeing on your website landing page?** Is there a clear call-to-action to sign-up for your newsletter or one next step to engage further, and is it relevant to the audience coming over? Are your welcome autoresponders fresh and current? Are your about page and bio updated?

4. **Is there something special you would like to create for this audience in particular?** One common technique is to say, "Welcome {publication} readers (or listeners)," briefly re-introducing yourself, and offering follow-up content related to what you were featured for on the larger site or show. Perhaps you would like to offer a special discount or opportunity to engage with you further, maybe even setting up a free workshop a few weeks out that this new audience can enroll in to get to know you better. In other words, how can you roll out the red carpet for this group?

5. **Are you ready to filter out the scrutiny that an influx of strangers might spark?** Going mainstream requires a thick skin. You will be exposed to new people who do not already know and trust you, who might be having a tough day, or who might decide for no good reason that they don't like you. Create a plan for moving past, or ignoring, unhelpful criticism from the peanut gallery, people who would rather poke holes in your business than provide constructive feedback, while still making room for your inner circle to point out what you might be missing.

The point of this thought exercise—reviewing these five big break considerations—is not to pin all your hopes on one special savior, but rather to foster an ongoing state of readiness that energetically invites—even courts—opportunities to come your way.

Are you the bottleneck limiting your income potential? Are there areas hiding in your operations where things could break at the worst possible moment? Think through surges in advance, step by micro-step. Imagine you are running an emergency preparedness drill with your team: Does every person know what to do if and when a big interest wave hits?

Seven Scale-Building Levers

Archimedes was an ancient Greek of many talents: mathematician, physicist, engineer, astronomer, and inventor, famous for his *eureka!* exclamation. He also discovered the *law of the lever*. Think of a seesaw, or prying a boulder off the ground. The lever is a bar that pivots on a fulcrum, where the bar rests. Depending on where that fulcrum is located, the lever can lift heavier weight. In business, this translates to achieving greater leverage with less force, by applying effort strategically.

Below are seven levers you can consider when looking to create greater scale, so that you can capitalize on increased interest, or generate your own momentum:

1. **Services:** If you offer services, you can experiment with format for greater reach or consolidating delivery, such as half- or full-day deeper dives in what *Systems Saved Me* owner Jordan Gill calls "Done in a Day" intensives, also commonly referred to as VIP Days. You can train others to deliver your services, so that if inbound inquiries increase to ten or one hundred times their current volume, you are not the bottleneck for working with new clients. Another example is train-the-trainer (TTT); instead of just offering workshops, teach others how to deliver those same sessions, either as an extension of your facilitator network, or internally within larger companies.

2. **Products and Pricing:** Extend your reach through affiliate partnerships and setting up programs that provide recurring revenue, such as subscriptions or retainers. You can "productize" your most commonly requested (and most lucrative) service, as author John Warrillow teaches in *Built to Sell*, streamlining processes for delivery. You can also offer "skip the line" VIP pricing, as theme parks do, for an accelerated start date when you have a waitlist, or for increased access to you. It may surprise you how many clients may be happy to pay for this higher-touch experience.

3. **Platform:** The larger your platform, the more you become *discoverable*—like two Bluetooth devices connecting—to new opportunities, press, and inbound interest. This creates added leverage for catapulting your business into bigger opportunities and growing your network.

4. **Advertising:** Methodically test paid advertising so you know exactly how much it costs to acquire a new customer. Compare your *cost per acquisition* (CPA) to your average *customer lifetime value* (CLV) to identify your ad-spend sweet spot. Those who really nail this are able to pour money into advertising because they have discovered, for their unique offerings and onboarding sequences, how to spend one dollar to get the proverbial two in return.

5. **Organic:** Intentionally build word-of-mouth moments into programs and products. Set-up systems for requesting referrals, as John Jantsch outlines in his book *The Referral Engine*. You can also work to improve retention of current

customers by asking about, then building, what they need next to meet their biggest challenges.

6. **Sales:** Capture talking points and repeatable processes, improving both over time to increase inbound inquiries and conversion rates. Jeb Blount shares many effective systems for sales and negotiation cycles in his book *Inked*. If you are currently handling all the sales conversations for your business, create a guide in your Manager Manual to open the opportunity for someone else to help with this someday.

7. **Systems:** You can also increase your capacity to scale or handle a surge of interest by increasing efficiency throughout your back-end systems and operations—the crux of this book!

Returning to Sarah's story, typically landing a *Shark Tank* appearance requires standing in snaking lines at a public casting call or submitting a video online, surely to be lost among tens of thousands of monthly submissions. Sarah was already building momentum of her own when the *Shark Tank* team called her out of the blue. Her "mission readiness" mantra—whether serving in Iraq, starting a fitness company, tending to her family, or responding to that *Shark Tank* phone call—means that Sarah actively plans to be ready for her big break, building with excellence and preparing ahead of time for all possible consequences and outcomes.

When I asked if she was happy with how she performed during her two-minute opening pitch, the one she had been rehearsing for 90-minutes each morning for over one month, Sarah replied, "I was so happy, I cried. I mean, I absolutely crushed it."

The *Shark Tank* experience was not merely a random chance. "It was a beautiful culmination of the first two years of my experience as a founder and

FitFighter's founding story," Sarah said. "I am grateful for that and what has resulted, and how it has planted our feet firmly on the ground to grow into the next billion dollar health and wellness brand."

How did the rest of the pitch go?

Spoiler alert: Sarah received FitFighter funding from Kind founder Daniel Lubetzky, someone aligned with the values she so clearly articulates for herself and others.

CHAPTER 14 RECAP

Scale: Be Ready for a Big Break

Two-Sentence Summary

Make it easy and inviting for thrilling opportunities to come to you. Be ready before the wave, not scrambling or fumbling after the crash.

Give Yourself Permission
To fantasize where your big break could come from, what you would be featured for, and what new possibilities would open up in your life and business as a result.

Ask Yourself
Imagine your future self and business receiving this increased interest: How are you handling it smoothly and joyfully? What are you grateful to have done to prepare?

Do (or Delegate) This Next
Identify your biggest limiting factor, or *limfac*, and take steps to increase your capacity to scale in this area.

15

Use Life-Giving Language

We don't create users, we create evangelists.

—Julie Rice

One morning I was listening to a business podcast, and the host kept talking about *cold traffic*, in reference to all the people that had reached her randomly outside of ads. I couldn't help but scratch my head. *That's me.* She was talking about me and others as if we weren't in the audio room.

Meanwhile, another podcaster described his audience-building quest as "a war for attention." On a reality TV series about hiring a VP of operations, the company founder and show's star said "I need a killer," then described her current assistant as "a silent assassin." A well-meaning guest on a systems podcast compared customers to fruit, encouraging business owners to "put that fruit in a juicer" and squeeze the remaining value out.

In a span of several weeks, as a listener, I had been reduced to descriptors like "cold," "traffic," and produce to be pulverized. Suffice it to say, none of that language resonated with me as a potential customer.

The words you use publicly and behind the scenes matter. They carry energy. Your clients and community members are not cold *anything*, no matter how they found you, and no matter how new they are to your corner of the world. They are living, breathing people who you can look forward to working with when there is a mutual fit.

I can hear the correction chorus now: *These are* business *podcasts, after all, what did you expect? These are common business terms.* I don't care. Calling people I respect "users" and "fans" just does not make sense. For this reason, I chose not to sign up for a leading email service provider because I didn't want readers to click on newsletter links and see an irksome word (the provider's name) in redirects before landing at the destination URLs.

Jacquette M. Timmons, the financial behaviorist you met in the Design stage overview and host of the *More Than Money* podcast, shared a common financial phrase that grates like nails on a chalkboard for her. She illuminated the historical context making the imperative to "charge what you are worth" so harmful:

> My heritage is Jamaican American. My ancestry is tied to people's humanity being connected to a dollar. So when people say "charge what you are worth," I don't know if they fully understand the visceral reaction that creates for some of us. Instead consider the value *you deliver. How are you helping someone answer a question, solve a problem, or get their desire fulfilled? What are you bringing to the table? You are charging for your education (formal and informal), your perspective, your gifts, your skills, and your years of experience. You are not charging what you, as a person, are worth.*

Stewart Butterfield, CEO and co-founder of Slack, wrote an internal memo to his team just before the first version launched in 2013, illustrating how a shift in language leads to different results. In it, he said:

> We are an exceptional software development team. But, we now also need to be an excellent customer development team. That's why I said "build a customer base" rather than "gain market share:" the nature of the task is different, and we will work together to understand, anticipate and better serve the people who trust us with their teams' communications, one customer at a time.

For another example of the impact language can have, consider the showboating in business circles about founder stories. When you hear someone boasting about how much they earn, or bootstrapping their business without outside funding, what was their relationship to risk given the privileges of their birth? Did they know, like me, that their family would not let them end up homeless? Were they tasked with working throughout high school to support their siblings, or able to take ideal internships? Do they discuss these advantages among their other heroic traits?

I love celebrating qualities like tenacity, ingenuity, and perseverance. I am fascinated by the behind-the-scenes of how others achieve what they do, *and* it is still important that we acknowledge our visible and invisible privileges.

As Robert H. Frank reminds readers in *Success and Luck*, "Although success is extremely difficult to achieve without talent and hard work, there are nonetheless many highly talented and hardworking people who never achieve any significant material success."

Perhaps one of the best answers I heard on a business podcast when asked to explain his notable career accolades was someone who answered, "I was born lucky. I won the family lottery," before launching into his efforts toward building a successful business.

Some have faced unspeakable trauma and adversity in their upbringing, and still they persevere. How many of us were fortunate to grow up with a roof over our head, clean water, no roaches or rats scuttling about, good schools, and/or parents who supported our ambitions? I respect when leaders acknowledge their hard work, luck, *and* privileges—as success is almost always a combination of these and more.

Language represents our values and beliefs, and becomes the foundation for the internal narrative that drives our actions. Consider how language maps to processes in your business, and your resulting motivation (or lack thereof) to follow them.

For example, typical "biz speak" around acquiring new customers goes something like this:

1. Notice I said *acquiring*, as if you're an object to be bought or caught.

2. Write a *sales page* that emphasizes pain, fear, and FOMO: What will prospective customers be missing out on if they do not engage further?

3. Warm up *cold* prospects with a *lead magnet*, a sampler to sign-up for your newsletter.

4. Create a *tripwire*, a low-cost offering to see who might purchase higher-ticket items next.

5. *Convert* those prospects as they travel farther through your *funnel*, where as soon as the "purchased!" box is checked, you can refocus on step one, to acquire all those customers you haven't snared yet.

Is it any wonder many of us are turned off by this as a way of doing business? The language is all wrong. It is dehumanizing and demotivating, especially if you are a Heart-Based Business owner. Now imagine the *path to inviting* new members or clients, rephrased as follows:

1. **Instead of acquiring, we are inviting** others for whom there is a mutually beneficial fit.

2. **Write a letter to your ideal community member.** What are they feeling and where are they heading? How would you write to a friend sitting across from you in a coffee shop, making them feel seen and heard? What are they struggling with, and how can you help?

3. **Delight your potential friend by offering something immediately practical and valuable.** How can you build trust and demonstrate the value you bring through free offerings? What complimentary gifts are you excited to give?

4. **Invite commitment** through offering the next step as a product, even at a low investment, so they show up for themselves as much as you. Half the value of hiring a coach is in the accountability created when hard-earned resources are at stake.

5. **After building trust through delivering value, provide ongoing opportunities** for new community members to engage even more deeply, aligning their needs with your next offerings, helping them meet their most important goals along the way.

I am a builder, not a natural marketer. In order to launch programs with ease and joy, I need to flip the script as I did above into something that intuitively makes sense to me. Instead of "acquiring customers" I think of it as making friends. I imagine figuratively holding people's hand as they traverse a four-stage path into my business: aware, explore, join, stay. I also note how I want people to feel as they navigate each of those four stages: ease, utility, delight, and deeper commitment. Let's go through each one in more detail.

1. Aware: First I need people to know I exist. I achieve this through ongoing public original thinking, primarily my podcasts, weekly(ish) newsletter, and websites for each book. When people first encounter my work, I hope they experience a sense of *ease*; possibility and permission instead of pressure.

2. Explore: Once people know where to find me, I make it easy to explore my offerings. I deliver free templates (and have, since my earliest days as a blogger in 2005), host free workshops, and create evergreen content that is helpful to specific goals, such as writing a book or launching a podcast. My hope for people in the exploration phase is that they experience immense *utility* through practical tools that provide immediate relief.

3. Join: If they are an ideal community member, which means they will benefit from what I offer and Heart-Based Business resonates with them, presumably they will have already received tremendous value and joy through my work. Inviting them to join a course or community is not burdensome (for me) or obnoxious (for them); rather, it's the next natural step. Once people join, I want them to feel *delighted!* A mixture of small, quick wins combined with a powerful sense of vision and possibility.

Part 2: Design

4. **Stay:** Finally, for the inner circle of community members, there is a sense of continuity and *deeper commitment* on both sides. I build in listening opportunities, so I can continue creating content that most meets their needs. Fellow community members multiply each other's impact by connecting with each other even outside of more structured interactions. At this stage, we are all sticking around for an ongoing, rewarding, long-term relationship and Heart-Based Business community.

The path and desired outcomes I outline here may differ from yours. The point of this exercise is to free yourself from traditional marketing constraints and "corp speak," instead reimagining resonant paths toward relationship-building with your future community members. How would you describe your ideal customer journey in a way that a five-year-old would understand? And not just understand, but be excited by?

Much of this book is about systems and principles for running a Heart-Based Business, and taking a stand for how you will operationalize those values in your day-to-day activities. If you have not already done so, take time to clarify your position regarding specific practices for fostering diversity, equity, inclusivity, and accessibility. For example, when pricing services to expand reach, some business owners offer scholarships, "pay what you can," donation-based, or sliding scale prices. Some block out names on resumes, so unconscious bias does not factor into hiring decisions.

No business operates in a vacuum. We weave into broader systems of society, visible and invisible. Many of these systems have long-standing bias and dysfunction embedded into them that we must actively work to correct, such as through our education, criminal justice, political, medical, and financial systems. This is an ongoing work-in-progress, not a box we check and mark complete, then move on. It is a lens for viewing every process—whether hiring, marketing, or community-building—to ensure that we are taking forward-looking steps to be accessible and inclusive in our language and actions.

Words are meaningless if they are not backed by process and internal action. Upon hiring me for a speaking engagement, one company asked to review my slides for potential accessibility issues prior to my keynote. I was grateful that they took the time to add text descriptions to every image for those with vision impairments.

Another organization I worked with conducted an internal audit of how much they paid vendors. When they noticed a discrepancy between how much they were paying female contractors compared to their male counterparts, even though none were full-time employees, they raised compensation across the board for the female-owned businesses.

These are teams that are walking their talk. Beyond generic corporate PR statements, they are putting diversity, equity, and inclusion (DEI) practices in place, engagement by engagement, even with outside vendors like me. What unexpected steps can you take toward improving others' lives through the resources, privileges, and advantages you already have?

When she was just twenty-four years old, Karen Pittelman made a radical move. She dissolved her trust—all three million dollars of it—to co-found the Chahara Foundation, a fund run by and for low-income women activists in Boston. Karen also served as the first program coordinator for Resource Generation, a "Community of young people with wealth and/or class privilege committed to the equitable distribution of wealth, land, and power," and co-authored their book *Classified*.

As Karen pointed out during our *Pivot* podcast conversation, redirecting her financial privilege did not give away her *class privilege*. Of her decision, she recalls asking herself, *"Am I going to be complicit with the system that created me, or find a way to align my life with my values?"*

"Some people work three jobs just to survive," Karen said. "I had a three million dollar trust fund just for being born. I didn't have to do anything for that, and that changes everything, even though I gave it all away."

Today Karen works as a writer, writing coach, co-founder of the Trans Justice Funding Project, and singer-songwriter for her queer country band, Karen & the Sorrows, while still actively championing wealth redistribution.

She encourages those with privilege to take action by not only redistributing their wealth, but also the decision-making power over those resources by giving to community-led funds.

"It's easy to take this to heart and think it's about you personally," Karen said. "Instead, remember that we are tiny drops in bigger institutions surrounding us, shaping our lives."

Beyond the language you use throughout your business, consider: What action can you take to become the kind of organization you want to see more of in the world? As you grow and succeed, how can you share some of those resources to help others do the same?

CHAPTER 15 RECAP

Use Life-Giving Language

Two-Sentence Summary

The words we use publicly and behind the scenes matter and carry energy. This is not a box we mark complete once, then move on; it is a lens through which we consider every process and product.

Give Yourself Permission

Ditch language that demotivates you or that doesn't feel aligned with your brand. Speak to potential customers as you would to friends.

Ask Yourself

What specific practices will ensure that your values around diversity, accessibility, equity, access, and inclusion are reflected in how you conduct your day-to-day business?

Do (or Delegate) This Next

Map your new community member's path through your business with the four stages—aware, explore, join, stay—or modify to create new ones that resonate.

Part 2: Design

Align > **Design** > Assign >

_____

Process

Beyond the ideal outcomes and impact of new projects, ensure that you and your team are intentional about designing the processes required to make that work happen before you assign to team members. Be strategic with your time: bake in batches by saving similar tasks to be done at a regular cadence in sprints during designated time blocks, particularly actions that are small and not time-sensitive. Batching helps eliminate task bloat that comes from reacting unconsciously to low-priority items. Email and messaging apps can also be processed in batches, so you and your team are not splintering your attention all day, checking and reacting as a default state. Design your default state to be intentional, active focus. Ensure that your calendar has plenty of spacious time for strategic, creative thinking. No task needs to be repeated the same way twice if you are paying attention and willing to do a bit of extra work up front. For any recurring task or message, take small actions today that will save time in the future. This has the added benefit of preventing knowledge from being stored only in one person's mind.

In this section, you will:
- Design deep work containers
- Time block and bake in batches
- Automate what you repeat

16

Design Deep Work Containers

Alone had always felt like an actual place to me, as if it weren't a state of being, but rather a room where I could retreat to be who I really was.

—Cheryl Strayed

Cal Newport, who you met in the "Solve for Sisyphean Systems" chapter (Chapter 12), put words to an atrophying quality in the modern working world in his book, *Deep Work*. This quality is one that many of us crave: "The ability to focus without distraction on a cognitively demanding task." He calls deep work a "skill that allows you to quickly master complicated information and produce better results in less time . . . [providing] the sense of true fulfillment that comes from craftsmanship."

You deserve to have uninterrupted, focused time to do dynamic work, at times you are most creative. We all know how elusive that dynamic focus can be, making it all the more important to systematize deep work time amidst a world of fractured, digital distraction.

For example, at the end of each year, I block out deep work days (two per week), weeks (one per month), and months (two per year) on my calendar for the following year, knowing that it is much harder to create these containers once my schedule is full. These are blocks of time that prevent anyone from scheduling over them, including my team and scheduling tools. The hardest person to prevent overrides from? *Me!*

As soon as I have one meeting scheduled on a given day, even if it is at 2 p.m., my whole day coalesces around it, as one person remarked, "like mosquitos to my bare arm." I set timers, I am anticipating the call, starting to prepare, and I am far more likely to fritter time away the closer the meeting time gets. My whole day changes and magnetizes toward that meeting. For me, a deep work day means *nothing* gets scheduled in advance, not even coffee with a friend. I can always decide something spontaneously that day, once my focused work is complete. This set-up allows me to enter a flow state on whatever I choose to do that day.

At the start of a deep work week, I queue up my biggest project, the one activity lever that, if implemented, would have the most positive impact on my revenue or creative output. It is typically something that I need to fully immerse myself in. I don't want to get interrupted or have to context-switch and pick up the phone. Context-switching creates *return-time costs*, the time it takes to get back to the level of depth prior to the distraction. Sometimes the designated week becomes a time for desperately needed deep *rest*, and I could not have known that in advance until the free, open calendar time arrived.

The early drafts of this book came together spontaneously on a series of unscheduled Mondays. I was free to jump on *aha!* moments and big ideas, then spend the day working them out, unplanned yet focused and immersed. I compiled the first draft on one of these meetings-free Mondays, flowing with momentum from my weekend work. To my relief, the next day I only had one call, which meant I could keep going, lost in a whirl of time, totally dialed in.

When I checked RescueTime, it showed four hours and twenty-two minutes of computer time. I did a double take. *That can't be right!* I counted the hours on my hand. It was true; what felt like double the time was really double the focus, and quadruple the output. Not just how much I was able to get done, but the feeling of accomplishment from going from "zero to one" on a project that was so important to me. I did not open my inbox once; in prior years that would have seemed radical or impossible. In addition to keeping my phone perpetually on silent mode, while writing I turn on my computer's "do not disturb" feature, put up an email autoresponder for anywhere from one week to one month, and do not pressure myself to respond to texts the day they arrive.

While finishing final edits, I blocked off two *months* for mostly focused work, something I was unable to do with my previous two books. This coincided with summer, the slowest season in my business. Although my income did drop while I dedicated such singular focus to the book, I also knew the trade-off would be worth it for a project that could create abundant new opportunities across the next several years.

How We Free Time at JBE

These are best practices I share in our Manager Manual to encourage team members to work strategically, even if they are not accustomed to working this way with other clients:

- What is truly urgent? We only rely on text messaging and Slack when items are time-sensitive. If a team member emails or Slacks after hours, feel free to respond during your next work window, unless the message is noted as urgent.
- If you are choosing to work on a weekend, but don't need a reply on the weekend, you can start messages with "For Monday" or "For Next Week."
- Work from wherever you want, just about whenever you want! Barring major deadlines, meetings, or customer service hours, we do not care when or where you work.
- We will never *set* deadlines on evenings or weekends, but that doesn't mean you cannot work at those times if they fit your energy and workflow.

- If you will be out of office (OOO) for one day or more, add that to our shared calendar. It is rarely an issue; rather, it helps the team know where and when to pick up the slack without stepping on toes, and to not assign you tasks due or ask questions on those days.
- If previous work or weekly check-ins are scheduled for the day/s you are out, please complete those in advance or renegotiate the deadline.
- Each of us has a right to call out bureaucracy and busy work, and help eliminate it!

Due to my disdain for distracting pings for things that aren't time-sensitive, my team and I use instant messaging tools very selectively. In no way would we want to create, or subscribe to, a never-ending stream that we are each monitoring all day. We reserve texts and phone calls for relative emergencies, or if it is clear the person has missed an earlier message and an important deadline is fast-approaching.

The second way we implement more "instant" messaging is what we call "Pop-up Slack" when working quickly during an important launch week with more moving pieces and customer inquiries. The team and I create a channel for the launch, then agree to monitor it more closely than usual, responding as quickly as we are able. Outside of these use cases, it is preferable for us (and for organization's sake) to communicate about specific tasks or projects in the Notion work area for that project, tempting as it may be to fire off emails or Slack messages in the moment.

When it comes to designing deep work (and rest) containers, consider your energy bank account. If you are making too many withdrawals from your natural way of working and interacting with others, soon your balance will be zero.

As an introvert, I think about low energy as an iPhone turning red on ten percent or less battery. When I find myself in too many situations with other people, especially if I am already feeling run down, I simply cannot get to a full charge unless I take measures to say no. It is often the case that I don't realize I am on empty until it's too late, when resentment starts bubbling or I become a *Grumpy Monkey*, the name of a wonderful children's book by Suzanne and Max Lang.

Even if you do not mind frequent interactions, for your more introverted team members, too many meetings and inbound pings may be costly for their energy bank accounts. Brainstorm together: What has worked best for them in the past? What if the entire team had one day a week with no meetings? Asana, a team productivity software company, observes No Meeting Wednesdays with over 100 employees. The Muse named theirs "Winning Wednesdays" where no one on the team is allowed to schedule meetings from 9 a.m. to 1 p.m. Not only will your introverted team members appreciate this, ambiverts and extroverts can also benefit from days without distractions.

More radically, you might try holding meetings just *one* day a week, leaving the rest of the week strictly meeting-free. In a *Forbes* profile, Ophelia co-founder and Columbia Business School faculty member Mattan Griffel shared how helpful it was to hold *all* of his meetings on Wednesdays. It helped preserve his focus time and filter out unnecessary requests.

Sometimes no matter how much time we set aside for deep work, we still wake up on the wrong side of the bed and can better use that time for recharging instead. The *Grumpy Monkey* children's book mentioned above teaches through the lens of Jim Panzee, who wakes up one day in a world where "the sun was too bright, the sky was too blue, and the bananas were too sweet." His mood matches the title of one of my favorite comedy podcasts, hosted by siblings Alex and Christine Schiefer, providing commentary on irreverent one-star reviews: *Beach Too Sandy, Water Too Wet*.

The moral of *Grumpy Monkey*: "In a world full of *shoulds*, sometimes we just need a day to feel however we need to feel."

CHAPTER 16 RECAP

Design Deep Work Containers

Two-Sentence Summary

We are not brain surgeons; little is truly urgent. Be mindful to prevent small, compounding withdrawals from your energy and focus bank accounts.

Give Yourself Permission

Stop scheduling so far in advance, and holding calls on five days of the week (*if not three or four!*). Permission to turn on "Do Not Disturb" mode on your laptop and phone all day, especially during your deep work windows.

Ask Yourself

What calendar constraints could you devise to create spacious freedom?

Do (or Delegate) This Next

Starting from the next available "blank" weeks on your calendar, block out deep work containers. Think of this like setting up bumpers at a bowling alley, so the ball stays between the gutters. Whether one week a month, two days per week, or even an entire month in the summer and over the holidays, get a jump on this before your calendar fills by default through lack of action and planning. New meetings will bump off these lane boundaries and stay right where you want them.

17

Time Block and Bake in Batches

There is no salvation in time. You cannot be free in the future.
Presence is the key to freedom, so you can only be free now.

—Eckhart Tolle

Our relationship to time is imprinted upon us from an early age, and it affects the boundaries we set, or fail to, as business owners.

You may be used to a default *time blueprint* that influences how you approach blocking categories of time on your calendar, such as for your projects, for clients, or for your team. Without inquiry, this blueprint is often set by default based on your upbringing, how your parents related to time and work, or habits that formed back when working in the military, college sports, or a corporate environment (if you didn't jump straight into entrepreneurship after school).

Limbic imprinting refers to how experiences shape our emotional map, beliefs, and values. Early experiences are stored in our brain's limbic system, influencing our lives at a subconscious level far beyond infancy. Some scientists believe our first two years inform the psychological development of our lifetime.

I didn't know there was a word for it at the time, but I was a latchkey kid in elementary school, with a house key hanging on a string around my neck. When classes ended and my parents were still at work, I either lounged with my younger brother and a babysitter at home, or I dog-eared books I hadn't paid for while sitting on the floor in the corner of Green Apple Books in San Francisco.

It was not every day, but I also remember taking San Francisco's MUNI bus, the kind with big lumbering poles to conduct electricity as they navigated hilly streets, over to a community center where my afternoon activity stack would begin: gymnastics, piano, ballet; working on homework in-between, or for an odd and short phase, selling chocolate bars (if I sold three, I got one free).

My mom picked me up on those days when she got off work, around 6:30 p.m. Between school days and jam-packed afternoons, my schedule set the tone for working full-time, for always being on. For learning, yes, but also for meeting others' expectations for attendance and performance.

When reflecting on my harried life as a working adult, I realized the crux of my unconscious over-scheduling conundrum: I had been practicing stacking my day full of "meetings" since I was a kid. A crammed calendar seemed normal to me. It was the energetic blueprint of how I spent time. It started with rushing from one thing to another at eight years old. I was constantly monitoring when I needed to be where, what time things were starting, when I needed to be picked up. Even then, I had a side-hustle: *The Monthly Dig-Up*, a newspaper I started out of my living room when I was eleven years old, that I continued producing—sometimes under great self-imposed stress—throughout high school.

While at Google, I created a Craigslist post to earn money on the side as an HTML and CSS tutor for small business owners, so they wouldn't have to hire an expensive designer to make simple updates on their website. I did this for years, while also starting a blog that I managed on nights and weekends. I was raised under what we now see as trends of my generation: providing kids with a week full of scheduled activities—yes, for personal enrichment and professional advancement—but also for the benefit of allowing both parents to work.

Don't get me wrong: I learned so much from these coaches, teachers, and side hustles. I learned discipline from athletics and how to meet tight deadlines from journalism. I learned independence from managing my own suite of activities after school. But I also accepted feeling time-stressed and overstuffed as a default state. There was always somewhere to be or a deadline to crunch on. This feeling was imprinted early via *nurture*, and it was partly inherent, if you consider my *nature* has its own built-in motivation. If there *wasn't* an impending time crunch, I quickly found ways to fill my time.

Free time felt uncomfortable, until I got sick from the stress and had to confront that discomfort. As psychologist Mihaly Csikszentmihalyi, author of *Flow*, writes, "The popular assumption is that no skills are involved in enjoying free time, and that anybody can do it. Yet the evidence suggests the opposite: free time is more difficult to enjoy than work."

I remember looking ahead at every calendar week as a brick wall of meetings when I worked at Google, walking from one to the next with my still-open laptop resting in the crook of my arm. *Hey, I could even type while in the elevator!* Even when I first became self-employed, I could not understand why I set goals to create more schedule space, but then conceded dozens of small "yeses" each week that left the following one jammed again . . . and the one after that, and the one after that.

As the saying goes, "Don't write a check that your body can't cash." Was it a coincidence that I developed Graves' disease, a hyperthyroid condition marked by bulged eyes and shaky hands, when I started working full-time as an adult? Was it a coincidence that, after years of monthly blood tests and treating it with medication, what was supposed to be a lifelong condition—necessitating removing my thyroid and taking a daily pill to replace it—normalized as soon as I could set my own hours and daily cadence as a small business owner? Thankfully, due in large part to these lifestyle changes, I skipped the radioactive iodine pill one doctor tried to pressure me into taking, keeping my thyroid intact.

It was not until several years into self-employment that I connected the dots. I realized how deep my neural pathways went, well-worn grooves that reminded me time is meant to be filled, stacked, managed, and juggled. What was completely unfamiliar: spaciousness and simplicity. Those were luxuries beyond imagining.

Only as an entrepreneur did I start tuning into my actual energy requirements, not the perception of how much energy I *should* have for meetings on a given day. After more than three phone calls in one day, I started to become drained and impatient, resentful that I couldn't get back to my creative work.

I did not invent the concept of time blocking, dividing the day into specific segments to complete discrete activities through concentrated focus. But I can tell you this: *knowing* is one thing, and *doing* is another. We all have bad calendar habits. You will not block the time expansively if you still hold yourself to an outdated energetic imprint of what a calendar means, and how it should be managed. I don't have the stamina I had as a child, as a teenager, as a twenty-something, and I no longer want to.

John Lee Dumas, author of *The Common Path to Uncommon Success* and podcaster mentioned in the chapter on nonlinear breakthroughs, blocks off just four days per month for conducting interviews for his daily podcast, batching about eight conversations per day. He allocates a fifth day to being a guest in a marathon stack of twenty back-to-back fifteen-minute interviews, with five minute buffers in between, for when he is invited to other people's shows. We may not all have JLD-level stamina for this level of time blocking consolidation, but it is worth considering all possibilities.

Or consider Antonio Neves' time blueprint shift. He spent ten years as a TV journalist before striking out on his own. When Antonio was single, he could work around the clock guilt free. But once he and his wife had twins, everything changed. Routines and boundaries became central to a smoothly running household and business, as he wanted to be present as a husband and father. He needed to release his fears of hiring help, whether due to the financial investment or trusting other professionals to handle aspects of his business.

Antonio didn't anticipate what happened when he did set clearer boundaries around his time and tasks. "I found that making those decisions opened me up more for creativity, and *increased* my income as opposed to decreasing it," he said.

Another benefit was greater credibility with his clients, even though he was hesitant to release his role in "high-touch mode" on new speaking engagements. Soon, scheduling, planning behind the scenes, and logistics were being handled by someone else.

"When I stopped being the main point of communication for my speaking, something energetically shifted there," he said. "When I showed up the day of the engagement it was different than previously when I was the one doing everything. The dynamic was more special."

Many of my own realizations came from road-testing. When I first started coaching, I set up *project-based* or *time-bound billing*: nine sessions in three months. But calls would get rescheduled, three months would somehow stretch to seven, and I never knew who I was billing and when, or how much I would earn in a given month. When I switched coaching engagements to retainer-based billing with weekly sessions at the same recurring day and time, and invoices sent automatically on the first of every month, my cash flow immediately improved.

However, I discovered that it became difficult to plan a vacation, as there was nowhere to put that week's calls, and it did not make sense to coach with someone twice in one week. So I shifted active clients to three weeks on, one week off. When I had clients in "maintenance mode" of calls twice a month, I stacked them; the "A" and "C" weeks of the month had calls, the "B" and "D" weeks did not. This became more refined over time, when I started holding coaching calls only on Thursdays during those A and C weeks.

As much as I loved it, eventually at the end of 2019 I stopped taking on new coaching clients at all, realizing I needed even more time and space to work on my business, instead of jumping from call to call. This felt radical at the time, given that coaching had been my most consistent source of income for ten years, but it opened up necessary space to envision what to create next. Unbeknownst to me, it also cleared space to navigate the emotional rollercoaster of the soon-to-arrive pandemic and global shut-downs.

Bake in Batches to Eliminate Task Bloat

Once you have blocked out your deep work time, be strategic about how to achieve more in less time *within* those blocks. How can you manage ongoing content production, a process that does not have a fixed end date, without letting it overtake your entire business? Batch your time by doing similar activities together, even planning them in advance on a quarterly basis, rather than scrambling at the last minute to meet deadlines.

For example, batching bookkeeping to a monthly check-in makes much more sense than logging in every time you create a new expense just to categorize things one by one. Or recognizing there is no benefit to updating the press section of your website every time a new featured link comes in. Instead, set up a monthly recurring task; note the links within that task throughout the month, and update the website on a monthly recurring basis. This helps set a default state of intentional focus.

By collecting smaller tasks over time, then working on them in batches during intentional, planned windows, you can ensure that they do not take disproportionate and unnecessary effort in terms of time, attention, and context switching.

Because I find it helpful to know exactly how others set up their schedules—a popular content category known as *time voyeurism*—these are my time and content batching guidelines, subject to change and evolution. I do not always stick to them perfectly, but this overall template helps me hit an easeful work target most of the time:

- **No meetings:** Monday or Friday; before 11 a.m. or after 3 p.m., with rare exception for time-sensitive client requests or to accommodate time zones. No meetings during the fourth week of every month. No meetings in August, inspired by my European clients, whose strict adherence to this gave me the courage to try it stateside. No meetings from mid-December through mid-January.

- **Maximum number of meetings:** Four per day, ideally three, with at least thirty-minute buffer in between each.

- **First two hours upon waking, prior to computer work:** Reading non-fiction books and *The New York Times* with coffee, sitting near a window or in a comfy chair in the living room (not at my desk).

- **First computer-based work hour of every day (at a minimum):** Creative and strategic business projects. I do not check email before spending at least one hour on these.

- **Mondays:** All day for creative projects or errands and admin, catching up on communication channels.

- **Tuesdays:** Client meetings and networking calls.

- **Wednesdays:** Interviewing guests for my two podcasts, *Pivot* and *Free Time*. One Wednesday each month: private live Q&A call for podcast supporters, and stack-scheduling people who are interviewing me.

- **Thursdays:** Internal meetings, such as one-on-ones with team members, all-hands team meetings, and mastermind calls with friends.

- **Email batching:** Thirty to sixty minutes, one hour prior to first call on Tuesday through Thursday.

- **Afternoons:** Exercise and/or dog walk, ideally both. I do not check email after signing off in the afternoon. I wind down my mind, otherwise there is no hope of turning it off, as I will become anxious upon reading new messages, working on the business in my sleep.

Content creation is another area of the business ripe for batch baking. Even if you enjoy it, it can have a consuming, ongoing nature that makes it challenging to juggle publishing regularly while managing the rest of your operations. Map out your content quarterly to create content in batches while still keeping it fresh and timely.

Then, delegate next steps to your team to handle in batches for more efficient production on next steps. For example, once you have drafted content, ask them to format it for an email newsletter, blog, or social media post. Rather than assigning these content bits haphazardly on a one-off basis, set yourself up to work in sprints to produce five or ten at the same time, allowing them to complete next actions all at once. Not only will you be more focused and productive this way, but your team will appreciate packets of similar tasks rather than scrambling to meet last-minute deadlines for something they could have completed much faster, in advance, without your time-anxiety sprinkled on top.

As I shared in the sidebar, baking in batches helps increase focus and performance. Podcasting only on Wednesdays allows me to get in the zone and stay there, to gear up for the mode of deep listening and interviewing, and not switch my attention to anything else or worry about being so "on" during the rest of the week.

When I was in a groove of delivering virtual keynotes, I stacked two or three on the same day within a given month, so I only had to fuss with hair, make-up, wardrobe, and tech set-up (ring light, clicker, external mic) once.

Part 2: Design

Although those were long days, I could gear up for them and keep my energy high by staying focused on the same type of task. If anything, each session helped generate momentum and enthusiasm for the one that followed.

So little is truly time sensitive, even if other people have to wait. Keeping this in mind prevents you from slipping up and reflexively saying yes just to be accommodating. Remember, open blocks of time allow you to spontaneously say yes when that addition would be joyful, and joyful *on that day*, given your remaining energy once your strategic work is complete.

Author Elizabeth Gilbert taught herself to see email requests from strangers as people entering her home uninvited. Upon realizing how odd this would be, she dropped the guilt that she couldn't reply or accommodate their request. Adapted from Byron Katie, "Thank you, and no," became her go-to response for such inquiries, no further explanation needed.

As Elizabeth's friend and fellow bestselling author Ann Patchett shared with Jonathan Fields on his *Good Life Project* podcast, her books are her offering, and that is enough. On Ann's decision to stay off social media (and cell phones in general), she said:

> *I don't want to knock seven new doors in my house. I don't want to give you seven new ways to get a hold of me. I write novels. Every single thing you need from me, everything that I would ever have to give you that is worth anything, is in* The Dutch House. *So, if you are interested in me, in what I am thinking, and what I am doing, that's the very best of myself. I don't need to interact with the world any more than that.*

CHAPTER 17 RECAP

Time Block and Bake in Batches

Two-Sentence Summary

Rethink calendar-cramming habits that no longer serve you; open blocks of time allow you to spontaneously say *yes* when that addition would be joyful, and *on that day*, given your energy. Bake in batches by grouping similar tasks so you can make more progress in any given work session.

Give Yourself Permission

Relentlessly protect your favorite time of day (and days of the week) for your best work. Stop reacting to suggested meeting days and times by default. Set your parameters and create a scheduling link that matches, through a service like Calendly.

Ask Yourself

Look at your calendar for the next month: How could you better cluster commitments of a specific type? What blocks or new batch baking rules can you create?

Do (or Delegate) This Next

First on a piece of paper, then later in a scheduling tool, map out ideal criteria for different event types. For example, catching up with friends, sales calls, interviews. Specify what day/s of the week you prefer to hold these types of meetings, what time of day, the format (phone, video, in person), the buffer time before and after, and the duration.

18

Automate What You Repeat

The best thing about your life is that it is constantly in a state of design. This means you have, at all times, the power to redesign it. Make moves, allow shifts, smile more, do more, do less, say no, say yes—just remember, when it comes to your life, you are not just the artist but the masterpiece as well.

—Cleo Wade

If this, then that **(IFTTT) is programming shorthand that went** mainstream when co-founders Linden Tibbets and Jesse Tane launched a website called IFTTT to help people navigate their burgeoning social media habits. You may be familiar with theirs, or with a similar service called Zapier. Both help software services interface with each other, like a tech relay race with one app passing the information baton to the other for next steps. Or as Chris Davis, founder of Automation Bridge, puts it, Zapier is like digital super glue for "whenever apps don't talk (or stick) to each other."

Example workflows, or *Zaps*, include: When someone submits a Typeform survey response, add a new row to the Google spreadsheet collecting replies. Or, each time you post a new article on your website, automatically share the link on Twitter.

Beyond the service itself, IFTTT represents a way of thinking for repeatable tasks in your business. No task needs to be repeated the same way twice, at least if you are paying attention and willing to do a little bit of extra work up front to define *if this, then that* rules.

Josh Kaufman, author of *The Personal MBA* and *The First 20 Hours* who you met in "Serendipity as Business Strategy" (Chapter 11), finds joy in discovering what he can automate. Inspired by a learning experiment, he taught himself computer programming so he could get better at automating complex business tasks. Ten years later, Josh credits this skill as a daily time saver.

"[Programming] helps me build the systems I need to save myself future work, things that would potentially take an enormous amount of time, energy, and attention capacity," he said during our *Free Time* podcast conversation. "I can just write a little program, and all of that [work] goes away."

Programming also allows Josh to run a Delightfully Tiny Team. By automating as much as he can, he stays focused on the work he loves most: building, not managing others who are doing the building. He referenced an engineering adage from Larry Wall, "Develop the three great virtues of a programmer: laziness, impatience, and hubris." Josh's impatience at repeating the same task keeps him motivated to hone his automation skills further.

Sometimes automating actions are more analog, and they show themselves through doing extra work, the absence of a clearly defined *if-then* rule-of-thumb. For example, there is a household habit that perplexes me: tea bags in the sink. *What's the big deal? Hey, at least they are not creating small puddles across counter tops!* My issue is inefficiency, doubling the work even at a tiny scale. Those tea bags in the sink require two touches: from mug to sink, then sink to trash; sometimes hours later, and by two different people. Why not just move the teabag straight from the mug into the trash? Then one person has only touched it once.

Continuing with our household case study, recycling is another clearly defined system. You only touch things once, putting them into bins for trash, plastics, paper, and maybe compost. Imagine throwing everything into the trash first, then going back through to sort those items later on before garbage pick-up days. *What a smelly waste of time!*

Here are some simple IFTTT processes I shared with Michael, my husband, when we moved in together. I didn't realize I had them until it became clear that he didn't:

- When you see a product running low in the house, add it to our shopping cart the moment you notice. You won't have to remember or think about it again.

- Set-up four-month recurring subscriptions for: trash bags, dish soap, laundry and dishwasher pods, and toilet paper.

- When you want to purchase a big-budget item, add it to a wishlist. Review the wishlist once a month and prioritize next purchases.

- Keep a set of travel-sized toiletries in your suitcase. If you run out of something while on a trip, replace it as soon as you are back, so you don't forget before heading out again.

If there is one meta systems principle I live by more than any others, it is the title of this section, borrowed from the world of agile software development, as I shared in Chapter 2: "Each time you repeat a task, take one step toward automating it." This inspires so much of what I do, even developing the four-stage Pivot Method to help people navigate change. My motto for that book: "If change is the only constant, let's get better at it." That is the agile development mantra in action. I knew the pace of career changes was (and continues) accelerating, and with that, there must be a better method for navigating changes than fumbling through each time we hit a pivot point, or plateau.

One IFTTT practice I ask my team to take: Save message templates for everything in our shared TextExpander account. TextExpander is a tool that allows you to program short snippets, or codes, to populate text. This comes in handy all the time, for any text you will repeat, whether your website address, hex codes for your brand colors, emojis (I can't help myself), to longer messages for frequent business activities.

For example, with TextExpander running in the background, when I type the abbreviation *;address*, it populates a text snippet with my mailing address. If I type *;directions*, it populates more detailed instructions on how to get to my house. I learned to add the semicolon (no space) from my friend Mitch Joel, who pointed out that there is never a time in day-to-day typing that we otherwise write that way. I have thirty-five TextExpander categories for every area of life and work, with dozens of time-saving snippets within each, and I discover more to add every week.

When messages are part of a sequence, such as new client onboarding, save them with numbers in the title of what order each message typically appears. As I tell my team, personalize these messages and make them your own; the goal is not to sound robotic, but to provide a head start in your approach.

You can also set meta-rules that save time. For example, I tell my team: If I send an email that is actually a task, create a new task in our tracker. If I give feedback on something before it goes live, add it to our style guide if it is not already there. If we develop a new process, or update an old one, make sure the Manager Manual reflects that. These can also relate to external tasks. If a podcast episode goes live, email the guest and provide the link.

How satisfied are you with the current level of automation in your business? For those who worry that "if we automate everything, no one will have jobs anymore," I think about it differently. I don't want anyone on my team doing routine maintenance work that can be automated or systematized. We are constantly figuring out how to automate work so that their role can become even more oriented toward their strengths. Automating through software, even with a subscription fee, reduces your personnel costs; not just your own time, but your team's time too.

While working on this book, I piloted artificial intelligence (AI) scheduling software from a company called Clara Labs. Figuring it was worth a shot, despite my trepidation about potential errors, I set "Clara" up with an email address on my company's domain, and I looped her into emails as if she were a team member, even though most of her work is programmed via algorithm. Within two weeks, I was hooked!

Although "she" costs several hundred dollars each month, it ends up being close to what I would be paying someone, and more accurate. Clara's scheduling skills are nearly flawless; nothing falls through the cracks, nothing is added in the wrong time zone, and she schedules within my pre-designated blocks and buffer-time preferences between calls. Clara's human team members are available upon request as backup to assist with any requests that are too complex for her to understand. An added touch, she wishes recipients a good morning, or says "have a good evening" when signing off later in the day, even suggesting proposed times in *the recipient's* time zone, delighting me with all these small refinements.

Regarding the concern that AI is taking jobs away from people, Deborah Lahti on my team shared her take. As an executive project manager with decades of experience, she still does significant scheduling for other clients who appreciate the "high touch" of a team member (her) personally scheduling, rather than using tools like Calendly or Clara.

"But I don't do that for you," Deborah said. "It could potentially be a real time drain, and while it does take finesse, Clara seems to be doing well. Now I'm doing other things for you that I have never done before, like booking new speaking engagements."

When one of our speaking clients thanked her for being "such a great agent," Deborah did a double-take. "I'm an agent?!" she said. "I didn't even know that was a thing, and I love doing it. It taps into my project and vendor management skills that I have honed over many years. That role is worth the money you pay me, rather than scheduling, which Clara can do."

I also experienced a secondary, unexpected benefit from working with Clara: she defaulted to thirty-minute phone calls, based on my pre-defined preferences, which assuaged the pressure and micro-guilt I sometimes feel to schedule certain calls for one hour. All of a sudden, I was not the bottleneck any longer for getting catch-up call requests out of my inbox and onto the calendar. I returned to a steady cadence of catching up with friends and colleagues, and never felt bad if I looped Clara in late at night, on weekends, or on very short notice, the way I might have with my own team. When a reporter reached out for a time-sensitive media interview, Clara coordinated with her and added the meeting to our calendars within an hour. I would have had to ask a team member to drop what they were doing, likely something more strategic in the business, to do the same.

When Deborah joined my team, the first project I assigned her was selling the condo I owned in California, but that I hadn't lived in for ten years since moving to New York. I asked her to handle all communications with the real estate broker, managing movers remotely, figuring out if we needed storage, setting up staging, and many other smaller subtasks. Although I was nervous to delegate such a big project, and had my own emotional attachments after twelve years of ownership and many memories there, at that time given my other responsibilities, there was not a way that I could work on the sale while operating the rest of my business.

Deborah echoed these sentiments, saying that for many of her clients, having someone handle tasks with emotional attachments made decisions and communication easier.

"My clients often remark how helpful it is to have me schedule something or perform certain tasks because they get frozen by the emotion—hurting someone's feelings, or feeling bad about negotiating something because it's so personal," Deborah said. "When I do it, I don't have the emotional attachment, so it's much easier for me and I don't put those tasks off."

One of Deborah's clients wanted to make a memory photo and text book of her late father's life, but had been delaying for years, getting lost in reflection and so emotional that she couldn't move forward.

"I never met her father, so I could simply look at it as a creative exercise; what photos would look best with the text, and how to lay it all out so it looked good and read well," Deborah said. "I got it done in a couple weeks, even with the long conversations I wound up having with her as she shared memories with me."

CHAPTER 18 RECAP

Automate What You Repeat

Two-Sentence Summary

Automate small, repetitive actions through software. Engineer simple systems to prevent failures of memory, energy, overwhelm, decision making, and delegation.

Give Yourself Permission

Stop remembering or repeatedly fussing with small recurring tasks, every time they are due. Automate or delegate, then celebrate!

Ask Yourself

What process could you put in place for recurring tasks, at home or work? For these recurring items: What if you worked *on* the process, not just *in* the task?

Do (or Delegate) This Next

Bring to mind one thing you often forget that you would like to better remember. What is the simplest system you could put in place? Bonus: Create a repository of message templates and text shortcuts that you can add to as you work. What makes the cut? Anything you would have the chance of sending again, which is most things.

Design Resources

For free tools and templates to help implement strategies from the **Design** stage, visit **ItsFreeTime.com/toolkit**.

A sampling of resources for this stage include:

- Sample TextExpander shortcuts for saving time with snippets

- New member path worksheet: to map joyful ways of growing your community

- Stuck email categories: to help you improve reply processes

- Notion walkthrough: sample video from our monthly Q&A for podcast supporters

- My scheduling parameters for tools like Clara and Calendly

Ass

ign

Overview

Just after *Pivot* launched, I headed down to Tribeca for a keynote speech and book signing. To my mortification, I realized only upon arrival—fifteen minutes before going on stage—that *I forgot to bring the books.* There I was, smiling from the flyers taped throughout the co-working space, taunting myself: "Book signing with Jenny Blake!"

My heart started pounding. *What to do, what to do, how to fix this?*

In the next ten minutes, I downloaded the TaskRabbit app and hired a "Tasker" for the first time, with no clue if it would work. TaskRabbit bills itself as a "same-day service platform [that] instantly connects you with skilled Taskers to help with cleaning, furniture assembly, home repairs, running errands, and more." Five minutes before starting my speech, the app assigned someone who picked up the books from my apartment (thank goodness Michael was home) and delivered them to a coordinator at the venue during the hour that I was on stage.

To my great relief, the books arrived during Q&A, ten minutes before I headed to the signing table. There they were, a stack of five glorious boxes. *Crisis averted.* Filled with gratitude, I happily signed and sold them all.

This story illustrates building the third muscle in the Free Time Framework: **Assign**. Once you are clear that the work you are tackling is *aligned*, and you have *designed* the ideal outcomes and process, then it is time to let go of as much of it as you can by *assigning* next steps to someone other than you. In this stage, you will set up structures that build trust in your team.

Assign, the third stage of the Free Time Framework, embraces three main ideas:

1. **Stretch yourself to delegate ever more:** There is no way you are good at everything or want to be. Rather than burying yourself in distracting details and tiny, tedious tasks, challenge yourself to assign *most* of what you can.

2. **For every *task, project,* and *responsibility*,** get clear on **who** will do **what** by **when**; how you will track, communicate, and renegotiate deadlines along the way.

3. **Ensure that you have a central task tracking repository.** Just as no information should live in any one person's mind, no task goes untracked. Similarly, no task data lives only in messaging tools, making it harder to track and search archives in the future.

In this section, we will cover the philosophy behind how to reach a cruising altitude of creative efficiency as a team. This is an ongoing process; there is no finished or perfect state. Everyone must regularly step back to see the bigger picture. There is always room for improvement, as technology and software tools continually increase in sophistication. Each team member must be adaptable and observant, willing to spot—and call into question—areas of friction to improve operations.

As I mentioned in the introduction, no one on my team works full time, at least in the traditional sense. Jenny Blake Enterprises operates with a small ecosystem of three core members at any given time, four including me. Each of the partners in my business ecosystem runs a small practice of their own, where I am one of several of their clients. This means we are all continually opting in to work together, given that there are no minimum time-bound contracts. If I was a tyrannical, demanding boss or client, assigning draining work that did not pay well, they would be gone in a heartbeat! I like knowing my team members have this option, and that they work with me because it is mutually beneficial as part of their small business portfolio.

Author Jim Collins shared a conversation with his mentor, the late Stanford Graduate School of Business professor Bill Lazier. "How do you know if you have a great relationship?" Bill asked him rhetorically. "If you were to ask each person in the relationship who benefits more, both would answer *I do*."

Free Time is not just about clearing the business owner's mind, while everyone else on the team juggles unruly projects and more work than they can handle. Each person can operate with ease and joy, while making a greater impact. This starts with being clear when delegating, not stepping on toes by micromanaging or taking back too much responsibility. No one needs to sacrifice sleep to meet unreasonable deadlines. You can set-up a system of calm communication best practices that do not necessitate anyone jumping frantically from ping to ping, fracturing attention through in-the-moment messages that are not actually urgent, and that become messy en masse, nearly impossible to sift through and make sense of later when needed, which may be years in the future.

If you and your team start applying these principles—truly applying them and making them your own—the sense of daily dread will subside. You know, that ambiguous anxiety of not really knowing what will happen by when, how you will know, and having it all rest on your shoulders to figure out. Instead of your team stuck taxiing on the runway, just waiting for you to loosen your grip on the areas they are responsible for, they will be cleared and free for takeoff.

The same mistakes won't happen more than a few times, because you will design systems-based solutions for them. Barring mal intent, errors are not anyone's fault when the system itself is broken. If aspects of the work were not handled well, there is a good chance unclear guidelines were at the root. This necessitates an important caveat: It is almost impossible to give feedback to someone who won't listen or take responsibility, who is not a fit for the role, or who does not have the desire to learn or the awareness to self-correct. Short of a major breakthrough, these people are not a fit for your business. You deserve a team—no matter how loosely formed—that is passionate about the work you do.

Align > **Design** > **Assign** >

Who

If you are the only person working in your business, you are far more likely to be the bottleneck and to be burdened by work that drains you. Your business may be negatively impacted by you trying to juggle all the details at the same time as forming the vision and addressing bigger challenges. Most of all, you may make mistakes or miss things by doing all the work, particularly work that you are not skilled at (and have no interest in becoming skilled at). Hiring help does not have to be overwhelming or break the bank. Start with the biggest opportunity areas related to freeing up your time and generating revenue. Build trust slowly, and increase time and team as you get more comfortable and see meaningful results. Be patient in the beginning. Onboarding, delegating, and documenting new systems always takes more time at the start. It will pay great dividends later, and position you to better respond when opportunities arise, since you won't be bogged down by details.

In this section, you will:
- Promote yourself from Chief Everything Officer
- Construct your Delightfully Tiny Team
- Double how much you delegate

19

Promote Yourself from Chief Everything Officer

Now that all your worry has proved such an unlucrative business,
Why not find a better job.

—Hafiz

Time for an inventory. **How many roles are you currently** fulfilling in your business? Circle all that apply:

CEO	Account Manager	Social Media
CTO	People Operations	Accounting and/or Bookkeeping
CFO	Customer Experience & Support	Content & Thought Leadership
VP of Product	Community Management	Add any missing roles:
VP of Operations		
VP of Sales		

If you circled three or fewer, *bravo!* You have successfully relinquished your role as Chief Everything Officer, and can skip this chapter. For many of us, we continue wearing far too many business hats. Staying *Delightfully Tiny* in team size is one thing (more on that in the next chapter); working entirely alone is another. Even if you are happy with the number of roles you currently juggle, treat this as a thought exercise: What *would* it look like to creatively take more responsibilities off your plate? How could you offload these confidently, without adding stress?

It's nearly impossible to do your *best* work when you're doing *all* the work.

Let me preface this chapter by saying: I am not naturally inclined as a team builder, though I did enjoy creating mini-businesses and holding leadership positions growing up. When I was in college, group projects made me cringe. When I read the proverb, "If you want to go fast, go alone; if you want to go far, go together," I remember thinking that my preference was to go *fast!* Even though, in reality, my happiest moments and proudest professional accomplishments always involved going together with incredible teams.

When I worked at Google, I remember looking up the hierarchy of middle management and pining for a simpler future. When I left Google to start my own business, I promised myself not to create a large company where I spent more time managing than doing creative work, while still scaling beyond the time-for-money trade as the sole service provider.

Herein lies the difference of being a solopreneur working on your own versus building a business that can operate at least partly without you. How can you stretch yourself along that spectrum so you create a lasting company, not one hinging only on your energy, effort, attention, and time? How can you replace outdated methods of working and thinking about time, while earning even more abundantly?

There is a chicken-and-egg problem in the early days of any business, at least those that are not venture backed. You need to earn more money in order to hire help, but hiring help is one of the only ways you can free your valuable time to do the highest revenue-generating activities.

John Briggs, the founder of Incite Tax and Accounting and author of *Profit First for Microgyms*, advises business owners to calculate the return on compensation for every current or potential team member. Even if that person's role is not directly tied to revenue-generating activities, such as sales, they should be freeing up time for whoever is generating the income. For example, if hiring an assistant at $30,000 per year frees up one thousand hours, will you be able to bring in *more* than $30,000 in that time without the responsibility of handling those activities?

"You want at least double the ROI to make it a true investment," John said in a podcast interview with Mike Michalowicz. "If they are just saving [your company] $30,000, you're not actually any further ahead, but you have more headache in managing more people."

I often have *should* moments around being a small business owner, particularly that I *should* enjoy hiring, team-building, and managing. If I am being honest, it is simply not my zone of genius, or even excellence. It took me ten years to admit that managing others falls squarely in my zone of competence, as Gay Hendricks describes in *The Big Leap*. I am *okay* at it. I love my team, but I do not love the day-to-day of "management," to the point where I thrive creating large, intricate teams and organizations. I prefer working closely with a small handful of people, ideally for many years once we have a solid foundation of trust, communication, smart systems, and abundant individual freedom to work in ways that suit each of us best.

If it is not obvious from the Design stage (Part Two), I crave stretches of uninterrupted, unscheduled deep work for strategic thinking, reading, reflecting, and creating. The less time I am on the phone and in meetings, the better. After more than three or four calls or meetings in a given day, I am completely fried, in desperate need of a context switch into something like reading or a workout, even in the middle of the afternoon.

As tempting as going solo seems for some, it is challenging for another central reason (that I learned repeatedly the hard way). Like the beached *Ever Given* across the Suez Canal, you *are* the bottleneck. *Always.* No matter how much you may love your craft, there will be aspects of running your business that are inherently draining.

For this reason, two team members are almost always better than one, even if you both work part time. Having a second-in-command, a right hand person, provides much-needed outside perspective, and someone to share the workload. With two, however, if one of you steps out temporarily, or your team member resigns, the team is broken and bottlenecked yet again. There is no redundancy. I consider a *Delightfully Tiny Team* to be at least three (more on this in the next chapter). Consider hiring a thought partner who compliments your skillset—they enjoy the work you do not—and an assistant or project manager who can take care of the details for both of you.

I admire colleagues who do this naturally, like my friend Laura Garnett, author of *The Genius Habit* and *Find Your Zone of Genius*. She becomes giddy when growing her team. Team building is part of Laura's genius, because it allows her to do even more of *her* best work coaching leaders and teams. She loves the process of understanding others deeply, including her team members, and is inspired by the unique skills and possibilities each new person brings.

"I love being able to provide someone with their dream job," Laura said, "while having their support as I work to help more people experience the joy and delight that comes from being who they are."

When Laura works with outside specialists, such as a branding agency or marketing assistant, she feels "boosted by rocket fuel." When she hires "top-of-their game" players, she can relax, knowing that they will deliver something far better than she could think to request.

Over nearly fifteen years of running her business, Laura became clear that she only wants to hire people for whom her business offers them an ideal role, not one that serves as a stepping stone. Laura is also committed to creating a team where every person is working in their respective zone of genius. When team members no longer enjoy the work, she helps guide them toward what *would* suit their strengths best, even if it is outside of her organization.

Despite my passion for solitude and default inclination to work alone and *overfunction* by doing everything myself, I know I am better off—and that our work and clients are better served—with a tiny team in place. Still, going solo is an ongoing impulse I strive to resist. I expand slowly and reluctantly, first looking for ways to streamline and simplify. One of my favorite quotes comes from Irish novelist James Joyce: "He was alone. He was unheeded, happy, and near to the wild heart of life."

CHAPTER 19 RECAP

Promote Yourself from Chief Everything Officer

Two-Sentence Summary
Promote yourself from Chief Everything Officer. Take the pressure off you and your business by hiring at least one person, even just for a few hours each week.

Give Yourself Permission
To not always love the day-to-day of managing a team. Find ways to at least *appreciate* it by considering all the work you no longer have to do.

Ask Yourself
What would expanding your team free you up to do?

Do (or Delegate) This Next
Throughout the next two weeks, keep a list of all the tasks and projects, large and small, that you would be elated to delegate—even if you do not yet know who will help you with them.

20

Construct Your Delightfully Tiny Team

The leap to "three" takes us over a threshold and through *past polarized limits of the Dyad. Wherever there are three, as the three knights, three musketeers, three wise men, or three wishes, there is* throughness, *rebirth, transformation, and success.*

—Michael Schneider

eflect on your career and the different team sizes you have managed. When were you happiest?

Most business literature and research examines ideal team size in terms of *output*, what produces the highest volume and what is most efficient. I prefer to examine team size based on leader preference, culture, and cohesion. What size is most *joyful* for you and your team?

What makes a team *delightfully* tiny is up to you, the leader, to decide based on the intersection of three things: your strengths and energy, your current strategic projects, and desired outcomes for your team or business.

For creative entrepreneurs, ones for whom high net freedom is equally important to revenue growth, there is a Goldilocks quality to designing a Delightfully Tiny Team, a *horseshoe of team happiness*. If your team is too big *or* too small for your personality and preferences, you may feel dread, despair, depressed, drained, or distracted. Let's look at both ends of the horseshoe in more detail:

Too small, and you are taxingly tiny: In many cases fewer than three people, but certainly if you are entirely solo, the burden constantly falls on you. It is hard to get the rest and recharging you need to do strategic work. You risk exhaustion and burnout from overwork and from processing the minutiae you dread, not to mention the cognitive cost of being the one in charge.

On the other end of the horseshoe, if your team is too big, you may feel burdened by pressure and complexity. Unless building a large organization is your ambition and you love managing people, recurring meetings start to overwhelm your calendar. Time spent responding to questions, switching between team members' projects to help where they are stuck, adds up. Meanwhile, you are still on the hook for higher overhead; profit margins may be thinner despite—or because of—the growing team.

Delightfully Tiny Teams help you reach a personal sweet spot of efficiency and freedom as the owner, enabling you to focus on your best work. The perfect team size *for you* feels, on the whole (even if not every day), delightful. You delegate the details, and have automated and systematized enough of them that even your team is not overwhelmed by minutiae. Processes are clearly defined, and team members are clear on their role and responsibilities, freeing them to take on more creative projects in the business.

When it comes to constructing your ideal team size, there are some guidelines to keep in mind. According to Bob Gower, author of *Agile Business* and co-author of *Radical Alignment*, the rule of thumb for agile teams is four to nine members. Beyond this size, you will face far greater complexity. In the Connection Nodes diagram, note the difference in complexity and potential for confusion between a three-person team and a ten- or fourteen-person team. Complexity is indicated by the number of intersecting lines connecting each node to the others.

Team Size: Connection Nodes

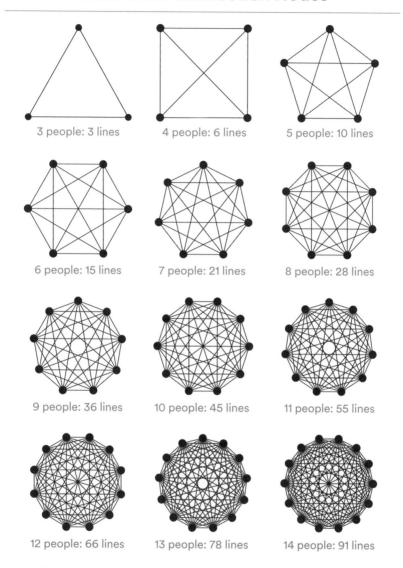

3 people: 3 lines   4 people: 6 lines   5 people: 10 lines

6 people: 15 lines   7 people: 21 lines   8 people: 28 lines

9 people: 36 lines   10 people: 45 lines   11 people: 55 lines

12 people: 66 lines   13 people: 78 lines   14 people: 91 lines

Part 3: Assign

Delightfully Tiny Teams are big enough to share strategic work according to each person's strengths, but not so large that they create drag and friction, for the manager or the team. High-functioning Delightfully Tiny Teams are resourceful. They know how to leverage technology, automation, and systems for their benefit. From a systems perspective every person matters, bringing unique perspectives and strengths that can improve processes with fresh eyes. If documentation is a regular practice, then *brain drain* becomes less of an issue. Most of all, Delightfully Tiny Teams enjoy their work! They work with joy and ease. Otherwise they would just be tiny teams: strapped, stressed, and stretched too thin.

When constructing your team, consider that triads are more stable than dyads, where one absent person means halting shared work and collaboration. With three, even if one is out, you have back-up. With teams of three to four, you stay between three to six lines of communication.

Once you reach a group size of five, with ten lines of communication, an operations manager may become necessary. In his book *Rocket Fuel*, author Gino Wickman describes one model for a successful partnership in leading a fast-growing organization: a relationship between the freedom-loving *visionary* (the CEO) and the more structured *integrator* (COO). The visionary is full of imagination, infusing the organization with motivation, drive, and excitement. The integrator ensures "all the trains run on time" and prevents the visionary from overwhelming the team with new ideas, interfering with their ability to meet their stated mission.

With teams of six or seven, you can start to organize by functional groups or project "pods." For example, if you run a design agency, you may set up a sub-team structure where every client is assigned a project manager, creative director, and copywriter.

One likely result of teams that are too large? Brook's Law says it best: "Adding manpower to a late software project makes it later." And I would add: less joyful, unless you *need* a minimum number of people to drive particular projects or a greater vision forward, such as scaling a business that produces tangible goods to meet growing demand. Even larger companies, or countries for that matter, still rely on a core executive team at the center.

Gallup studied engagement levels of three million teams. On average, teams with fewer than ten members have the highest *and* the lowest engagement. According to Robert Sutton and Huggy Rao, authors of *Scaling up Excellence*, "After devoting nearly fifty years to studying team performance,

Harvard researcher J. Richard Hackman concluded that four to six members is the best team size for most tasks, that no work team should have more than ten members, and that performance problems and interpersonal friction increase exponentially as team size increases."

For large organizations, bigger teams equal greater capacity, theoretically translating to more productive output. However, this does not account for the *happiness* and *aptitude* of the managers sandwiched in the middle of the org chart. No matter how passionately they care about the company's mission, many pine to run their own businesses just to escape the minutiae of management, and the overwhelm from leading too-large teams. In one Gallup survey, 67 percent of employees said they wanted to start their own businesses someday.

In a Google *re:Work* study of over 180 teams (115 project teams in engineering and 65 pods from the sales organization), named "Project Aristotle," a "tribute to Aristotle's quote, 'the whole is greater than the sum of its parts.'" The authors discovered that "what really mattered was less about who is on the team, and more about how the team worked together." This came down to five primary ingredients, in order of importance, all of which can be improved by applying the principles throughout this book:

1. **Psychological Safety:** Team members feel safe to take risks and be vulnerable in front of each other.

2. **Dependability:** The team reliably completes quality work on time.

3. **Structure and Clarity:** Team members have clear roles and goals.

4. **Meaning:** Work is personally important to team members.

5. **Impact:** Team members think their work matters and is making a difference.

Although team *size* did not significantly impact team *effectiveness*, Project Aristotle provides culture-related caveats as it relates to team *satisfaction*. In their research of scholarly journals they found that teams with fewer than ten members "experience better work-life quality, work outcomes, less

Part 3: Assign

conflict, stronger communication, more cohesion, and more organizational citizenship behaviors."

We are in the era now of the New LLC, every employee a company unto themselves. Although LLC technically stands for Limited Liability Corporation, we could rethink it in today's terms under a new definition: LLC as short for *limited loose connections*. Or *location-independent lattice contractors*, lattice defined as "an interlaced structure or pattern."

Although I run a private community for small business owners, it is bigger companies that hire me for Pivot programs such as keynotes, train-the-trainer, and licensing. As part of these engagements, I get a peek into how large organizations are thinking about the future and their people operations. I hear from many employees about how things are going and what they anticipate for the future. It is not uncommon for the person hiring me to ask about how to set up a consulting practice someday. Many who do this are excited to have their current employer as their first client, and their employer is equally excited to continue work with the former employee in the way that best suits their strengths and previous contributions. Of course it stings to lose a linchpin team member, but usually people see that it is for the best. I am thrilled to still work with Google, even a decade after leaving my full-time role, and not just from time-to-time; I am honored that Google selected *Pivot* as their global career development framework.

My team comprises its own unique ecosystem of interlocking LLCs, and the size varies depending on what services and strategic projects I focus on. When I mentioned this concept of latticed contractors to Brenna Barry-Martinez, project manager on my team, and asked her if she would prefer to be full time instead, she said no.

"I love what we do, the structure we have built, and the systems we have," Brenna said. "I don't feel any pressure that I need to be full time. If the relationship works for both of us as is, then there is no need to force that extra time when it isn't necessary for our projects."

CHAPTER 20 RECAP

Construct Your Delightfully Tiny Team

Two-Sentence Summary

We are in the era now of the New LLC, every team member a company unto themselves. Construct a stable, Delightfully Tiny Team that lowers complexity of communication.

Give Yourself Permission

Not to expand your team just because you *should*. Grow when it is delightful and the right thing for your business, in a way that fits your innate people preferences and relieves friction. Create more ease, not more stress.

Ask Yourself

When in your career have you been happiest in terms of team size or structure?

Do (or Delegate) This Next

What role is missing from your team, even part time? Envision your ideal next hire: What would they help you with? Will the role be ongoing or project-based? Write a one-page job description in Google Docs with a link that you can easily send to others. Bonus: reach out to someone you respect, who you know works with a specialist you need. Ask if they can make an introduction. If so, send the job description you drafted. If you end up working together, send a thank you note or gift to your friend.

21

Double How Much You Delegate

If you want to fly, you must give up everything that weighs you down.

—Denzel Washington

Jordan Harbinger had been podcasting for eleven years, building a top-rated show, until a rift with his business partners sent him into emergency mode.

Due to legal complications, he would have to start over from scratch, and they would not allow him to announce the news to his current audience, given that lawyers were still sorting out who owned what. Jordan did not have the luxury of planning or doing everything himself. As the main source of income for his family, he and his wife, Jen, needed to rebuild quickly, increasing the new show's subscribers and download numbers significantly enough to keep their current advertisers.

Thankfully, he did not have to rehire. Jordan's Delightfully Tiny Team came with him, including a podcast producer, audio engineer, and Jen leading operations. He had the listeners, who needed to do a little work to find the newly relaunched *The Jordan Harbinger Show*, and he had the interviewing chops from over a decade of releasing multiple episodes each week. But perhaps one of the biggest keys to Jordan's successful business pivot was the skill he had honed in continually doubling how much he delegates, getting as much off of his plate as he can.

Jordan starts delegating by looking for places where performance degrades. When Jen started to get bogged down by juggling too much within their day-to-day operations, they hired an assistant allowing her to also jettison time-consuming tasks. Regarding how he spends his time now, during our *Free Time* podcast conversation Jordan said, "I can't imagine going back and having to do all this stuff myself, because it just wouldn't be possible."

Even if he were to make the time, working sixty- to eighty-hour weeks—something he is unwilling to do with small kids at home—he knows his performance and reputation as host would suffer. Jordan is known for punchy, in-depth, well-researched interviews with guests that are often hard to find and book.

"You might be in a different business than me, but it's a performance any way you look at it," Jordan said. "No one says, 'Hey Bieber, can you go grab that pallet of Coca-Cola? We need that in the concession area.' Because he's going to perform and we don't want him tired from setting up and cleaning stadium aisles."

Business owners have the same need to be fresh for center stage. But for various reasons we resist delegating, relegating ourselves to stage hands doubling as performers. Jordan delegates every aspect of producing his podcast except for what he and only he can do: be known as a highly prepared interviewer, source interesting guests through his unique curatorial lens, and conduct engaging interviews that keeps audience interest top of mind. He doesn't do much on social media, which makes the time listeners spend with him through his main channel more special. If he was everywhere, all the time, he would risk turning himself into a commodity, just another person podcasting, rather than providing what he knows is more polished output. Or to use his term, to deliver a *star performance* with every episode.

Even if you think you already delegate effectively, I bet you have room for even greater efficiency and resulting peace of mind, whether on the home or work front. Remember, our angel of favorite tasks and projects is someone else's devil, and vice versa. That means there is someone out there who can delight in the devil of your details. With roles tied to revenue *and* tied to freeing your mind and time, you can far outearn the cost of creating a team that you know you can rely on. Hiring more help, while it can dent the budget in the short term, has almost always helped me surpass the investment.

Recall Emily Heyward's advice to see brand strategy as an investment not a cost. *Costs* add up, particularly if you are not closely measuring their impact. *Investments* multiply your earning power. Even your team members can get more done in less time than you might think, without breaking the bank, if you can outsource tasks that aren't a match for their skills or energy.

That said, when you have mounting issues, merely throwing money at the problem won't work. Hiring the wrong person, at the wrong time, or for the wrong role, can be disastrous if it quickly gobbles up resources without providing the relief or revenue you need. Start on a project- or part-time basis, and build trust and responsibility as you go. Document whatever time you invest in training, so that if your new team member transitions out sooner than expected (which is always a possibility, even through no fault of your own), you are not repeating yourself when onboarding their replacement.

Most leaders know they need to delegate. That is why you hire a team in the first place. But even if you delegate 80 percent of the work you know you do not *need* to do, there is a good chance that you are still secretly hoarding an unnecessary, and unproductive, 20 percent. Why do we clutch so tightly to this remaining 20 percent? For a few reasons:

- Sometimes we are not even aware we are doing it.

- Trust issues: If you want the work done right, you feel you need to do it yourself; maybe you have been burned in the past.

- Uncertainty about how to delegate or to whom.

- Resistance to investing more energy up front by finding and training someone (so much faster to just do it yourself!) even if you know it will save time in the long run.

- "I'm special. So special that no one could *possibly* learn how to do what I do!" *Is that true?*

- What Chris Drucker, author of *Virtual Freedom*, calls Superhero Syndrome: heroically doing all the work until you crash.

- What author Sarah Young describes as "seagulling" instead of "eagle-ing" by flying *too* low to your team, hovering and micromanaging, leaving droppings along the way.

Even if you chalk it up to just plain-old procrastination, this delegation ceiling is likely contributing to, if not entirely responsible for, some of your biggest bottlenecks. What would happen if you doubled the amount you currently delegate?

Conduct a Five T's audit to determine what to offload next:

1. **Tiny:** Tasks that are so small they seem inconsequential to tackle but they add up. They are never important or urgent, and even if they only take a few minutes they end up taking you out of the flow of strategic work.

2. **Tedious:** Tasks that are relatively simple, but tedious, are not the best use of your time. Straightforward tasks can be clearly documented, and should be handled by others.

3. **Time-Consuming:** Tasks that, although they may be important and even somewhat complex, are time-consuming and do not require you to do the initial research. You can step in when the task is 80 percent complete and give approval or direction on next steps.

4. **Terrible At:** Areas where you are ill-equipped; you take far longer than people skilled in this area, and produce a subpar result. For example, if you don't have a knack for visuals, hiring a professional designer to update your slides for an upcoming presentation.

5. **Time Sensitive:** Tasks that are time-sensitive but compete with other priorities. There isn't enough time to do them all at once, so you delegate work to be completed in parallel.

After offloading these Five T's, what's left? Ideally your most strategic tasks. Here are three approaches for delegating these effectively:

- **Todd Herman**, author of *The Alter Ego Effect* and creator of the 90 Day Year, looks for **"$10,000 tasks."** To cement this further, he coaches people to track the level of their activities on any given day across four columns: $10 tasks, $100 tasks, $1,000 tasks, and $10,000 tasks. What $10,000 tasks are already on your radar? Which ones are hiding in plain sight? You can invent your own moniker for these high-value tasks, so you and your team members can ensure that every day they allocate their time where their expertise yields the best results.

- Upon realizing she was the bottleneck in her organization for information, the only one with full strategic visibility, **Brené Brown**, author and social science researcher, implemented a new system. Before starting work or making a request, she asks her team to clarify The Five Cs: connective tissue (relationship to other work streams), color (added nuance), context (why it is important), cost (of doing the project), and consequence (of not doing it).

- Similarly, author **Dan Sullivan**, founder of Strategic Coach and prolific systems-thinker, says "Almost all the trouble you'll get yourself into as an entrepreneur will come from trying to sell someone on something you're not sold on yourself." The best thing he can do is set aside thirty minutes before delegating any project to fill out one of his Impact Filters. Similar to The Five C's, this is a one-page PDF that outlines the project's purpose, importance, ideal outcomes, best and worst results, and success criteria. Only after Dan fills out this Impact Filter is the project ready for a team member to take over, upon whom he bestows full autonomy to solve smaller problems along the way.

This relates to a saying Dan helped popularize, from an off-the-cuff remark his friend Dean Jackson made: focus on *who not how*. Dan and collaborator Dr.

Benjamin Hardy turned this phrase into a book, *Who Not How*, that encourages leaders to shift away from "the time-and-effort economy" toward the "results economy." The title alone is an imperative: instead of focusing your energy on *how* to solve your problem or tackle a next project, look for a "who" who is more skilled than you. As the authors write, "*How* is linear and slow. *Who* is nonlinear, instantaneous, and exponential."

Run a Hiring Pilot at Home

Some systems-minded entrepreneurs who want to free-up time for their entire family hire a chef who comes in two days a week, buys groceries, then prepares lunches and dinners according to their dietary needs.

As my godmother, Martha Schwartz, who has been running her landscape architecture business for over forty years while raising three kids, once told me about her set-up: "I bring *home* the bacon, I don't *cook* the bacon."

The financial investment of hiring help at home might surprise you, in a good way: When you tally the costs of eating the way you are currently, for many families it adds up to less than what they already spend on delivery and meals out. It also frees any one person from responsibilities they may not always enjoy, and provides healthier sustenance through planning and consistency instead of last-minute scrambling. In addition to the family benefits, you will also free-up energy to devise expansive ways of increasing income through the business to joyfully pay for these services!

Back in 2013 my friend Andy, a lifelong entrepreneur, posted the following ad on Craigslist. His ad is still as useful and inspiring today as I found it then.

Part 3: Assign

Andy's Craigslist Post

Looking for: Talented home assistant to help with cooking, cleaning, grocery shopping, laundry, etc.

Hi there. I'm looking for a long-term personal assistant to help me around my home.

- You are highly organized, detail-oriented, and serious about organization and cleanliness. You have probably done event planning or bookkeeping because you are good at logistics and details. *I need your help because I'm a creative person who is extremely unorganized!*
- You love to write and work from checklists and are dependable. (I'm talking about very dependable, not the "This usually doesn't happen, but it happened again" type).
- You like doing a variety of roles and enjoy working alone.
- Bonus points if you are happy, easy-going, self-motivated, and trustworthy. :-)

Your role will be five to ten hours per week to start, and includes:

- Grocery shopping
- Meal prep (following the Paleo diet)
- Laundry
- Cleaning up home (nothing major)
- Running errands (such as shipping packages)
- And other odd jobs

If this goes well, there will be opportunities for more hours. Pay is $20/hour to start. If you are interested, please email me your resume, your salary expectations, and your availability during the week using the subject line, "Let's do this!"

For years, I was only comfortable delegating the small stuff. I kept ah-hoc sales processes for big ticket items like speaking engagements close to the vest, handling everything from sales calls to scheduling to invoicing, and of course, delivery.

As my brother, Tom, pointed out when encouraging me to take myself further out of the equation:

> *If you go to the dentist's office, you don't make an appointment with the dentist. You make it with the receptionist. Then a dental assistant sees you first and handles routine maintenance before the dentist arrives. There are two or three people before you ever meet with the dentist, and we never expect otherwise.*

How much is your time worth? Calculate it. What is your billable rate if you break down your income on an hourly basis? Here is how I estimate:

1. How much would you be *thrilled* to earn this year? _____

2. How many work hours per week is *ideal* for you to achieve that? ____

3. Multiply that number by 42 weeks (to account for time off) = _____

4. Divide line 1 by line 3 to get your ideal billable hourly rate: _____

Does it still make sense for you to spend hours researching flight costs and travel dates only to save $150 on the ticket, if you have spent $1,000 worth of your time? What would you rather have done instead? Where else could you have directed that big brain of yours to have earned an extra $1,000 instead of earning the frustration of frittering that time away?

Even when I was going through my "apocalypse year" in life and work in 2013, my virtual assistant quickly became the one expense I was not willing to cut. I had just signed up with her at $250 a month, significant for me at that time. With business stalled, I didn't buy clothes or fancy dinners, I bought my time. It was, and continues to be, the best purchase I can make every month.

You can hire someone for as little as $150 each month for five hours of time. Start there, or by hiring someone on a project-based trial period, like Dave Crenshaw, who you met in the Continuously Bust Bottlenecks chapter.

Dave hires three people in parallel from freelancer networks like Upwork for a small, paid, temporary project. This helps build trust and determine who matches what he is looking for, reducing doubts about who will be the best fit before committing full time. It is beneficial for potential contractors too, to see if they resonate with the work and are qualified for the role.

You may be surprised at how much can get done in just a few hours each week, and how much more you start wanting to assign. Personal assistant services are also becoming a main vehicle for many others to create flexible, remote, stay-at-home businesses. By doing this, you are helping to give someone else a job, to create a freedom-based business of their own.

Start with your network: Many people employ virtual assistants or project managers part time, and would be happy to ask if they have extra capacity to take on another client. This way you know that the person can be trusted to do great work.

Consider, who is your ideal next team member? Do you want help with in-person tasks or virtual? Or both? Write a description of what the role entails, even if you are not yet sure where or how you will find this person. Who would be the perfect fit, and how will they know? What one hire would make the biggest impact on your efficiency? Your happiness?

Still not quite ready to add to your team? Try hiring someone to help at home, as described in the sidebar, such as a house cleaner, culinary school student, or subscribing to a pre-cooked meal (or meal kit) delivery service. Track everything you *could* delegate over the next two weeks. You will be surprised at how many small ideas arise as you go about your day-to-day, in contrast to trying to think of tasks up-front, in the abstract.

Double How Much You Delegate

Two-Sentence Summary

Dig deeper: what can you and *only* you do? Look for ways to assign the rest, doubling what you currently delegate, even contemplating how you could offload the work that seems impossible to let go of.

Give Yourself Permission

To stop doing everything yourself! Take risks by moving ever higher-stakes responsibilities off your plate.

Ask Yourself

What is the most tedious task currently on your to-do list? Who can help with it? (If you don't have a specific person in mind, imagine the *type* of person or team that is needed.)

Do (or Delegate) This Next

Check out the sample delegation observation tracker in the Free Time Toolkit online. Pen and paper works too, and sometimes better since you can keep adding to the list reminding you by sitting right on your desk. Create an assignment for one tedious task you identified, even if you start with a voice memo or screen walkthrough in lieu of writing it down step by step.

Part 3: Assign

Align > Design > **Assign** >

What

Look for person-to-project alignment as you facilitate ongoing conversations with your team. Look for ways to delegate, automate, or drop the draining work. Sometimes another person on the team will jump at these tasks (happily!), or perhaps you can outsource. Feedback isn't personal; it is about improving the business and helping each other grow. As book mentor Michael Larsen taught me to say when soliciting input, "Don't spare me, spare the reader." Translation: If someone (or something) has business "spinach" in their teeth, say something! Learn from mistakes that don't seem to be your fault. Remind your team: Instead of playing Question Ping Pong, asking someone else to answer because it's faster, first take your best guess. Explain your logic with proposed timing for moving forward if you don't hear back by a certain date. The Manager Manual is a living document. Keep it open and updated while working with instructions for everything, except for sensitive information such as passwords and credit cards. Everyone should be continually trying to "work ourselves out of a job" to focus on increasingly more sophisticated work.

In this section, you will:
- Make yourself replaceable with the Fiji Test
- Identify, discuss, and solve for drainers
- Take responsibility for *all* frustration

22

The Fiji Test:
Continually Make Ourselves
Replaceable

Don't be irreplaceable. If you can't be replaced, you can't be promoted.

—Scott Adams

For years I worked through hypothetical business scenarios starting with the premise, "If I were to get hit by a bus tomorrow . . . "

Eventually, rather than spending another minute worrying about a terrible outcome I didn't want, I shifted the thought-exercise to what I call *the Fiji Test*. As in, what if any one of us were whisked to Fiji on a moment's notice for a three-week unplugged vacation, and told to leave all of our devices at home? Instead of ruminating about getting terminally ill or hit by a bus, this lightens things up, still keeping the thought exercise's benefits. After all, as the saying goes, "Worrying is praying for something you don't want." (That said, I do have disability insurance for worst-case scenarios.)

The *whisked to Fiji test* means setting up systems and documentation to support one core question: Can a stranger to the business step in tomorrow, in any role, and run things smoothly?

This goes for everyone, including the CEO: we all continually work ourselves out of our individual jobs. In doing this, we paradoxically make ourselves more valuable to the business. If a team member is sick or transitions off the team, others can seamlessly step in with only minor disruption. Remember, that includes you, as the owner. Get as many of your steps and systems out of your head and onto the page.

One of my colleagues, Leah, ran an experiment to hire a salesperson for her services. I give her kudos for delegating something stretchy and edgy, something she previously assumed only she could do as the owner of the business. Hiring someone always feels a touch risky financially, even if their role is theoretically revenue generating. But when Leah's salesperson left four months later with nary a new client, the bigger missed opportunity became clear: All that effort to train her and teach her how to sell the services was lost. The thousands of dollars spent on her trial period solidified as a sunk cost, with no documentation to show for it.

For this reason, I suggested Leah ask the salesperson to spend the last month of her trial period documenting all that she had learned so far, strategies she had tested and ones she planned to, and clear notes on who she had spoken with. That way, at least Leah would have invested money into creating an asset in the form of documentation to help the *next* salesperson get up to speed more quickly. Imagine Leah stepping away from her business tomorrow, with little notice (*whisked to Fiji!*). If the salesperson had created this process asset, Leah could rest assured that someone else could quickly step in to pinch hit during her absence.

The Fiji Test emphasizes qualities I love about software coding. Coding centers on creative problem solving, yet within clear boundaries. Something either works as intended, or it doesn't. Troubleshooting becomes part of the fun, as does documentation and clean code. Many engineers take pride in clarity and documentation for the next person who will be working with it, even if most end users will never see what's behind the code curtain. Without this documentation, anyone who has to work with that code later is left to do their own guesswork.

When it comes to your own Fiji Test, your Manager Manual becomes the documentation linchpin where every process (and the values, philosophy, and logic behind each one) has a home. To provide perspective on the utility of this beyond mine as the owner, I asked current and former team members to share how we use our Manager Manual, and how it came in handy during one of our biggest business transitions that I described in the introduction.

After five years working closely with me on all aspects of the business—starting as an intern when she was a junior at Yale—as her skills and sophistication grew, Marisol Dahl wanted to transition out of day-to-day maintenance and into a more strategic role.

"This meant offloading and re-delegating what felt like a gazillion tasks and systems, activities that I had been doing nearly every week since we started working together," Marisol said. "With a growing team, this is when we really went all-in on the Manager Manual. Writing down each process helped us identify opportunities to simplify and automate, and it made onboarding new team members a dream, since they were able to hit the ground running with little oversight."

Stephanie Huston, our newest team member at that time, was taking over the community director role from Marisol. "The Manager Manual single-handedly made the biggest impact for my seamless transition," she said. "When I first started it was almost weird because I legitimately did not have to ask one question on how to complete any task! I was set up for success and able to step in and do the work from the very first day."

Stephanie acknowledged the effort put into creating the manual, and noted that it did take effort on her part to keep it updated on a weekly basis. But even with those extra steps, she said, "I have no doubt in the priceless ROI of the Manager Manual now that I have experienced it myself! I have complete confidence and a wonderful peace of mind that if I had to take any abrupt time off (or went on a month-long hiking trip) that someone else could easily step in to help without issue."

For Brenna Barry-Martinez, who started as a virtual assistant and quickly moved into a more strategic project manager role, getting the hang of working with us was a refreshing change from starting with most of her other clients. "The Manager Manual made not only onboarding but my day-to-day tasks drastically more efficient," she said. "It gives time back to every team member to focus on their strengths, rather than digging around for details and processes, or waiting on others to answer questions."

In *Clockwork*, author Mike Michalowicz operationalizes this further, with the help of Adrianne Dorison, CEO of the related Run Like Clockwork business. They encourage business owners to actually schedule, and take, a "Four-Week Vacation." The Four-Week Vacation becomes a beacon and an assessment. How well have you "clockworked" your operations? How smoothly can your business run without you, not just in by-the-skin-of-your-teeth, here's-hoping-nothing-catches-fire-without-me maintenance mode, but perhaps your team even *growing* the business while you are out, increasing sales and supporting new clients?

Put another way, experiments like a Four-Week Vacation or the Fiji Test are *not* just for the health of the founder. They are beneficial for the health of the business. By you, the owner, getting out of the way of the day-to-day, the business has an opportunity to grow as a result. Your team members can become even more empowered to step up and solve problems, particularly without you hovering over them micromanaging. *Yes, you*—we all fall into this trap sometimes. After intentional systems building, it may seem counterintuitive, but consider time away as necessary oxygen for expansion.

CHAPTER 22 RECAP

The Fiji Test: Continually Make Ourselves Replaceable

Two-Sentence Summary

If any team member were to get whisked off to a three-week surprise vacation, with no devices and no ability to give notice, could the rest of the team seamlessly step in and take over the role? To achieve this, each person works toward making themselves replaceable every day.

Give Yourself Permission
To try a tiny Fiji trial: Go offline for double the duration of what is typical for your time away from the business, and see how your team responds. Give them a heads-up to go into "first responder" mode by taking extra initiative during this time, not just waiting for your approval upon return.

Ask Yourself
If an outsider were to step into any role in your business tomorrow, would they be able to run things smoothly? What would function, and what would fail?

Do (or Delegate) This Next
In your preferred cloud-based software establish an area called "Manager Manual." If you have help now, or will in the future, ask team members to update this while working, with clearly documented steps for projects and tasks, particularly recurring ones. *Note: Do not keep passwords here; I recommend 1Password for secure storage.*

23

Drained? Let's Discuss

Don't spend time beating on a wall, hoping to transform it into a door.

—Coco Chanel

Although my official job title two years into my five-year Google tenure was Senior Strategist and team lead, I had become a glorified PowerPointer. Instead of facilitating training for dynamic rooms full of eager new hires, I was sitting behind my laptop shifting bullet points by the pixel while massaging ever more data. I remember sitting with my manager at the time, a business school grad and former consultant, reviewing "v5" of a strategy deck that I had been working on for weeks.

I held my breath as my manager walked through yet another round of never-ending feedback, swallowing my disagreement that we needed further edits before presenting to senior leadership. At that moment, I felt like I was slowly dying inside. The level of effort to output did not make sense to me. No amount of learning in this area was helping me enjoy it more. I hated every slide, I resented my lack of visual acuity in designing better diagrams, and most of all, I loathed spending (*wasting!*) months of time, energy, and attention on preparing something that *might* get fifteen minutes of stakeholder attention.

It was this type of task that, as it swallowed more of my projects pie at work, had me start taking steps toward an internal pivot. I loved Google, but I barely recognized what had become of my day-to-day work. I pined for the days where I was energized, fully immersed in delivering training that I received glowing feedback on, making a real difference in people's lives—rather than bumping up against arbitrary, abstract tasks where I never felt skilled enough. Between back-to-back meetings, never-ending emails, and perpetually in-progress management tasks, I knew I was only operating in my greatest strengths 20 percent of the time, at most. My projects were simply not aligned in a way that allowed me to give more, despite my best intentions and hopes of doing so. Thankfully, shortly after these realizations I was able to move into a different role on the newly formed career development team, one I ended up thriving in.

The Pivot Method comprises four stages for mapping what's next, repeated cyclically, as pivoting is a continuous process: Plant, Scan, Pilot, then eventually, Launch. The Plant stage focuses on strengths and vision, akin to setting your current and desired locations into Google maps, before solving for how to get there in the Scan stage.

To assist with strengths discovery, in *Pivot* I suggested a tracking exercise along the lines of the hotter/colder exercise that many of us played as kids. Across three columns, jot down some notes about work that feels cold (like a drag, induces dread), lukewarm (meh, got it done), and hot (time flew, deeply focused). Think about your day-to-day work from the last month: consider all the moving pieces, the people you interacted with, your overall responsibilities. Review the month ahead, consider new projects on your plate, meetings on your calendar, and items on your to-do list.

The "hot" column is what author and #lovework co-founder Josh Allan Dykstra calls *true strengths*. As Josh taught me during their certification program about energy intelligence, typically when you hear the word "strengths," you think of *competencies*, what you are objectively skilled at and praised for. However, those are not always the same activities that energize you most. Just because you are good at something does not mean you enjoy it.

To return to my example, even if you have well-developed presentation skills, maybe you hate the process of building slides, and therefore decide to start hiring out for that. Conversely, you may be energized by something that you are not yet very good at, such as learning a new language.

Your *true strengths* are areas you are already skilled at *and* that energize you. Better understanding your *energizers* can also help you navigate your *drainers*, Josh's term for soul-sucking work that drains your energy instead of charging you up.

For example, when I took #lovework's Strengthscope assessment, my lowest energy-strength by a landslide was *collaboration*, clocking in at a measly one-and-a-half out of ten on my enjoyment scale. If that's the case, *what are you doing writing about Delightfully Tiny Teams and encouraging people to hire help, you ask?* Well, there is a reason my favorite teams are tiny and reliant on smart systems! My highest energy-strengths were creativity and efficiency, measuring ten out of ten on my enjoyment scale.

Regardless of whatever *skill* I may or may not possess in terms of collaboration, collaborative projects with too many meetings drain me by default, unless they are facilitated skillfully with people whose expertise directly complements my own. I groan when people I don't know reach out saying they would "love to partner" on something long and complex, particularly when it is clear they are mostly looking to boost their own reach.

As Josh and his team advise, once we know what our energizers are we can apply them as keys to unlock solutions for this more draining work.

For example, I might ask, "How can I approach collaboration through my highest energy-strengths, creativity and efficiency?" Unskilled collaboration that is disorganized, plodding, and stuffed with wandering conversation makes me cringe. But when I can design working relationships and shared projects with creativity, clear deadlines, and efficiency in mind, I enjoy collaboration more.

Energy-strengths can vary significantly even within those sharing the same job role or title, as illustrated during an event I spoke at, a global conference for administrative business partners working at a large

Part 3: Assign

233

technology company. This group was responsible for supporting executives and teams, keeping everything running by juggling a number of complex responsibilities and schedules. Technically, these hundreds of people shared the exact same job title. But when I asked about what aspects of the role they enjoyed most, there was incredible variety in the room. *How many of you love working with spreadsheets?* A dozen arms shot up to the ceiling, while others *tsk-tsked*, crossing their fingers and shaking their heads to say *no way.* When I asked how many love event planning, an entirely different set of hands raised, while others recoiled at the cat-herding nature of coordination as they mimicked pushing that work to their coworkers who were happier to handle it.

Seeing energizers and drainers so clearly spelled out can provide helpful insight into why you work the way you do, and can lead to fruitful conversations with team members. I hold the somewhat radical belief that none of us should be doing work that drains us. It isn't productive and the results are never as good. Contrary to the belief that *someone's gotta do it*, when it comes to unexamined drudgery, there is no benefit to *anyone* being drained at work. Keep in mind that sometimes responsibilities that were exciting at first become draining once they enter maintenance mode.

As a result of the #lovework training and assessment results, when Marisol was still the main right-hand person on my team, she and I set-up a conversation we nicknamed "design your role." Managers confused by how to best approach career coaching, take note: This conversation can be as simple as *two* powerful questions, a few helpful follow-ups, and deep listening.

Marisol and I focused on just two questions:

What projects and tasks energize you most? Which ones drain you, that in an ideal world you could move off your plate?

Be sure to copiously sprinkle a few key follow-ups throughout: What else? What else? What else? Tell me more. What specifically do you enjoy about that type of work, or what drains you most about that?

Do not try to solve for the drainers in the same sitting. Just listen to what they are, so that you have maximum information to work from moving forward. By moving the conversation from typical performance management topics like strengths and "areas for opportunity," there is nothing personal at stake. Everyone can speak objectively about the work. What energizes you and what drains you are not value judgements, they are observations.

There is a reason Marie Kondo's book, *The Life-Changing Magic of Tidying Up*, became an instant mega-bestseller. It focused on one simple question: Does this spark joy? Kondo was referring to objects around the house—books, travel trinkets, junk drawers, clothes, etc.—but this process and guiding question can just as easily apply to our suite of work tasks. Keep what energizes you and your team members, then methodically work to get rid of the rest. Maybe not right away, and maybe not *everything*, but this will open up creative possibilities and greater person-to-role alignment along the way.

Returning to my *design-your-role* (DYR) conversation with Marisol, for one hour we stayed with this one topic of what energized her most and what drained her. I let her know that I might not be able to move the drainers off her plate right away, but together we held the intention of dropping them eventually, first by documenting them to delegate to a future yet-to-be-hired team member, and in some cases systematizing and automating them, which led to searching for software-based solutions so that no one had to do them.

We scheduled a follow-up meeting three weeks out, and I asked her to draft an ideal role description in the interim to help me better understand her vision moving forward. In the meantime, we also drafted a role description of the work she was ready to delegate. After five years of honing her craft in these areas, and developing new strategic skills with her other business and clients, she was understandably ready to keep moving.

In Marisol's case, we knew more about what we were moving off than what she would be keeping or starting moving forward. She had the courage to let go of 80 percent of her scope of work and transfer it to new team members, trusting that together we would find new projects for her to tackle. We both acknowledged the transition would happen over several steps and several months, and that there would be uncertainty along the way.

Even when Marisol fully transitioned out of my business one year later, after six years of working together, we continued to collaborate. She is the co-founder of Together Agency, the branding company I hired for the *Free Time* book and podcast, now building out her own Delightfully Tiny Team as head of operations.

Given the nature of Together's detailed strategy and design work for clients, she and co-founder Adam Chaloeicheep are building toward a team of ten. At three, they were overly stressed and strapped for time. When they had expanded to over twenty team members in the past, Adam and Marisol felt bogged down by administrivia, removed from the more creative and strategic work that energizes them.

Here is how to tackle these design-your-role conversations, even with new or part-time team members:

1. **Kick-off conversation:** What are your energizers and drainers? Homework: Continue observing over the next two weeks, capturing additions large and small.

2. **DYR follow-up conversation:** What is your ideal role or job description at a high level? What do you love that you would like to do more of?

3. **Documenting and rethinking our current workflow:** Update the Manager Manual to capture current knowledge, such as small tasks on autopilot, while researching new ways to automate. Then draft a role description for work your team member would like to delegate. Ask around among your network to find new potential team members to fill the open roles.

4. **Onboard new team members:** The transitioning team member spends two to four weeks walking through more complex tasks, paralleling and guiding the work as the new person completes more complex sequences for the first time. This also helps the owner avoid answering too many questions during the transition time.

5. **Open space:** Only at this stage is there more room to think. Let the transitioning team member take time here to continue reflecting. With the older and routine work removed from her plate, Marisol could think more creatively about the business and most pressing problems. We determined that her interim title would be Director of Special Projects.

6. **Define your next role or projects for this person:** Do not underestimate the power of the special projects role; for someone freed up from routine tasks, they are available to tackle high-level projects with a discrete start and end date.

What if no one wants to do the draining work?

This is often a signal that it can be automated or dropped altogether, in more cases than you might think. I tell my team to aim for a 70/20/10 ratio: ideally we love 70 percent of what we do, 20 percent is neutral, and no more than 10 percent drains us. For the drainers, we continually question how we can free up that time through elimination, automation, and delegation.

CHAPTER 23 RECAP

Drained? Let's Discuss

Two-Sentence Summary

Tell your team not to be shy about speaking up if the work becomes tiresome or draining. It is not personal; it means you have not yet found the best person-to-project match.

Give Yourself Permission

Empower your team (and yourself!) to drop drainers, creatively solving for how to do this on an ongoing basis.

Ask Yourself

What's the work you hate doing? Make a list of your top ten. How can you drop, delegate, automate, or trade just *one* of these to quickly provide relief?

Do (or Delegate) This Next

Ask your team to schedule you for a one-hour conversation to discuss their biggest energizers and drainers. Remind them: you cannot offend me with this information! It is all helpful, even if we don't know how to resolve it right away.

24

Frustrated? Take Responsibility

I have learned to avoid the care and feeding of Gordon's monkeys by using an anti-straddle reflex *that is instantly provoked by the word "we." When I hear the phrase "we've got a problem," I visualize a straddling monkey with one leg on my back and the other on Gordon's back. I say to Gordon, "**We** do not have a problem, and **we** will never have one again. I'm sure there is a problem, but it is not ours, it is either yours or mine."*

—William Oncken, Jr.

was set to speak at a **Women@Google summit on March 12, 2020.** During a planning call the week prior, they let me know it would be postponed, and that all Googlers had just been asked to work from home. This was a business canary in a coal mine, the first of my speaking engagements to topple that year. I knew the rest of my speaking engagements would soon vanish, and disappear they did.

Within two weeks, 90 percent of my projected income for the next two quarters was gone. *Cancelled.* Entire teams of people I had been in contract negotiations with were furloughed. I was one of the fortunate ones. I was healthy, I had a roof over my head and food to eat, and I could work remotely from home as I generated replacement income. I had monthly recurring revenue from a private community I had been running for five years for Heart-Based Business owners. Ironically, it was the *smallest* businesses that kept mine afloat in 2020, while my big corporate clients were busy stabilizing (as they should), helping employees figure out how to suddenly work remotely. Soon the world would know our sweatpants secrets.

It would have been easy to wallow, to feel sorry for myself. I did, for about a week, as my stomach lurched with every next cancelled check. A pandemic is not any one person's fault. It happened to all of us, globally and collectively, as we all *got* pivoted on a daily basis.

I also knew that the best thing I could do as a business owner was re-center and take full responsibility, then act accordingly, one small next step at a time. Together, my team and I steered through tremendous uncertainty. If I had been waiting for a hero, someone to come fix things or save me, I would have been waiting for a long time. Besides, there were many people in far greater need. Handling this would be on me.

Whether you run a business, lead a team, or work for someone else, the only path to sanity is to take full responsibility and to be open to feedback. Nobody wants to catch a hot blame potato: "It's not my fault, you fix it!" This means everyone, from the newest team member to the one with the longest tenure.

Have you ever been in a room with an A-list celebrity? It is incredible to watch just about everyone who crosses their path fawn over them, lavishing them with praise. Ironically, this puts them in a challenging position, as it is tougher to get honest input on ideas when everyone is ingratiating themselves to the star, telling them only what they think they want to hear. CEOs and business owners have the same problem: they create a power distortion field. It is harder to solicit authentic reactions when people are worried about how their comments will be perceived. Leaders must go out of their way to invite commentary, and set-up systems to do so.

When I am sharing a new project with my team or early participants, I make a point to say how helpful feedback is and how much I appreciate it. I need it! We all do.

When *delivering* feedback, provide the logic behind your comments. Instead of just pointing out a problem, or blaming the person, focus on the potentially faulty process behind it.

Note also, where praise falls short, even when it is for something positive. Praise would be saying to someone, "Great job on your presentation today!" Far more helpful is to provide details on what factors enabled it to be great, adding, "I loved how clearly you outlined our onboarding process, the slides were simple and compelling, and your delivery was perfectly paced. Bravo!"

Invite Debate, Disagreement, and Feedback

I stared out into an airport-hangar sized room as hundreds of people streamed in, filling over one thousand seats in the room. That meant at least two thousand eyeballs staring ahead, just waiting for me to ensure this hour would be worth their time. As my heart thumped out of my chest, I took a few deep breaths, then began my keynote.

Oh, how far I had come from the days of breaking out in hives.

If you have ever felt nervous before a speech, big presentation, or client meeting, you too probably felt it was a personal shortcoming or flaw, that you could have done better if only you were born with the elusive "public speaking" gene. I assure you, this is not true. If it were not for an annoying-at-the-time yet valuable piece of feedback, and what I did after receiving it, I might not have been on that stage at all, figuring I was simply too nervous to be a professional speaker.

When I was a freshly-minted manager at twenty-four years old, I delivered an important presentation to a room full of senior level directors. I thought the meeting went well since I delivered my content clearly, but afterward my manager gave me some feedback. My talking points were solid, he said, but my whole face, neck, and chest turned red during my presentation, which made me appear nervous. I was mortified.

The worst part? The feedback had been passed down to him from one of the directors in the room! *Don't shoot the messenger,* they say. No matter. At first I was fumingly angry . . . *How dare they?! Talk about a rash on my chest, something I have no control over, as a professional area of development?! What were they doing looking there anyway?!* Then I became deeply embarrassed, turning bright red all over again. I could not deny it was true. I felt betrayed by my own body. *How would I fix this fatal flaw? Could I? Does this doom my public speaking dreams?*

For the next *three years*, I wore turtlenecks on days I led important meetings or workshops. Ultimately, the feedback and ensuing embarrassment motivated me to find a better way. So I picked up a book called *Confessions of a Public Speaker* by Scott Berkun and started laughing with relief at a passage from the first chapter:

> *Our brains, for all their wonders, identify the following four things as being very bad for our survival:*
>
> - *Standing alone*
> - *in open territory with nowhere to hide*
> - *without a weapon*
> - *in front of a large crowd of creatures staring at you*
>
> *In the long history of all living things, any situation where all of the above were true would be very bad for you. It meant*

the odds were high that you would soon be attacked and eaten
alive. Our ancestors, the ones that survived, developed a fear
response to these situations.

Ah ha! No wonder I felt so nervous! My body was doing its job, engaging my fight-or-flight response as a survival instinct during what it perceives as a very dangerous situation.

After leaving Google, keynote speaking became my primary source of income for the next ten years. I learned strategies for giving that surge of adrenaline a job in order to release it: taking three deep yogic breaths, clenching and unclenching my fists while backstage, or pacing outside prior to going on (many speakers make the mistake of pacing nervously while on stage). I learned to keep moving through the momentary panic that still sometimes strikes me when doing something as simple as introducing myself among a small room of twenty people.

Even still, sometimes my voice quavers or my leg shakes. But now I know how to breathe into it. If I panic, make judgements about myself, or worry that the audience can tell, adrenaline production only accelerates.

Inviting critique, holding feedback as more precious than our pride, means we are constantly looking for better systems to help our business butterflies fly in formation, as the saying goes.

In the end, I am grateful for my manager's candid comments, delivered with a kind heart, no matter how jarring at first. His words changed my relationship to my professional calling by encouraging me to build skills around managing my nerves when on stage, rather than assuming I was born without the right genes (and turtlenecks) for public speaking.

As a business owner, if I did not have a cash runway to support me even during something as unpredictable as a global pandemic, that's on me. Government-mandated shut-downs alongside skyrocketing rents and unforgiving landlords did send a devastating number of restaurants, coffee shops, hair salons, and brick-and-mortar retailers into a death spiral. No one can say that those mandates were those owners' fault. But some got creative in spite of these crazy circumstances.

Michelin-star restaurants started offering doggie bags for delivery, or "do it yourself" kits for heating the perfect gourmet meal. Dani Zoldan, co-owner of Stand-up New York, a comedy club on the Upper West Side, started offering shows on the one-train subway, and other scrappy stand-up comics brought mic-and-speaker sets to Central Park. One restaurant just north of the park built a walk-up bar for patrons to take drinks to nearby picnics while social distancing.

Even for someone in my line of work, with travel and in-person keynote speeches comprising significant annual revenue, I had always known that the economy could crash at any time and that I needed to be prepared. The way I saw it: if I had not set-up diversified streams of income that were counter-cyclical, anticipating an inevitable recession, *that's on me.* I purposefully wrote *Pivot* with boom and bust times in mind. I knew that if the economy crashed, even more people would need help pivoting, and that ended up being true. Book sales spiked in May of 2020, selling ten times more than in a typical month.

Learn from mistakes or things that are not your fault but happened anyway. Reflect and ask every team member to take responsibility:

- What happened?
- How can we resolve the current situation and fix the larger systems issue that created it?
- How can we each own the outcome, no matter who was technically responsible?
- What can we do differently next time?

- What new systems, checks, or communication can we put in place as a result? How can we ensure this happens more smoothly next time?
- Report back to the group and document the above; so we all become more skilled.

You will be so much happier in the long run if you take responsibility for everything that happens, good and bad in your business. We are not going to get into the *life* side of this. If something terrible happens, we certainly do not want to blame victims for circumstances beyond their control. That is not what we are talking about here.

When running a business and a Delightfully Tiny Team, taking responsibility means that your success is a result of your efforts, even with healthy servings of serendipity and luck. It also means that *everything* that frustrates you, that you don't like, is still your responsibility to handle. You may not have created the problem, but as the owner, on some level it is still yours to fix, even as you may delegate solving the smaller details to your team. *All* issues are ones that you and your team members can learn from with the right mindset.

Remember, business stress is a systems problem. Otherwise you are always going to be looking to blame other people in ways subtle and overt. Even if you are someone who *thinks* you already take responsibility for your life and your business, you might be surprised.

Let's work through a few scenarios to understand the subtleties of this. If a client does not pay, or pays so late that this negatively impacts your business:

- Were your processes clearly outlined? Your policies?
- Did you ask for a deposit or payment in full before starting?
- Did you follow up?
- Do you have systems in place for collections?
- Do you enforce consequences of late payments?
- Was your energy aligned with this client when they signed on?

- In what ways are you attracting clients that are no longer a fit?

- On a subconscious level, how and why are you experiencing this exact situation? What lessons are you meant to learn?

- You could go deeper, asking: In what ways am I insecure about my worth? My prices? How can I step into my confidence as a business owner?

- Do your website and marketing materials clearly communicate who you most enjoy working with?

- What can you do differently, or what systems can you put in place, to *prevent* a situation like this? To handle it even if it still arises again?

Your team member completes a task that is not up to your standards:

- What did you miss in terms of assigning the task clearly?

- How can you build better delegation skills?

- Do you have the right team member/s on board, and are you assigning tasks that match their skills and interests?

- How can you more clearly communicate the deadline and the completed result that you are looking for?

- How well-documented are your systems, processes, style guide, and delivery standards?

- Have you asked team members to document and improve on those systems as they go?

- What can you learn from this? What do you need to do differently?

As a team member, you receive feedback that a project was not done up to par:

- Did you ask for clarification when you received the assignment?

- Did you anticipate what success would look like in the larger context of this task? Did you understand why it was being assigned at the start?

- Were you clear about what you needed to deliver by when, and did you honor that commitment?

- Did you get a head start on scope and plan for how you would complete it, or did you wait until the last minute to ask for help?

- Did you research solutions or fill your own skill gaps before reflexively asking for input?

- If you had a technical question, did you do a quick Google search or reference that software's help center to assist with troubleshooting?

- Did you ping another team member who might have helpful context?

- Did you proactively address possible follow-up questions and next steps from the person assigning the project, before you handed it over?

- Did you improve the confusing aspects of documentation behind-the-scenes for future projects or tasks like this one?

Now, of course, if you work with a toxic manager as I once did, where multiple team members got physically ill from the daily gaslighting, pressure, and imposing presence, you must make bigger moves. If you have a team member who does not pull their weight and clearly does not respond to feedback, they will not last on your team. Taking full responsibility is what allows Delightfully Tiny Teams, already lean by design, to function well together, each anticipating the other's needs, and taking responsibility to fix things that might not seem like anyone's fault at first glance.

If your clients are frustrating you, what do they all have in common? *You.* What is it about your sales page, your marketing materials, your consultation calls, that are attracting people who are not a fit? Or maybe these are your ideal clients, but you are doing something or interpreting something that they are doing in a way that reflects a boundary needing to be set.

For example, if your clients are texting questions in between regular coaching sessions and you are frustrated thinking, *none of my clients have any respect. They text me night and day, always wanting more—more advice, more attention. Ugh, they are so needy!* Well, maybe they have worked with another coach who loves corresponding with their clients over texts! But you have not yet set this explicit preference or boundary with your clients that texting is not the best way to reach you. Take this as an opportunity to set guidelines for "How to communicate when we are in between sessions." I asked my coaching clients to track homework, questions, and updates at the bottom of our shared Google Doc. That way I could get caught up asynchronously before each session, while allowing them to keep a helpful record of their progress throughout our coaching engagement.

Still, we all know that sometimes it does feel cathartic to blame someone else and vent. There is something refreshing about letting out steam by saying, "How dare they!" Getting mad is convenient, but ultimately counterproductive once you have had time to process, vent, and get over it. By staying mad, you skip the even harder work of looking at yourself and what you could do differently. In the long run, though, this is the only sustainable way to run your business.

CHAPTER 24 RECAP

Frustrated? Take Responsibility

Two-Sentence Summary

Learn from every mistake, even things that do not seem on the surface to be your fault but that happened anyway. Nobody wants to catch a hot blame potato; reflect and take responsibility, knowing that *all* slip-ups can spark systems inquiries.

Give Yourself Permission

Stop dwelling on difficult people. What can *you* do differently next time?

Ask Yourself

What are your three biggest business frustrations at the moment? Make a quick list.

Do (or Delegate) This Next

Now, take responsibility. For each issue ask, "How have I played a part in creating this?" What is this exact situation, at this moment, asking you to learn or do differently? How can you grow? Why are you noticing this as a problem, and why now? How will the business benefit from creating a solution? How will your team benefit?

Align > Design > **Assign >**

When

When you work matters as much as how you work, and how much. It does not benefit anyone, or the business, to fracture attention by jumping at messages all day the moment they come in. Most messages can wait; set parameters for your communication cadence, and how you will indicate when something is truly time-sensitive. Communicate in thoughtful, non-reactive ways when sending and replying. Choose communication channels that are most appropriate for the long term; don't choose channels based on what is quickest or more convenient in the moment. Be clear with commitments. Tell your team, "If you will not meet a deadline that you have set or that is in our task tracker, it is not usually a problem—just check in with updated timing." Do not let tasks slip without any communication, as that creates confusion and breaks trust. Renegotiate deadlines if needed to tackle truly time-sensitive and important, strategic tasks. Be mindful of arbitrary or conflicting deadlines that do not meaningfully contribute to the most important work. Document all feedback, questions, and answers to save the team (and customers) time, confusion, and hassle.

In this section, you will:
- Track every task and assign one clear owner
- Answer less: every question lives three lives
- Save someone next steps

25

Track Every Task and Assign One Owner

Faulty memory and distraction are a particular danger in what engineers call all-or-none processes: whether running to the store to buy ingredients for a cake, preparing an airplane for takeoff, or evaluating a sick person in the hospital, if you miss just one key thing, you might as well not have made the effort at all.

—Atul Gawande

Have you seen my [keys, wallet, phone]? This is a common refrain in our household, and you can guess who, between me and my husband, is doing the daily searching versus the methodical finding. In a survey of over 3,000 adults, people reported spending an average of ten minutes each day looking for lost items. That's 3,680 hours—153 days—over the course of their lifetime.

Imagine how many *more* minutes you spend each day looking for lost digital items: where you stored that file, where you read that quote, a vague recollection of something you know you assigned to a team member, but no clue what or when, or whatever happened to it.

For some with information-organizing intentions, every new attempt at setting up the latest newfangled time-management tool becomes a graveyard of forgotten tasks and projects. Without going all in on any one, there is no trust or real need to return to it.

Every product in your business contains a series of sub-projects and systems. Like the oil change on a car, most systems need ongoing maintenance: checking trends of key metrics, such as enrollment numbers, to indicate the health of that product, or activities like fixing bugs, responding to customer inquiries and feedback, making updates, correcting typos and broken links, and archiving what is no longer relevant.

Without a central task database to capture every single activity, large and small, your externalized mind will fail. Your Manager Manual, documenting how to run various processes, will become fossilized and forgettable without a task-tracking system running in parallel.

Nowhere is this entropy more evident than in older homes or ones in nature. I remember staying at a cabin in the Catskills, where I could see right before my eyes all forms of plants and animals encroaching on the once-pristine house. Without upkeep, a dead tree teetered precariously toward the roof, weeds started overtaking the grass, spiders made themselves comfortable in bathroom corners, giant carpenter ants traversed the kitchen counters, and we spotted a garden snake crawling into the crevices of the outdoor hot tub.

Entropy, defined as a gradual decline into disorder, is intrinsic to all organic systems, and it is happening in your business, too. As author Lex Sisney explains in *Organizational Physics*, all systems are subject to this disorder or disintegration.

"An organization's available energy first flows to manage and counter the disintegrating force of entropy," he writes. "If entropy in the system is high, it costs the system a higher amount of available energy to maintain itself and get work done."

To my delight, there is a term for the opposite phenomenon, *negentropy*, which means things are becoming *more* orderly, more organized than their surrounding space. Sisney describes this opposite pole to entropy as *integration*, the amount of new energy made available from the surrounding environment, such as gaining new customers, resources, or even prestige.

As a business owner, you are already juggling a tremendous amount of responsibility, personally and professionally. Sometimes there is no need to sweat the small stuff, and at other times one missed task sends the Jenga tower toppling.

You will benefit greatly by building a task management system you can trust, so you can focus without worrying that you are forgetting things. Every single task that happens in your business should live somewhere. Having a central, shared task repository is crucial to creating a collective consciousness for your business. It becomes part of the shared mind that everyone trusts to keep track of all the details: what you are working on, who owns that task or project, any dependencies, and who will do what by when.

It is easier to get sloppy when you are alone. Once you hire help, the cognitive load of relying on memory becomes burdensome. *What did I assign? When was it due? Who is taking care of that? Oh, what happened to that thing I mentioned last week?* If you are the team member, you might be asking, "What was I supposed to do this week again? Did so-and-so ever get back to me on that item preventing me from moving forward?"

Email is not equipped for project or task management; it is chaotic, reactive, difficult to sort and track by priority and deadline, and harder to search for information related to those tasks and projects later on. With task tracking software (we currently have a database within our Notion dashboard for this), you can easily pull in outside collaborators and give them restricted access to their specific project. This frees your mind—and your team's—for what it does best: strategizing, imagining, creating, and delegating, *not* trying to remember details and deadlines.

Over time, task tracking software can become cluttered. Low-impact, low-priority tasks that will never make the top of anyone's list. I suggest creating a tag or project for these. You can review anything tagged "Fix It" quarterly, and either conduct a one- or two-day Fix-It sprint with your team to clear them out, or delete them altogether. I also like adding "New Ideas" and "Next Up" tags, so that as team members come up with solutions while working, everyone can add to those lists without interrupting projects in progress.

Tidy Tasks

Task-tracking software can quickly spiral out of control, defeating the entire purpose, because you can't bear to go into the basement where everything is a mess, forgotten and moldy. You will lose trust in your system if you and your team do not maintain good task hygiene. Here are a few of our rules-of-thumb:

- Every project and task goes in our task tracker, with one clear owner and a delivery date.

- For any given project, the owner (me) is never the owner—except in rare cases—even when you are waiting on me for feedback.

- You can assign subtasks to me as *co-owner* when you are waiting on me for review. I will assign the task back to you once that step is complete. If I forget to review on time, please make a note to remind me and stay on the case, as you are still the project owner.

- If an email arrives that is actually a task, and you do not complete it right away, add it to our tracker. If you happen to be processing email and can quickly address it, no need to create a task just for the record, unless we expect more like it to follow.

- Group similar tasks, processing them in batches if they are not time sensitive. For example, placing orders, updating links, or buying tickets.

- Unless otherwise noted, aim for a one-week turnaround time as a default for most tasks.

- We strive to *precrastinate*: every single task that can be completed leading up to a launch should be, as far in advance as possible. This frees our energy up for responding to new opportunities and challenges in the moment during the launch itself.

- Feel free to cc others, but only one person should be leading and on the hook for any task or project. This reduces confusion, and helps us all stay attentive without doubling up on work (i.e., more than one person with the cognitive load of remembering due dates).

- Streamline content creation by using cloud-based software whenever possible, as it makes information readily available from any device, and easier to track revision history.

- Consider the most efficient format for delivery for all involved, minimizing versions and copies. For example: When sharing transcripts or templates, avoid Word or Excel attachments. They are not on "systems" brand with our efficiency value, since each recipient has to take time to download their own separate copy, spawning many different versions in the process.

- If we receive an attachment that we want to make public, like a transcript, first import it to Google Docs, move it to the relevant folder in our team Drive, then publish the link in view-only mode.

Let's look more closely at one of the most important rules-of-thumb from the sidebar on Tidy Tasks: *The owner is not the owner.* More specifically, if you own the business, avoid owning the tasks and projects within it. Ask your team to take responsibility for tasks *and* outcomes.

This problem is not uncommon, and we all get overwhelmed at times, team members included. One day film executive Peter Guber, running a Hollywood studio at twenty-nine years old, vented to Jack Warner, president of Warner Bros. Studios, that he was overwhelmed and "left with a million problems" at the end of every day. Warner replied:

> *Don't be confused. You're only renting that office. You don't own it. You're the zookeeper in a zoo. Every person arrives with a monkey. Think of that monkey as their problem. They're trying to leave it with you. Sometimes you have to discover where the monkey is. It's hidden or dressed up. But remember you're the zookeeper. You've got to keep the place clean. So when you walk them to the door, be sure they've got their monkey by the hand. Don't let them leave without it. And if they come back, make sure it's trained, i.e. they have solutions to their problems. Otherwise at the end of the day, you'll have a screaming, jumping troop of monkeys . . . .*

The monkey story above originates from one of the most popular articles in the history of *Harvard Business Review* magazine, a 1974 piece called "Management Time: Who's Got the Monkey?" that was later turned into a book, *The One Minute Manager Meets The Monkey.* Article co-authors William Oncken and Donald Wass describe a common problem for managers: team members enter their office with a monkey on their back (a problem or question), then leave. The monkey is left behind on the manager's desk. If every team member nonchalantly leaves their monkey on the manager's desk when they encounter roadblocks, the manager is quickly running a raucous zoo, unable to complete bigger-picture work.

To prevent this, two things must happen: The manager must not accept monkey babysitting duties, and team members must take greater initiative. Instead of reflexively solving every problem because in the moment it seems easier than delegating, Oncken and Wass counsel managers to take a clear "no monkey left behind" stance. They describe five degrees of initiative, with one being the lowest and five the highest:

1. Wait until told;

2. ask what to do;

3. recommend, then take resulting action;

4. act, but advise at once;

5. and act on [one's] own, then routinely report (highest initiative).

Encourage team members to strive for levels three through five, and notice when you fall for the trap of accidentally or automatically accepting monkeys. *It happens so quickly!* I once "returned" a monkey by retracting my initial reflexive offer to help someone out, noting that upon reflection I was too time-crunched while working on final edits of this book. They proceeded to solve the problem themselves within minutes. *Voilà!* It was an empowering moment for them too.

As my husband, Michael, said when I shared this concept, "So what you're saying is, you can't hoard the monkeys. You need to give them away, help them find better homes." Otherwise, he noted, they move from your office into your kitchen: "not just drinking your wine, but mischievously breaking bottles on the floor," descending into overwhelming chaos.

In a reissue of the HBR article twenty-five years later, author Stephen R. Covey recounts how Oncken lived his message while on the lecture circuit. "Like the Dilbert comic strip, Oncken had a tongue-in-cheek style that got to the core of managers' frustrations and made them want to take back control of their time," Covey writes. "The monkey on your back wasn't just a metaphor for Oncken—it was his personal symbol. I saw him several times walking through airports with a stuffed monkey on his shoulder."

CHAPTER 25 RECAP

Track Every Task and Assign One Owner

Two-Sentence Summary

If you own the business, don't own the tasks. Your mind is a terrible place to track tasks and projects; every task—large and small, personal and professional—must have a home in an externalized mind, your central task-tracking database, with an assigned owner and delivery date.

Give Yourself Permission
Stop taking care of everyone else's monkeys!

Ask Yourself
Where are you stepping in too quickly instead of helping others solve problems on their own? What systems or practices could you put in place to track tasks more clearly?

Do (or Delegate) This Next
Identify how many monkeys are sitting on your desk right now. Who do they actually belong to? Assign one clear owner—that *isn't* you.

26

Answer Less: Every Question
Lives Three Lives

*The cost of a thing is the amount of what I will call life which is
required to be exchanged for it, immediately or in the long run.*

—**Henry David Thoreau**

Disorganized documentation around common questions in
your business triples the work—and the frustration—for your
team and customers.

Consider my friend Shogo's experience upon embarking on a year-
long project with a decidedly *un-delightfully tiny* team. Every time he asked a
question about their process, or for a timeline on what to expect next, they
failed to answer clearly. When they did, it was with brief answers trapped
in one-off emails, providing scant information without any forward-looking
guidance. These spawned dozens of clarifying follow-up questions for Shogo
to get the answers he needed. The team regularly missed delivery deadlines,
and work quality was poor.

Fed up on all sides, Shogo escalated these collaboration challenges to
the senior-level leader who had promised the world before he signed on.
Eventually, the team relented and sent a document with minimal details to

outline next steps. This is something that: a) could have easily been spelled out in advance for a smoother onboarding experience, b) could have been posted to an internal webpage or project management system for future customers to reference rather than sent as a one-off attachment, and c) should have already existed to save the company's team members from annoyance at repeatedly answering the same questions via email.

This company caught a case of *botching the basics,* failing to deliver the baseline minimum expected customer experience, cementing it as a deal-breaker for Shogo (and me) to refer future clients. Their team members are probably not any happier. With many missed documentation opportunities, it is likely they too are struggling with overwhelm, inefficiency, and festering frustration.

Years after relinquishing my Chief Everything Officer role, I realized I had unintentionally taken on another position weighing me down: All-Seeing Question Answerer.

A few summers ago, I was excited to expand my team from one person to a Delightfully Tiny three, four including me. Although some business books suggested hiring an operations person as the buffer that all team members report into, this did not seem necessary: With three people in their own distinct roles and projects, I did not need someone to manage them and report to me. What I did need was a system to stop the new crush of the inbound: *questions,* particularly ones from within our team (I share a process for capturing questions from customers in the second half of this chapter).

In the beginning, answering questions seemed like a good use of my time. I enjoyed it because it meant I was no longer attending to the details of getting work done. *Every question was an accomplishment!* But as soon as the team expanded, the volume of incoming questions became cumbersome.

When my team doubled, the number of questions tripled. I was quickly overcome with question fatigue. I remember days of frustration from constant interruptions, pulling me away from the more immersive work that I had theoretically hired these new team members to allow me to do. I started to get annoyed at every new question, especially ones that seemed small or where the person asking had missed an opportunity to take their best guess. Although I was happy to be doing less work *in* the business, I grew tired of having to ask simple follow-up questions, like how much the next tier of software would cost when responding to whether to upgrade after maxing out our current level.

This was no one's fault but my own, of course. It was death by a thousand question cuts, a tragedy of the questions commons. No one team member could know how frequently I was getting pinged, and no *one* question was the end of the world. There was no way my team could have known the conflict I felt between wanting to provide a quick and helpful response versus staying focused on my own projects. Besides, two team members were new; it was only fair that I give proper energy toward onboarding them. Despite having processes and documentation in place, I was still missing two crucial steps.

First, I needed to commit to retiring from my role as All-Seeing Question Answerer. Second, I needed to communicate to my team that I was retiring from this role. They should present *recommendations*, not questions—and even better, what action they would take, and by when, if they did not hear back. That way, my failure to respond to a question would not create a bottleneck: any resulting consequences would be "on me." The team would need to take more responsibility and greater risks with their best guesses.

In a quest to retire from her role as question answerer for her team, Nilofer Merchant, author of *The Power of Onlyness*, discovered one question that she says changed everything.

For twenty years, Nilofer assumed that when her team asked her for something, they must have really needed her. She never questioned it. It made her, too, feel more valuable as a leader to jump in and help. As a result, more decisions flowed her way, even though she had a highly skilled, experienced team. She could not understand why the ball continued ending up in her court.

Now she knows why, and she takes a beat before responding to see if her team member *really* needs her or not. She asks, "Have you done everything you need to do? Have you taken this as far as you can take it?"

Sure enough, once she started asking this question before reflexively jumping in, team members started to look at her a little sheepishly and pull the work back off her desk, taking it to a much higher level before returning it to her.

"The first couple of times I said it, I worried that I sounded mean," she said. "And yet what was interesting was how much they were not carrying the ball as far as *they* wanted to go, because they thought I needed to do a check-in."

Nilofer encourages all leaders to reflect: How much do we take on because we are not letting other people fully own their assigned work?

Work Asynchronously:
Our Approach to Calm Communication

With so many apps, it can sometimes get confusing where to look and when, and how to best get in touch with each other. Here is a look at the communication hierarchy within my team, one that helps us set a day-to-day cadence of what is truly time sensitive versus what isn't. Each tool has a logic guiding the best practices to help people understand *why* we set things up this way, not just what to do.

Notion: JBE Operations Dashboard—tasks database and Manager Manual, the first place to look and respond so all conversations stay within their associated project.

- Logic: Keeps everything central, organized, linkable, and trackable.

- Best practices: Create a new task for everything, especially anything that will have more than one round of back-and-forth, or quick tasks we may repeat later. Tag team members in Notion with task-related questions, rather than in email or Slack, where the conversation will no longer be

Part 3: Assign

directly tied to the task's history, and more intuitive and centralized for searching in the future.

- Ideal turnaround time for notifications: One day for important tasks, a few days for everything else; aim for within the week if unsure.

HelpScout: Team inbox for communicating about, assigning, and responding to emails.

- Logic: Track conversations by message and sender, assign to each other with notes, search archives, and track multiple communications from the same sender.

- Best practices: If discussing something sensitive in content or urgency, we can ping each other on our #email channel in Slack. Familiarize yourself with HelpScout shortcuts; this will make things much faster! You can also forward messages from your individual Gmail account into the team mailbox, and set up workflows to automatically take action based on keywords or message type.

- Ideal turnaround time for notifications: One day for important emails and emails from current clients and customers, within the week for the rest.

Slack: For time-sensitive, topic-sensitive, or quick requests.

- Logic: Slack archives are harder to track by project, owner, and deadline; not using Slack as go-to allows us to reduce notifications overall. When we do see a Slack message, we know it is more important than usual, or that we have missed something in Notion. Ideally this is used sparingly, for sensitive or quick topics (i.e., nailing down a #scheduling date with a client), or for quick direct messages.

- Best practices: Check to see if there is a relevant Notion task or page; write in the comments there first. Default to Notion unless this requires a same-day response. If so, include the link to the Notion page in your Slack message.

- Ideal turnaround time for notifications: One hour, latest by end of day.

Text Messages: For the most time-sensitive, important issues.

- Logic: Back-up channel if you need a fast reply. By not using this as our first choice, we can keep work communications separate from personal phone and text.

- Best practices: Try to reach out in Notion or Slack if it is not urgent. If it is urgent, text away! Recipient will try to drop what they are doing to respond.

- Ideal turnaround time for notifications: ASAP.

Gmail: Emails that go directly to your individual Gmail account, instead of into the team inbox.

- Logic: Do not let others' timelines set your urgency meter. For example, you have probably gotten a random pitch for something, from someone you have never met. When you don't respond in two days, they automatically follow up. After one week, they follow up again. Does this mean it is time to leap into action? *No!* Their urgency and obnoxious persistence has nothing to do with our actual timeline based on our chosen business priorities.

- Best practices: In our *Pivot* podcast about his book *Indistractable,* Nir Eyal and I discuss his approach to email. He applies two labels: today and this week. He spends one hour per day on "today" emails, and does a batch every Monday for those marked "this week."

- Ideal turnaround time for notifications: Two to three days if not time sensitive. *Caveat: I put the "snail" back into email, often taking much longer, and my team knows this!*

In addition to clarifying your preferred cadence for communication channels, consider how you could build or shift programs to serve customers asynchronously.

Steven Forrest, a well-known author and astrologer, offers such readings, albeit with a nine-year waitlist. "When your turn comes, Steven contacts you to confirm [details] and gather any last-minute questions," he shares on his website. "He then records the [session] and immediately emails you a link to the MP3 sound file."

As for the long wait, he explains his logic in a section called "General Statement," itself inspiring for freeing up Founder Time:

> Steven is in his 70s now. He views this work as a calling and plans to continue doing personal readings as long as he is alive and mentally competent, but with his age and the lengths of the waiting lists, there are no guarantees. He is also putting more time into "legacy work"—writing and working with his school, the Forrest Center for Evolutionary Astrology. Need a reading now? Try one of the wonderful astrologers Steven has personally trained.

Caveday provides another example of creative ways to serve customers. Caveday is an organization co-founded by Jake Kahana, Jeremy Redleaf, and Molly Sonsteng committed to "improving our relationship to work" by facilitating coworking sessions in person, virtually, and asynchronously.

Their core business is inviting people to sign up for a "Cave" at their desired duration, either one or three hours. A moderator walks the room through light warm-up rituals, including setting intentions about what participants would like to accomplish, then leads timed sprints with breaks, followed by a completion exercise.

Adapting this format to an asynchronous offering, Caveday created an automated version of their guided sprints. They achieve this with Typeform's survey software embedded onto their website, where participants can indicate what they want to work on, rate their current focus level, note what they want to leave out of "The Cave," and select preferred background music.

The coolest part is what happens next. Based on your selections, you press play on a video that is the length of your desired duration, and that contains the background music you chose, such as white noise or flowing water. A voice-over walks you through the starting rituals, then you start working on your project. At the end of the video, the music fades as the voice-over returns to guide you out of the sprint, asking you to complete a few closing questions to wrap up. Despite not being live with participants or facilitators, the entire experience feels dialed in and does as intended: helps you accomplish something meaningful. I even wrote this story from a self-guided Cave! So I can confirm that their innovative approach to asynchronicity works.

When it comes to scaling asynchronous customer support to answer fewer questions, consider strategies developed by Lee LeFever and his wife, Sachi. Co-founders of Common Craft, they created the first "explainer" videos with simple animations to illustrate complex topics such as RSS feeds.

As he shared with me in a *Free Time* podcast interview, when starting their company fifteen years ago Lee and Sachi asked themselves, "What if we designed the business so that we don't ever have to have any employees?"

This constraint became a catalyst for many of their creative decisions, inspiring them to answer demand and incoming inquiries far more creatively than if they took the more traditional route of building out a small agency, hiring more people in proportion to the number of new clients. This meant designing a scalable business, but within limits.

"That constraint informed a lot of our business decisions and strategies, because we could look at something and say, well, if that idea works, we are going to have to hire people," Lee said. "So maybe we should keep looking at other ideas."

At the same time, their videos were finding viral success, and demand for custom videos was quickly surpassing their capacity as service providers. Every time they noticed a surge in questions and requests from their audience, they listened, creating new income streams in the process. They created a membership-based library for companies, now reaching Fortune 500 companies in over fifty countries. When companies started inquiring about bespoke videos that would live internally, Lee and Sachi created a referral network who paid them a small membership fee to handle those requests. When enough creators asked them how to create the individual graphics, or assets, they decided to create a subscription-based database full of images, over 3,300 "Common Craft Cut-Outs," that anyone could pay to access.

At each step, Lee and Sachi went far beyond answering any one question from potential colleagues and customers. They mapped out ways to build scalable solutions that would answer those questions far into the future, so long as it was a fit for where they were trying to go and their original vision to stay *Big Enough*, the title of Lee's most recent book.

Similarly, when *Pivot* was launching I built a light shell website. Each time someone asked me a question via email, such as for a speaking engagement or a workshop, I built that page out and sent a link instead of a detailed reply. This saved me the step of writing emails from scratch, or from repeatedly sending the same information out. It had the added benefit of making new information public on an as-needed basis.

I call this *answering out loud*. Answering out loud can also include collecting advice-seeking questions sent to you privately via email, then with permission, answering in a one-to-many format such as a newsletter, article, or podcast episode. That way many people can benefit from the answer you take time to provide.

Every question, from a team member or a customer, lives three lives:

1. **The first time a question is asked and answered** via email, conversation, or project correspondence.

2. **Document question and response in our Manager Manual,** so it no longer lives only in one person's mind or email.

3. **Add that Q&A to a public-facing resource,** reducing the need for others to ask that same question. This could include website or enrollment page updates, editing confusing copy, or creating a downloadable resource.

For Lee and Sachi, creating scalable solutions *and* documentation—beyond their individual ability to answer questions and demand one by one—is an important piece of building a business that enables their marriage to thrive. "*Otherwise, what's it all for?*" Lee writes in *Big Enough*. Everything they do revolves around maintaining that sense of freedom and partnership.

"You can be rich with time," Lee said in our podcast conversation. "You might not have a Lamborghini, but people with Lamborghinis often wish they had more time."

Lee recalled a conversation with a wealth manager working with clients who became extremely affluent. As the wealth manager said to him of these well-heeled clients, "Because their lifestyle just explodes with material things in tandem, they spend the last half of their lives trying to simplify, trying to figure out how to get their time back."

CHAPTER 26 RECAP

Answer Less: Every Question Lives Three Lives

Two-Sentence Summary

Every question, whether from a team member or a customer, lives three lives: the original "ask," the response (also documented internally), and a public-facing FAQ or clarification. Prevent questions and answers from descending into the email void by capturing and categorizing them.

Give Yourself Permission
Not to repeat yourself!

Ask Yourself
Where are we creating extra work for ourselves when corresponding with customers? How can we write clearer copy on our website from the outset?

Do (or Delegate) This Next
Add an internal FAQ section to each category within your Manager Manual. Bonus: add an external FAQ to your website, even if it is not listed in the main navigation; something you can send people the link to as needed.

27

Save Someone Next Steps

I don't think necessity is the mother of invention. Invention, in my opinion, arises directly from idleness, possibly also from laziness. To save oneself trouble.

—Agatha Christie

O r to amend Agatha Christie's sentiment: to save *others* trouble, a central theme of this book.

"Cate, give me the good news." That's what executive coach Cathryn Carruthers says to her business manager when facing an issue. If there isn't any, Cate knows to sort it out and call back when she has some good news. Similarly, Cate does not cc Cathryn on emails. "I trust that she's got it covered. It empowers her and liberates me," Cathryn said.

Ask your team to get in the habit of looking beyond the initial details of a request. Run through a quick check before marking something complete, by anticipating what the assigning person will need to do next. How can you save someone the next few steps, even unanticipated ones? Is this task or project truly complete, or are follow-up details left unbuttoned? From earlier examples, if you help someone book a flight, do they also need help figuring out a ride to the airport? Every task includes strategic thinking about how to automate or systematize follow-up steps to save everyone time in the future.

It took many years for me to muster the courage to sit in the Upper East Side waiting room that I found myself in one summer day. I was there for a LASIK eye surgery consultation. I was always too afraid to consider the procedure, it was never the right time, and the contacts and glasses I had worn since seventh grade weren't *that* bad. Switching costs and fear held me back. My current state never seemed urgent enough to warrant action.

If you know anyone who has gotten LASIK, you know they rave about it, saying things like, *"It's not that bad! It only takes five minutes! You'll wake up and see clearly! It's the best thing I've ever done!"* Thankfully I had a friend in New York City, Dorie Clark, who had already vetted a renowned doctor for the procedure, having gone through it herself one year prior.

But alas, my palms were still sweating. As I went to fill out the potential patient paperwork at Mandel Vision, I accidentally drew on my new cream-colored wallet with their blue pen (the stain-prone color was my first mistake). From that moment the team leapt into action, and I could tell they had a special chemistry. Someone quickly retrieved an alcohol pad, and the pen mark wiped off without a trace. They were singing and joking while they worked, fluidly handing off calls and papers as they wove in and out behind each other traversing the small space. I was surprised by their camaraderie, in stark contrast to the mundane moods permeating the majority of medical offices I visit. This Delightfully Tiny Team legitimately seemed to be enjoying their work, and each other's company.

By the time I met with one of the nurses, I flowed through their well-oiled sales machine, and I mean that as a compliment. None of it was overly pushy. Step by step they removed all the friction potentially stopping me from moving forward:

- They answered my concerns about error rates and the potential for losing my vision.

- They explained why they are more expensive than competitors, making the intimidating financial investment seem insignificant compared to the costs of maintaining a lifetime of glasses and contacts.

- They walked me through every next step, and how the follow-up would work.

- Before I left the consult, they scheduled me for the surgery, and *all three follow-up appointments* that would occur within the next year. *Done.* No further scheduling added to my to-do list.

- As the nurse walked me back out to the front desk, they took my deposit for the procedure. *Done.*

- They offered to call my health insurance company to see if they could get me an even bigger discount. *Done.*

I left their offices exhaling with relief. I was finally doing this. My only remaining to-do was booking a hotel room nearby so I wouldn't have to travel across the city after my procedure.

On the day of the operation months later, as disconcerting as the smell of burning eyeball was—*nobody warned me about that!*—and despite significant pain that afternoon before I fell asleep, everything my friends and family said was true. Prior to LASIK, I could barely read the "E" at the top of vision charts. When I opened my eyes the next morning, for the first time in ages, *I could see.* I walked over to the window with glee. I could now make out the New York City skyline perfectly. It really was a miracle, and continues to be. I headed over to Central Park where I sat on a bench watching dogs take their owners for their morning walk, noting birds on branches and details in the tree leaves.

The operation took five minutes of my life for years of hassle-free mornings moving forward. Does that sound familiar? Systems design works the same way. My experience with Dr. Mandel and his team was memorable for several reasons, beyond the obvious personal transformation. They illustrated a number of lessons we can apply to our own businesses:

1. Their Delightfully Tiny Team was enthusiastic, and seemed to truly enjoy their work.

2. They interacted together seamlessly, dancing through the tiny office as if part of a well-choreographed Broadway musical about a medical practice.

3. They clearly and patiently answered all my questions, never making me feel rushed.

4. They took pride in their top-of-the-line technology, combined with decades of Dr. Mandel's experience, a specialist in his field.

5. The sales process was smooth, taking work *off* of my plate rather than adding more on.

6. I walked out with less to do than when I walked in. They saved me all but a few next steps, and they made those clear before I left their offices, sealing the deal. As the business adage goes, "Confused customers don't buy."

The more cynical among you might say, "Of course they 'saved' you the next steps! That's how they land clients, with the equivalent of a Buy Now button, even for a pricey procedure!"

But it worked. It did not feel sleazy, it was frictionless. Their efficiency and clear processes built trust that I would be in good hands, as did Dorie's glowing referral. By saving me all the next steps, I was far more likely to sign up, and to remember the experience as a positive one throughout, to the point that I am recounting it for you.

All the sales person *needed* to do was get me to say "yes" to surgery and ask me to leave a deposit. But by scheduling all three follow-ups then and there, they made the transaction effortless. No one needed to remember anything, from the moment I left the office.

Save someone the next steps is a systems mindset. It means zooming out from the task at hand to anticipate what subtasks will follow. Ask your team to think intuitively about what they would want to happen next if they were assigning the work.

Examples of anticipating follow-up tasks include:

- **If asked to register for an event, also add to calendar** with the event information in the description, and double-check time zones. If asked to book a flight or train, also ask about scheduling car service if needed. Even better, schedule car service directly based on previously outlined travel preferences.

- **Assume the ideal end state as your task**—e.g., number of books *arriving* at the event—rather than the starting assignment: *place an order* for number books. If something does not go as planned, such as the book order doesn't arrive or books are out of stock, be proactive about figuring out a backup option. Better still: Have the back-up option in mind from the outset.

- **Rescheduling our meetings:** If you need to adjust the time of our 1:1, no need to ask if it is okay via email and wait for my reply. Look at my availability, then update the invite directly, and opt to send me the calendar notice when you hit "save." If for any reason I can't accommodate that change, I will reply to that notice via email and let you know.

- **New? Help us welcome the next you:** Look for ways to improve our onboarding documentation as you get up to speed. With fresh eyes, you are best equipped to update processes that are out-of-date and add new FAQs, answers to questions that we didn't previously think to include. What else would the *next* new person find helpful?

Regarding onboarding and saving yourself next steps: stop recreating the wheel every time a new person joins your team, exerting equal onboarding energy for each. It should get *easier* every time; this will free you up to get to know each new team member personally, confident that the smaller details are already addressed.

If you do not already have clear guides, start by recording every onboarding or teaching call, then getting transcriptions. Some people create screen-capture videos for every aspect of their business and Manager

Manual: I am not a fan of this unless the steps are particularly complicated. Otherwise videos are hard to search, and become tedious to watch when you are in a time-pinch. You know the feeling if you have ever searched for how to do something simple on Google and the only helpful results are videos to wade through.

Let's close with two tactile examples of saving someone the next steps.

Every day I am delighted by the simplest of innovations: a small metal key that fits the width of the toothpaste container it came with. The bar, only three quarters closed, slides across the bottom end of the mint-green tube. A small tab handle allows me to rotate the bar, and therefore the end of the tube, just a tiny bit, neatly pressing the toothpaste ever-so-slightly up each time I use it. No more wringing, folding, rolling, or disorderly squeezing. Clean, simple, time-saving, and joyful!

The company behind it, David's USA, has a similarly streamlined website. Their tagline: "Natural toothpaste elevated." They list core values including naturally sourced and fluoride free, but their care for their customer is most evident in this free key sent with every tube. Imagine how much time and mess, no matter how small, they have saved across all the tubes in all their customers' households!

Another analog example: Melitta sells coffee filters that employ a different time-saving system: measure markings. Instead of measuring scoops by hand every morning to achieve the perfect water-to-grounds ratio, a set of horizontal lines printed across the inside of the paper cone indicate fill level options, allowing groggy consumers to eyeball quantity.

Every tiny interaction is part of a larger whole. Save someone even the *smallest* next steps, and they will thank you for it.

CHAPTER 27 RECAP

Save Someone Next Steps

Two-Sentence Summary

Ask your team to look beyond the surface of a team member's request to save the person asking the next steps, even ones they didn't think to ask about. Automate or systematize follow-up steps to save everyone time, customers included.

Give Yourself Permission

Relinquish managing details about next steps. Ask your team to take five minutes to think ahead to see if there is anything they missed, before turning work back over to you.

Ask Yourself

How can you solve someone's *next* problem, not just the most obvious one?

Do (or Delegate) This Next

Where in your business have you been picking up the slack in taking care of forgotten details that others didn't think to address? Look through your Manager Manual: How can you improve processes so team members save *you* next steps?

Assign Resources

For free tools and templates to help implement strategies from the **Assign** stage, visit **ItsFreeTime.com/toolkit**.

A sampling of resources for this stage include:

- Seventy-five tasks I have delegated in one year, with sample task descriptions

- Sample job descriptions for key roles

- Potential to Delegate: Task Tracker

- Design Your Role conversation guide

- Free Time Framework one-sheeter for planning new projects

- Weekly updates: information I ask my team to summarize and send on Fridays

Conclusion

The sight of any free animal going about its business undisturbed, seeking its food, or looking after its young, or mixing in the company of its kind, all the time being exactly what it ought to be and can be— what a strange pleasure it gives us.

—**Arthur Schopenhauer,** quoted in *Red-Tails in Love*

On many winter mornings, as I worked through ideas for this book, I was graced by the presence of two very special friends. One, or on my luckiest days, a pair traveling together, of red-tailed hawks. Like many birds of prey, they are exquisite to behold. With their cinnamon coloring, white underside, and a wingspan up to five feet wide, they soar majestically through the sky. These hawks might seem like an anomaly in Manhattan, but are famous among longtime birders. At the time of this writing, the city parks department had counted thirty-five red-tailed hawk nests throughout New York City.

On various mornings when I was fortunate to encounter the hawks, I stopped and marveled at their effortless flight. Symbolically, hawks represent vision, intuition, and higher perspective. Each time I saw them, these hawks stopped me from my typical morning routines atop a hill at the park. I alternated between throwing frisbees for my dog, Ryder, and picking up hundreds of small shards of grass buried in the dirt, embedded after years of broken bottles accumulating. Instead of focusing on the small details under my feet, I became giddy when I noticed one or both hawks flying overhead. *There they go!* Spotting them was awe-inspiring, and I loved knowing they were with me on those days.

This is our opportunity now. We must lift our focus from the ground—the dirt and shards—and pause. We can look up and out to experience a greater vision for our lives and businesses. We must give ourselves the permission and the space to soar.

The Free Time Framework—Align, Design, Assign—can help you spot and eliminate friction step by step, pulling your attention out of the weeds and back on your highest vision. For any given project, you can realign with why that work matters (sometimes phasing it out), then design a more streamlined process alongside your ideal outcomes, and finally assign it to someone on your team to shepherd its success.

Just before I made the decision to leave Google in 2011, after months of worrying, hand-wringing, and wavering, the image of a small bird in a cage came to me. I was the bird sitting inside the cage, and the door was open. I was frozen in place, staring at the open door, afraid to fly. I was terrified of taking the risk to go all-in on my emerging talents. I was not confident that my skills and interests could become the basis of a business at that time. As I thought about flying free, I worried: *What if I am wrong about myself? What if I am, in fact, better suited for an environment of thousands, not the life of a small business owner? What if no one cares what I have to say once I leave the comfortable shade of the big Google tree?*

Despite fears that I would not last longer than six months, I am now celebrating over a decade of self-employment, powered by my own Delightfully Tiny Team. But that is not what I am proudest of. I am proud of *how* I am working; how I redefined my relationship to time and work by decoupling the two. I am proud of sticking to my values of generosity and integrity in a world that says "business is war, you have to fight to stay alive." I saw how quickly my health bounced back from illness once I could set my own schedule, even with the inevitable bouts of stress and the undercurrent of uncertainty that accompanies running a business.

"Flying the coop" has little meaning if we do not grant ourselves space and freedom. Nor is leaving a larger organization the solution for everyone; many people love being part of bigger teams and companies. No matter the company size, I still see so many business owners sitting atop their own bird cages. They have returned to dysfunctional factory-style work structures. They are repeating the unrelenting, exhausting, overwhelming, illness-producing way of working that keeps them stuck and on the verge of abandoning their bigger vision, fracturing family time and health in the process.

One morning, I watched the hawks dancing together in flight, then landing on a perch together atop one of the northern red oak trees. Fifteen minutes later, as I was leaving I was stopped in my tracks—literally this time—by a hawk flying far lower than usual. Racing across my path, I saw, at my exact eye level, a large grey rat (whose lucky day it was not) in the hawk's talons. *Whoosh!* There they went. A successful hunt, and the hawk was off to savor his prize.

What does it mean?! I wondered.

For starters, again I was stopped from walking home on autopilot. The exhilaration of these hawks at work, seeing one whoosh by with a successful catch, was thrilling. We deserve to be enraptured by our work. We can design a business that provides us the thrill of the chase *and* the catch; balanced by the joys of coasting while we bide our time, not so tired we are unable to enjoy our successes. We have vast potential, but we have to give ourselves space to reach for it. Like the red-tailed hawks, we can do well in Delightfully Tiny Teams, working together with grace and ease.

As Daniel Pink writes in *Drive*, "Mastery is an asymptote." An *asymptote* is a curved line that approaches a straight line axis, but never actually reaches it. Business-building skills are similarly asymptotic. You may choose to exit a business you start by selling or closing it, but the larger container of entrepreneurship is an ongoing evolution.

Your business itself is more of an organic, emergent organism than a pre-programmed machine. Even if you grasp the core principles, your energy and interests will shift, the market changes, a pandemic hits, technology advances. Our opportunity is to remain curious. We can look for ways to love the learning, the mystery and the growth that comes with Heart-Based Business building, and the freedom that follows.

Do not feel bad—like you are behind or should know better by now—if you have not yet achieved *founder time nirvana*, enlightenment in the face of economic rollercoasters and business challenges. There is a reason renowned meditation teacher Jack Kornfield wrote a book called *After the Ecstasy, The Laundry*, interviewing over one hundred spiritual leaders on the challenges of returning to "householder" life.

My hope is this book will move you into action, immediately freeing your mind, time, and team, so that everyone can do more of their best work. I cannot wait to see what you do with the creative energy you release by dropping the *shoulds* and throwing out yesterday's business menu. Today's special? Freedom.

Freedom does not have to mean that you are self-employed, single, or a stuff-eschewing minimalist. It can mean many things:

- Freedom from self-doubt, fear, limiting beliefs
- Freedom from financial worry
- Freedom from overbearing social pressures
- Freedom to think, speak, and act with truth, integrity, and authenticity
- Freedom to make decisions and take actions in your business that serve the highest good

In commitment we find freedom. By committing to smarter systems and heart-based operating principles, we expand into even more of our immense potential, taking the extra steps now to help us soar far into the future.

This book opens with one of my favorite teachings from Zen Master and eminent Vietnamese monk Thich Nhat Hanh: "There is no way to happiness, happiness is the way."

There is no way to free time, free time is the way.

On Work

By Khalil Gibran, Lebanese poet (1883-1931)
Excerpted from *The Prophet* (1923)

Then a ploughman said, Speak to us of Work.

And he answered, saying:

You work that you may keep pace with the earth and the soul of the earth.

For to be idle is to become a stranger unto the seasons, and to step out of life's procession, that marches in majesty and proud submission towards the infinite.

When you work you are a flute through whose heart the whispering of the hours turns to music.

Which of you would be a reed, dumb and silent, when all else sings together in unison?

Always you have been told that work is a curse and labour a misfortune.

But I say to you that when you work you fulfil a part of earth's furthest dream, assigned to you when the dream was born,

And in keeping yourself with labour you are in truth loving life,

And to love life through labour is to be intimate with life's inmost secret.

But if you in your pain call birth an affliction and the support of the flesh a curse written upon your brow, then I answer that naught but the sweat of your brow shall wash away that which is written.

You have been told also that life is darkness, and in your weariness you echo what was said by the weary.

And I say that life is indeed darkness save when there is urge,

And all urge is blind save when there is knowledge,

And all knowledge is vain save when there is work,

And all work is empty save when there is love; And when you work with love you bind yourself to yourself, and to one another, and to God.

And what is it to work with love?

It is to weave the cloth with threads drawn from your heart, even as if your beloved were to wear that cloth.

It is to build a house with affection, even as if your beloved were to dwell in that house.

It is to sow seeds with tenderness and reap the harvest with joy, even as if your beloved were to eat the fruit.

It is to charge all things you fashion with a breath of your own spirit, And to know that all the blessed dead are standing about you and watching.

Often have I heard you say, as if speaking in sleep, "He who works in marble, and finds the shape of his own soul in the stone, is nobler than he who ploughs the soil.

And he who seizes the rainbow to lay it on a cloth in the likeness of man, is more than he who makes the sandals for our feet."

But I say, not in sleep but in the overwakefulness of noontide, that the wind speaks not more sweetly to the giant oaks than to the least of all the blades of grass;

And he alone is great who turns the voice of the wind into a song made sweeter by his own loving.

Work is love made visible.

And if you cannot work with love but only with distaste, it is better that you should leave your work and sit at the gate of the temple and take alms of those who work with joy.

For if you bake bread with indifference, you bake a bitter bread that feeds but half man's hunger.

And if you grudge the crushing of the grapes, your grudge distils a poison in the wine.

And if you sing though as angels, and love not the singing, you muffle man's ears to the voices of the day and the voices of the night.

Acknowledgments

Alan Watts once asked me, "Joe, what is your yoga?" I said, "My yoga is underlining sentences . . . all I know is what I read in books."

—Joseph Campbell

One of my favorite fridge magnets comes from the Strand bookstore in New York City: "BOOK ~~HOARDER~~ COLLECTOR AND PROUD OF IT." My husband and I make no apologies for the rainbow-colored stacks reaching toward our ceilings like magic beanstalks. Books have been my babysitters, my best friends, my business advisors, and my balm. They have given me countless gifts and priceless insights, at bargain prices for the value delivered. Every time my business sprung a leak, there was the next book to help me plug holes in my knowledge, skills, and understanding.

There are hundreds of authors to whom I owe credit and deepest thanks. I would like to specifically mention those who I have the honor to know personally, who have been instrumental in my life and work. Thank you for helping this particular project come to fruition: Penney Peirce, Michael Bungay Stanier, Seth Godin, Jonathan and Stephanie Fields, Sarah Young, Lindsay Pedersen, Laura Garnett, Charlie Gilkey, Julie Clow, Mike Michalowicz, Dorie Clark, Petra Kolber, and Christine Arylo. Your words, published and private, give me wings.

This book would not exist without frequent phone calls, voice memos, emails, brainstorming, and texts exchanged with Sarah, Michael, Penney, and Jonathan. Their books are cousins to this one, each of us writing and releasing in similar timing. What an honor to "bake" together!

To my JBE Delightfully Tiny Team, past and present: Marisol Dahl, Brenna Barry-Martinez, Stephanie Huston, Deborah Lahti, Lisa Orkin, James Ede, and dozens of specialists along the way. I couldn't do this work without you. Thank you for humoring me by putting all of these crazy ideas into practice and providing feedback!

To the publishing team: What a treat to work with you on a timeline that was as light and free as the principles in this book! I smiled the day Rohit told me, "Whatever you can think to ask, the answer is *yes*." Enormous thanks to the Ideapress team and extended network of editing experts for helping bring this book to life: Rohit and Chhavi Bhargava, Kameron Bryant-Sergejev, Marnie McMahon, Herb Schaffner, Lindsay Galvin, Christina Verigan, Lynsey Barry, Jessica Angerstein, Jane Cavolina, and Mamta Jha. To Sarah Lazin, Catharine Strong, and Adrian Zackheim: Thank you for discussing and helping to shape these ideas when they were still in the proposal stage, giving me the courage to go all-in on *Free Time*.

To the Together Agency: As you know, I refuse to create anything major without you! You are stuck with me. Adam Chaloeicheep and Marisol Dahl— what an incredible joy to celebrate over ten years of business collaborations and friendship. Phil Johnson, thank you for bringing your delightful expertise to this work. Adam, thank you for being like a brother to me all these years, and for always being in my corner for every next idea, breathing enthusiasm into each one like a big, gold balloon. Marisol, you set the standard for excellence at work. It has been such an honor to watch your path—and genius—unfold.

To Julie Clow, Ann Turi, Elisa Doucette, Becky Cotton, Niamh McElwain, Inna Aizenshtein, Allison Kluger, Bob Gower, Alexandra Jamieson, Katy Tripp, Vanessa Mayle, Monica McCarthy, Derek and Brittany Dolin, Edward Menicheschi, and Tara Adams: Since the day I met each of you, you have always been family, even as we spread across the globe. Thank you for filling my heart with friendship, wisdom, and encouragement.

To *Pivot* and *Free Time* podcast guests: Talking with you is the best part of every week. Turns out, podcasting is the perfect introvert's guide to networking and making friends! Each one of you said "yes," and you have made my life richer for it. Thank you for giving me the opportunity to learn from you, and to include your stories in this book.

To *Pivot* and *Free Time* readers and listeners: My favorite business activities would not exist without you! You make the joy + ease + revenue equation possible, and some of you have stuck around for fifteen years. Thank you for reading and listening, for your wonderful notes of encouragement, and for helping spread the good word.

To the Insider BFF Community (formerly MoMo): Thank you for helping me road test the ideas in this book, for weighing in with your wise perspectives, for submitting early feedback on aspects of this process, and for energizing me to do this work. I love you all, and I am so inspired watching you run your Heart-Based Businesses too.

To my family—Madre, Daddy-O, Gma, T-Bones, G-Bones; Gaby, Aida, and Chirine Karsouny, and Mala; to the Harringtons, Deinos, and Knoxes: Your unconditional love and support makes me the richest woman on earth! Thank you for cheering on my ideas and business risks. I love you all so much. T-Bones and Daddy-O: Where would I be without your detailed, sharp feedback on so many of the concepts in this book?! Every conversation we had enriched *Free Time* beyond measure. Gma: I love watching you and the YOLOs thrive; thank you for inspiring me to live life to the fullest. Madre: Thank you for providing crucial assistance to ensure this book made it to the finish line; and now, we are at a whole new beginning!

To Michael and Ryder: Michael, you are the greatest gift of all. Thank you for putting words to my formula for my life, planting early seeds for what would become this book: Love + Systems = Freedom. As you taught me from one of your favorite books, Antoine de Saint-Exupéry's *Little Prince*, a rose is special because you care for it, day after day. Thank you for the love you pour into our lives. To you and our little (*err, one-hundred pound*) furry friend, I include a final quote from Saint-Exupéry: "For true love is inexhaustible; the more you give, the more you have." I never knew this was possible, but now I do: I love you both more every day.

Finally, to you, dear reader: Thank you for breathing life into Heart-Based Business by reading this book. We know there is a better way, and together we *can* build business blissfully. Welcome to *Free Time!* I can't wait to hear what you do with it :)

Much Love,

Help Give the Gift of Free Time

As my first book mentor Michael Larsen told me, "Authors don't keep books alive, readers do." If you think others could benefit from *Free Time*, I would be grateful for your help in any way:

- **Rate and/or write a review** on Amazon, Goodreads, or the retailer's site where you purchased the book to help others decide whether to buy a copy.
- **Gift a copy** to a friend or to fellow team members.
- **Share your *ahas!*** on social media by tagging **#ItsFreeTime**
- **Send your favorite episode** of the *Free Time* podcast to a fellow Heart-Based Business owner.

Thank you in advance for your help keeping this message alive!

Resources

Send a Free Time Permission Slip

Take the pressure off of a fellow business owner by taking a photo of the permission slip template below with your phone. With the photo-editing feature, fill in the blanks; see the following page for a few suggestions to start with. Share your permission slip with other Free Timers by tagging #ItsFreeTime. To download a digital version and browse what others share, visit ItsFreeTime.com/permission.

free time
PERMISSION SLIP

I, _____

Hereby give _____

Permission to _____

_____

_____

Signed, _____
Date:

Sent with love from *Free Time: Lose The Busywork, Love Your Business* by Jenny Blake. Learn more at ItsFreeTime.com

Permission Slip Thought Starters

Here are twenty starting ideas you can prescribe to a friend with the template on the previous page, with a few examples of permission slips I have sent to friends on the following page:

1.   Drop everything but your deep work

2.   Do what's most delightful

3.   Sleep in tomorrow, even though it's _____day

4.   Take a social media sabbatical

5.   When in doubt, go without

6.   Give yourself a raise (or double your rates)

7.   Make serendipity a business strategy

8.   Invite a nonlinear breakthrough

9.   Eat ice cream in the middle of the day

10. Procrastinate

11. Stop worrying what "they" will say

12. Let it be easy, let it be fun

13. Rest

14. Say no to _____

15. Unsubscribe from _____

16. Drop your drainers

17. Go your own way

18. Join me at Hooky Headquarters (HHQ)! Let's take the day / week / month off

19. Be a slowpoke at email / Not to look at your inbox today (or this week)

20. Give the monkeys on your desk back to their respective owners

Examples: Permission Granted!

Free Time Framework Quick Reference

Where are you experiencing friction versus flow? For any business area or new project, run through the Free Time Framework.

Operating Principles Reflection Questions

Operating principles transcend specific tasks; they reflect your overall philosophy and unique approach to business. Categories to consider, from the Free Time Framework:

- **Align:** overall approach, values, strengths, energy
- **Design:** time, process, systems, automation, communications
- **Assign:** accountability, task tracking, documentation

Additional questions to help you articulate your underlying principles:

- What already guides your thinking? (Quotes, mantras, or sayings)
- How do you define professionalism or excellence in thinking, behavior, and output?
- What frustrates you? Why? What "rules" are being broken in those moments?
- What are your favorite companies? What makes them stand out in terms of customer experience? What do you perceive makes them great on the back end, behind the scenes?
- What are your own areas for improvement or bottlenecks that might be missing effective guiding principles? How do you decide what to drop, delegate, and automate?
- What helps you create more joy, ease, and efficiency in your work?
- What qualities do you admire most in coworkers, contractors, mentors, and friendtors?
- Bring to mind a business leader you respect. What do they credit for their success? How do they make wise decisions? How do you imagine they decide what to say yes or no to?
- Do you disagree with, or do things differently, from any practices in this book? If so, what is your twist or unique take?

Manager Manual Template

Build this out for each new section in your Manager Manual, for different areas of your business. Examples include: email, client onboarding, scheduling, website, gifting, and so on.

- **Purpose:** Higher level goals and desired outcomes.

- **Philosophy/Principles:** How do we uniquely think about this area and make decisions? What trade-offs are we willing to make? What operating principles does this area tie into?

- **Strategy:** How we will approach operationalizing this; setting a recurring cadence.

- **Step-by-Step Process and Guidelines:** Capture steps so somebody new to the business still knows exactly what to do. Check: is our process systematized, efficient, *and* delightful? Are we reducing decision fatigue and potential bottlenecks?

- **Potential Problems and FAQ:** Think through these in advance; add existing Q&As.

- **Additional Resources / Reference Materials:** Where we learned about this topic, resources where other team members can learn more through books, articles, and podcasts.

Visit ItsFreeTime.com/toolkit for an online version to easily duplicate this template. To purchase the done-for-you Free Time Manager Manual, visit ItsFreeTime.com/dashboard.

Free Time for Your Future Self: Systems-Thinking Steps

1. Is there a chance that I—or better still, the team—will repeat this?

2. Even if so, should it be done at all?

3. What larger system, function, process, or business outcome is this part of? Is this *nice-to-have* or *must-have*?

4. How can I save time when taking these same steps in the future? What can I automate?

5. What aspects currently live only in my mind that I can capture in our process docs?

6. Should this be recurring, even if it surfaced as a one-off?

7. What is the desired outcome of this process?

8. How can we design a process to achieve that outcome with ease? (Minimal effort, complexity)

9. Are there any remaining unknowns? (To ask another team member, or to experiment with)

10. Are there any subtasks that can be captured, and/or relevant and related links to include?

11. Can a person who is brand new to the business easily implement the steps? (Fiji Test)

12. If not, what FAQs and potential pitfalls can we anticipate? Is this all documented in our Manager Manual?

Additional Resources for Small Business Owners

There are many tools to support you in implementing the Free Time Framework:

- **Free Time Toolkit:** Templates, sample processes, glossary, online version of the Free Time quiz, and more. Access the free book bonuses at ItsFreeTime.com/toolkit.

- **Sign up for my weekly(ish) newsletter:** *Time Well Spent*, where I share behind-the-business updates and helpful articles, podcasts, and tools at ItsFreeTime.com/join.

- **Subscribe to the *Free Time* podcast** wherever you listen by visiting pod.link/freetime (If you enjoy it, I would be super grateful for a rating and/or review on iTunes!).

- **Author Toolkit:** Free resources for fellow authors on every step of the book process, from organizing, to writing, to editing, and launching. Visit ItsFreeTime.com/authors.

- **Start a Free Time book club or mastermind group** with facilitator guides at ItsFreeTime.com/leaders.

Private Community: BFF with Jenny Blake

For added support applying the principles throughout this book, I encourage you to join our close-knit insider community of smart, generous, Heart-Based Business owners. You will get access to a monthly Q&A call, a private podcast feed for call recordings and bonus content, and a community forum. Learn more and join us at ItsFreeTime.com/bff.

Free Time Business Dashboard

My passion is saving you time. If you would like to purchase the full Free Time Operations Dashboard to instantly populate the foundation for your externalized business mind in Notion, as I have described throughout this book, visit ItsFreeTime.com/dashboard. This will allow you and your team to hit the ground running with implementation, rather than traversing software learning curves and set-up headaches. In it you will find these detailed resources:

- Task Tracker
- Manager Manual
- Gifting Database
- Content Production Board
- Client Trackers
- Newsletter Set-up
- and much more, with regularly added updates

Free Time for Large Organizations

Scalable rollout options for conferences and large organizations include:

- Interactive keynotes for employees and for managers
- Discounted rates for bulk book purchases with optional customization, and
- Free Time Train-the-Trainer and workbook licensing

Visit ItsFreeTime.com/companies to learn more.

I look forward to working with you!

Notes

Introduction

9   *At a party given by a billionaire*: John C. Bogle, *Enough: True Measures of Money, Business, and Life* (Hoboken, NJ: John Wiley, 2008).

Free Time Framework

17   **state as effortless achievement:** Mihaly Csikszentmihalyi, *Flow: The Psychology of Optimal Experience* (New York: Harper Perennial Modern Classics, 2008).

17   **five times as productive:** Susie Cranston and Scott Keller, "Increasing the 'Meaning Quotient' of Work," McKinsey & Company, February 16, 2018, http://www.mckinsey.com/business-functions/organization/our-insights/increasing-the-meaning-quotient-of-work.

18   **Small businesses are an integral part:** Chamber of Commerce, "Small Business Statistics," June 21, 2021, http://www.chamberofcommerce.org/small-business-statistics/.

18   **According to VC firm SignalFire:** Yuanling Yuan and Josh Constantine, "SignalFire's Creator Economy Market Map," SignalFire Blog, https://signalfire.com/blog/creator-economy.

19   **Only 40 percent** and **52 percent of small businesses:** Ibid.

19   **86.3 percent of small business owners:** Meredith Wood, "What Is the Average Small Business Owner Salary in the U.S.?" Fundera, November 11, 2020, www.fundera.com/blog/study-finds-business-owners-earn-less.

19   **19 percent of small business owners:** OECD, "Average Annual Hours Actually Worked per Worker," OECD, 2021, http://www.stats.oecd.org/index.aspx?DataSetCode=ANHRS.

20   **throughout his decades of consulting:** George Knauf via Clubhouse, http://www.MyPerfectFranchise.com, January 27, 2021.

20   **Fortune 500 CEOs:** Brigid Schulte, *Overwhelmed: Work, Love, and Play When No One Has the Time* (New York: Sarah Crichton Books, 2021), 64.

25   **to tout "strategic laziness":** Andrew Wilkinson, "Lazy Leadership: The Flow Blog," Medium, July 12, 2018, http://www.medium.com/flow/lazy-leadership-8ba19e34f959; and Tim Ferriss, "The Art of Strategic Laziness," *The Blog of Author Tim Ferriss*, January 16, 2020, http://www.tim.blog/2014/08/25/the-art-of-strategic-laziness.

26   *Ideapreneurs* **require space:** Richard Harmer, "What Is an Ideapreneur?" June 1, 2014, http://www.richardharmer.com/blog/what-is-an-ideapreneur.

28 **In a 2009 TED Talk:** Stefan Sagmeister, "The Power of Time Off," filmed July 30, 2009, TED video, http://www.ted.com/talks/stefan_sagmeister_the_power_of_time_off.

Part 1: Align

Chapter 1: Embrace Agile Operating Principles: What's Your WiFi Password?

42 **reducing the *starting friction*:** University of Alaska Fairbanks Geophysical Institute, Alaska Science Forum, "Three Kinds of Friction," https://www.gi.alaska.edu/alaska-science-forum/three-kinds-friction, July 31, 2021.

44 **originators of the Manifesto:** "Manifesto for Agile Software Development," Agile Software Development, 2001, http://www.agilemanifesto.org.

Chapter 2: Create an Externalized Mind

47 ***As the old joke goes:*** Kevin Kelly, The *Inevitable: Understanding the 12 Technological Forces That Will Shape Our Future* (New York: Penguin Books, 2017).

47 **"Off-brand Minnie Mouse":** Corey Kilgannon, "Without Crowds, Is Times Square Really Times Square? Take a Look," *New York Times,* December 1, 2020, http://www.nytimes.com/2020/12/01/nyregion/times-square-nyc-coronavirus.html.

47 **"Times Square 'Creepy' Costumed Characters":** Elizabeth Rosner, et al., "Times Square's 'Creepy' Costumed Characters Are out of Control," *New York Post,* September 10, 2019, http://www.nypost.com/2019/09/09/times-squares-creepy-costumed-characters-are-out-of-control-survey/.

48 **we use Notion as our operations hub:** *Many thanks to Tara McMullin and Marie Poulin who introduced Notion to me in their podcast conversation.* Tara McMullin, "Going All In with Strategist Marie Poulin," *What Works,* podcast, June 16, 2020, http://www.explorewhatworks.com/going-all-in-with-strategist-marie-poulin.

50 **In our *Free Time* podcast:** Jenny Blake, "005: Brand Obsessed with Emily Heyward," *Free Time with Jenny Blake,* podcast, March 21, 2021, http://itsfreetime.com/episodes/005.

52 **In *The Extended Mind*:** Annie Murphy Paul, *The Extended Mind: The Power of Thinking Outside the Brain* (Boston: Houghton Mifflin Harcourt, 2021).

Chapter 3: Systematize the Spirit of Your Business

55 ***The first thing you should always sell is joy*:** "Dorie Clark & Robert Herjavec: How Your Business Can Thrive Through the Pandemic," YouTube video, interview by Dorie Clark, November 12, 2020, https://youtube.com/watch?v=UOeqZcCNAs4.

Chapter 4: Set Purposeful Intentions

65 **Oprah created a new policy:** "What Oprah Knows for Sure About Intention," Oprah.com, November 15, 2001, http://www.oprah.com/omagazine/what-oprah-knows-for-sure-about-intention.

65 **Before launching anything new:** Rebecca Muller, "The One Question Oprah Wants You to Ask Yourself at Work," Thrive Global, December 3, 2019, http://www.thriveglobal.com/stories/setting-intentions-meaning-work-question-oprah-winfrey-decisions; and Marina Khidekel, "12 Ways to Work Smarter, Not Harder," Thrive Global, January 3, 2019, http://www.thriveglobal.com/stories/how-to-tips-work-smarter-not-harder-focus-prioritization.

67 **podcast conversation for our Penney & Jenny series:** Jenny Blake, "34: Perception: Navigating Our Non-Linear Universe with Penney Peirce," *Pivot with Jenny Blake*, podcast, June 5, 2016, http://www.pivotmethod.com/podcast/perception.

67 **"You don't attract ideas":** Jenny Blake, "67: What Does Your Soul Know? Flow and Transparency with Penney Peirce," *Pivot with Jenny Blake*, podcast, October 7, 2017, http://www.pivotmethod.com/podcast/transparency.

Chapter 5: Let It Be Easy, Let It Be Fun

69 ***All our sweetest hours:*** Virgil, *The Aeneid*, Book XII, line 46, Gutenberg.org, https://gutenberg.org/ebooks/228.

Chapter 6: Give Yourself Golden Hour: What's Your Job Today?

77 **"Sitting has become the new smoking":** Nilofer Merchant, "Got a Meeting? Take a Walk," filmed April 29, 2013, TED video, http://www.ted.com/talks/nilofer_merchant_got_a_meeting_take_a_walk.

Chapter 7: Build Your Business Intuition

84 ***As long as we settle for thinking inside the brain:*** Annie Murphy Paul, *The Extended Mind: The Power of Thinking Outside the Brain* (Boston: Mariner Books, 2021).

86 **I was experiencing:** Tara Haelle, "Your 'Surge Capacity' Is Depleted–It's Why You Feel Awful" Medium, September 10, 2020, http://www.elemental.medium.com/your-surge-capacity-is-depleted-it-s-why-you-feel-awful-de285d542f4c.

88 **"This will probably sound strange":** Jenny Blake, "64: Only the Truth Sounds Like the Truth — with Former Starbucks President Howard Behar," *Pivot with Jenny Blake*, podcast, September 16, 2017, http://www.pivotmethod.com/podcast/truth.

89 **"Your life is always speaking":** Oprah Winfrey, "Whispers," *Super Soul Sunday*, podcast, April 7, 2021, http://www.omny.fm/shows/oprah-s-supersoul-conversations/whispers.

Chapter 8: Continuously Bust Bottlenecks

90 **the *Ever Given*:** Motoko Rich, Stanley Reed, and Jack Ewing, "Clearing the Suez Canal Took Days. Figuring Out the Costs May Take Years," *New York Times*, June 23, 2021, http://www.nytimes.com/2021/03/31/business/suez-canal-ship-costs.html.

93 **Dave Crenshaw started running:** Jenny Blake, "019: Most Valuable Activities with Dave Crenshaw," *Free Time with Jenny Blake*, podcast, June 18, 2021, http://www.itsfreetime.com/episodes/019.

96 **In *Fix This Next*:** "The Business Hierarchy of Needs," Mike Michalowicz, February 24, 2020, http://www.mikemichalowicz.com/the-business-hierarchy-of-needs; and Mike Michalowicz, *Fix This Next: Make the Vital Change That Will Level Up Your Business* (New York: Portfolio/Penguin, 2020).

Chapter 9: Embrace Imperfection: Cookie Dough and Tiny Streaks

105 ***We are, Thomas and I:*** Nick Cave, *The Red Hand Files*, newsletter, March 5, 2021, http://www.theredhandfiles.com/lockdown-start-carnage.

Part 2: Design

Overview

111 **"If success with money"**: Jenny Blake, "020: Pricing Psychology with Jacquette Timmons," *Free Time with Jenny Blake*, podcast, June 25, 2021, http://www./itsfreetime.com/episodes/020.

112 **To adapt a phrase**: Byron Katie, *I Need Your Love: Is That True?* (New York: Harmony Books, 2006); and http://www.thework.com.

Chapter 10: **Invite Nonlinear Breakthroughs**

118 *Planning rests on the idea that*: Bahar Noorizadeh, "After Scarcity," e-flux Video & Film, 2018, http://www.e-flux.com/video/374045/bahar-noorizadeh-nbsp-after-scarcity.

119 **That shift in strategy**: Jenny Blake, "017: Serendipity as Business Strategy with Leanne Hughes," *Free Time with Jenny Blake*, podcast, June 4, 2021, http://www.itsfreetime.com/episodes/017.

121 *nonlinear relationships* **are ones**: Donella Meadows and Diana Wright, *Thinking in Systems: A Primer* (Hartford, CT: Chelsea Green Publishing, 2008), 91.

Chapter 11: **Serendipity as Business Strategy**

125 *Let me release what wants to leave*: Tosha Silver, *Outrageous Openness: Letting the Divine Take the Lead* (New York: Atria Books, 2016).

129 **Josh Kaufman, author of**: Jenny Blake, "012: Generating Personal MBA Momentum with Josh Kaufman," *Free Time with Jenny Blake*, podcast, April 30, 2021, http://www.itsfreetime.com/episodes/012.

130 **"quietly do the next and most necessary thing"**: via Oliver Burkeman, *Four Thousand Weeks: Time Management for Mortals* (New York: Farrar, Straus and Giroux, 2021); *Letters of Carl Jung*, vol. 1, 1906-1950 (Oxford: Routledge, 2015).

Chapter 12: **Solve for Sisyphean Systems**

132 *I have configured servers*: Via Tim Ferriss, "Craig Mod: Writer & Photographer," Craig Mod, 2001, http://www.craigmod.com.

133 **Staying caught up with social media is impossible**: Jake Knapp and John Zeratsky, *Make Time: How to Focus on What Matters Every Day* (New York: Currency, 2018).

137 **Alexandra Franzen, co-founder**: Jenny Blake, "76: On Plan Z, Creative Finish Lines and the Graceful No—with Alexandra Franzen," *Pivot with Jenny Blake*, podcast, December 9, 2017, www.pivotmethod.com/podcast/alexandra-franzen, Alexandra Franzen; Alexandra Franzen, "10 Reasons to Quit Social Media," March 15, 2021, http://www.alexandrafranzen.com/2021/03/15/quit.

139 **"Your job is not email responder"**: Jenny Blake, "002: Eliminate Email with Cal Newport," *Free Time with Jenny Blake*, podcast, March 9, 2021, http://www.itsfreetime.com/episodes/002.

140 **"Don't make a hundred decisions"**: Jim Collins, "Ten Lessons I Learned from Peter Drucker," JimCollins.com, 2016, http://www.jimcollins.com/article_topics/articles/Ten-Lessons-I-Learned-from-Peter-Drucker.html.

Chapter 13: Always Be Listening

144 **Through empathic listening:** Ximena Vengoechea, *Listen Like You Mean It: Reclaiming the Lost Art of True Connection* (New York: Portfolio/Penguin, 2021).

147 **Volvo Cars certainly seemed:** "Care by Volvo: The All-Inclusive Car Subscription: Volvo Cars," Volvo Cars, 2021, http://www.volvocars.com/us/care-by-volvo.

Chapter 14: Scale: Be Ready for a Big Break

151 **like a lucky break:** Jenny Blake, "011: Pitching Shark Tank with Sarah Apgar," *Free Time with Jenny Blake*, podcast, April 23, 2021, http://www.itsfreetime.com/episodes/011.

152 **"More companies die":** Bryce Roberts, "Death by Indigestion - Bryce Roberts," *Medium*, May 3, 2018, http://www.bryce.medium.com/death-by-indigestion-aeod64e7648f.

152 **"hug of death":** Tim Ferriss, "My 10 Favorite Purchases in 10 Months," *The Blog of Author Tim Ferriss*, 2016, http://www.tim.blog/2016/04/25/my-10-favorite-purchases-in-10-months.

153 **With his online marketplace:** "All Our Best," AllOurBest.com, accessed May 30, 2021, http://www.allourbest.com.

153 **When someone purchases one of his NFTs:** Alex Williams, "Will NFTs Transform Tattoos Into Bankable Art?," *New York Times*, May 30, 2021, http://www.nytimes.com/2021/05/22/style/nft-art.html.

Chapter 15: Use Life-Giving Language

159 **We don't create users:** Julie Rice, "Make Sure Your Product Can Market Itself," *Wall Street Journal*, March 18, 2015, http://www.wsj.com/articles/BL-232B-3494.

160 **exceptional software development team:** Stewart Butterfield, "We Don't Sell Saddles Here - Stewart Butterfield," *Medium*, September 20, 2020, http://www.medium.com/@stewart/we-dont-sell-saddles-here-4c59524d650d.

165 **redirecting her financial privilege:** Jenny Blake, "114: Illuminating Invisible Privilege with Karen Pittelman (and Why She Gave Away Her $3 Million Trust at 24)," *Pivot with Jenny Blake*, podcast, August 26, 2018, http://www.pivotmethod.com/podcast/invisible-privilege.

Chapter 16: Design Deep Work Containers

170 **Alone had always felt like:** Cheryl Strayed, *Wild: From Lost to Found on the Pacific Crest Trail* (New York: Knopf, 2012).

Chapter 17: Time Block and Bake in Batches

176 **There is no salvation in time:** Eckhart Tolle, *The Power of Now: A Guide to Spiritual Enlightenment* (Novato, CA: New World Library, 2004).

176 **Limbic imprinting refers:** Liliane Desjardins and Douglas Ziedonis, *The Imprint Journey: A Path of Lasting Transformation into Your Authentic Self* (Ann Arbor, MI: Life Scripts Press, 2011); and Daniel Siegel and Marion Solomon, *Healing Trauma: Attachment, Mind, Body and Brain*, Norton Series on Interpersonal Neurobiology, 1st ed. (New York: W. W. Norton & Co., 2003).

179 **concept of time blocking:** Cal Newport, *Deep Work: Rules for Focused Success in a Distracted World* (New York: Grand Central Publishing, 2016); and Jake Knapp and John Zeratsky, *Make Time: How to Focus on What Matters Every Day* (New York: Currency, 2018).

179 **John Lee Dumas:** Jenny Blake, "010: Batching & Boundaries with John Lee Dumas," *Free Time with Jenny Blake*, podcast, April 16, 2021, http://www.itsfreetime.com/episodes/010.

179 **Antonio Neves's time blueprint:** Jenny Blake, "004: Take a Stand with Antonio Neves," *Free Time with Jenny Blake*, podcast, March 21, 2021, http://www.itsfreetime.com/episodes/004.

184 **Elizabeth taught herself to see email requests:** Tim Ferriss, "Elizabeth Gilbert's Creative Path: Saying No, Trusting Your Intuition, Index Cards, Integrity Checks, Grief, Awe, and Much More (#430)," podcast, *The Blog of Author Tim Ferriss*, recorded May 17, 2020, accessed May 18, 2020, http://www.tim.blog/2020/05/17/elizabeth-gilbert-transcript.

184 **On Ann's decision to stay off social media:** Jonathan Fields, "Ann Patchett: On Solitude, Writing & Indie Bookstores," *Good Life Project*, podcast, recorded June 25, 2020, accessed May 24, 2020, http://www.goodlifeproject.com/podcast/ann-patchett.

Chapter 18: Automate What You Repeat

186 *The best thing about your life:* Cleo Wade, *Heart Talk: The Journal: 52 Weeks of Self-Love, Self-Care, and Self-Discovery* (New York: Atria Books, 2020).

187 **taught himself computer programming:** Jenny Blake, "012: Generating Personal MBA Momentum with Josh Kaufman," *Free Time with Jenny Blake*, podcast, April 30, 2021, http://www.itsfreetime.com/episodes/012.

187 **"Develop the three great virtues of a programmer":** Larry Wall, Tom Christiansen, and Jon Orwant, *Programming Perl*, 3rd ed. (Sebastopol, CA: O'Reilly Media, 2000).

189 **(AI) scheduling software:** Clara Labs, http://www.ClaraLabs.com; via Kevin Kelly, "251: Tiffany Shlain," *Cool Tools*, podcast, November 5, 2020, http://www.kk.org/cooltools/tiffany-shlain-filmmaker/.

Part 3: Assign

Overview

199 **Jim Collins shared a conversation:** Jim Collins and William Lazier, *BE 2.0 (Beyond Entrepreneurship 2.0): Turning Your Business into an Enduring Great Company* (New York: Portfolio/Penguin, 2020).

Chapter 19: Promote Yourself From Chief Everything Officer

202 *Now that all your worry:* Hafiz, with renderings by Daniel Ladinsky, *The Gift: Poems by Hafiz, the Great Sufi Master* (New York: Penguin Books, 1999).

203 **calculate the return on compensation:** via Mike Michalowicz, "Ep 70: Building a Better Firm with John Briggs," *Mike Up in Your Business Podcast with Mike Michalowicz*, podcast, August 2, 2021, https://mikemichalowicz.com/mikespodcast/ep-70-building-a-better-firm-with-john-briggs/.

206 **Irish novelist James Joyce:** Clarice Lispector and Giovanni Pontiero, *Near to the Wild Heart: A Novel* (New York: New Directions, 1990).

Chapter 20: Construct Your Delightfully Tiny Team

207 *The leap to "three":* Michael Schneider, *A Beginner's Guide to Constructing the Universe: Mathematical Archetypes of Nature, Art, and Science* (New York: HarperPerennial, 1995).

210 **Gallup studied engagement levels:** Adam Hickman, "The 5 Tactics of Teamwork: A Blueprint for Team Management," Gallup.com, accessed January 25, 2021, http://www.gallup.com/workplace/275387/tactics-teamwork-blueprint-team-management.aspx.

210 **"After devoting nearly fifty years":** Ruth Wageman and Teresa M. Amabile, "J. Richard Hackman (1940–2013)," HBS Working Knowledge, August 2, 2013, http://www.hbswk.hbs.edu/item/7317.html.

211 **"67 percent of employees":** Jim Clifton and Jim Harter, *It's the Manager: Moving from Boss to Coach* (Washington, D.C.: Gallup Press, 2019).

211 **named "Project Aristotle":** Julia Rozovsky, "re:Work - The Five Keys to a Successful Google Team," *re:Work*, November 17, 2015, http://www.rework.withgoogle.com/blog/five-keys-to-a-successful-google-team.

212 **teams with fewer than ten members:** Google *re:Work*, "Project Aristotle," sources cited: Campion et al. (1993), Aube et al. (2011), Moreland & Levine (1992); Mathieu et al. (2008), Pearce and Herbik (2004).

212 **"an interlaced structure or pattern":** Joanne Cleaver, *The Career Lattice: Combat Brain Drain, Improve Company Culture, and Attract Top Talent* (New York: McGraw-Hill Education, 2012).

Chapter 21: Double How Much You Delegate

214 **Jordan Harbinger had been podcasting:** Jenny Blake, "006: Going Pro on Podcasting with Jordan Harbinger," *Free Time with Jenny Blake*, podcast, March 21, 2021, http://www.itsfreetime.com/episodes/006.

218 **looks for "$10,000 Tasks":** Todd Herman via Dan Martell, "The Way to Measure Your Productivity as an Entrepreneur," https://www.danmartell.com/scorecard.

218 **The Five Cs:** Brené Brown, "Brené with Priya Parker: A Meeting Makeover," *Dare to Lead*, podcast, May 24, 2021, https://open.spotify.com/episode/5Ky8LCMrZYY77CZzFn6Tcw.

218 **his Impact Filters:** Dan Sullivan, "Impact Filter," Strategic Coach, http://www.resources.strategiccoach.com/the-multiplier-mindset-blog/what-is-an-impact-filter.

Chapter 22: The Fiji Test: Continually Make Ourselves Replaceable

226 *Don't be irreplaceable*: Scott Adams, "Dilbert," comic, 1997, http://www.dilbert.com.

Chapter 23: Drained? Let's Discuss

232 **The Pivot Method:** Jenny Blake, *Pivot: The Only Move That Matters Is Your Next One* (New York: Portfolio/Penguin, 2016).

Chapter 24: Frustrated? Take Responsibility

239 *I have learned to avoid the care and feeding*: Kenneth Blanchard, William Oncken, and Hal Burrows, *The One Minute Manager Meets the Monkey: Free Up Your Time and Deal with Priorities* (New York: William Morrow, 1989).

Chapter 25: Track Every Task and Assign One Owner

252 **looking for lost items:** "Lost Something Already Today? Misplaced Items Cost Us Ten Minutes a Day," Daily Mail Online, March 21, 2012, http://www.dailymail.co.uk/news/article-2117987/Lost-today-Misplaced-items-cost-minutes-day.html.

257 **Warner replied:** *Don't be*: Peter Guber, "Cooking Up Purposeful Stories for Consumption," May 4, 2016, www.peterguber.com/jack-warner.

257 **The monkey story above originates:** William Oncken Jr. and Donald L. Wass, "Management Time: Who's Got the Monkey?" *Harvard Business Review,* November 1999, http://www.hbr.org/1999/11/management-time-whos-got-the-monkey.

Chapter 26: Answer Less: Every Question Lives Three Lives

262 **Nilofer Merchant, author of:** Jenny Blake, "264: Embrace Your Onlyness with Nilofer Merchant," *Pivot with Jenny Blake,* podcast, June 6, 2021, http://pivotmethod.com/262.

265 **Nir Eyal and I:** Jenny Blake, "131: Indistractable with Nir Eyal," *Pivot with Jenny Blake,* podcast, August 25, 2019, http://www.pivotmethod.com/131.

266 **nine-year waitlist:** Steven Forrest, "Astrology Readings with Steven Forrest," Forrest Astrology, accessed June 2021, http://www.forrestastrology.com/pages/readings.

267 **Lee LeFever and his wife, Sachi:** Jenny Blake, "016: IP Licensing with Lee LeFever," *Free Time with Jenny Blake,* podcast, May 28, 2021, http://www.itsfreetime.com/episodes/016; Lee LeFever, *Big Enough: Building a Business That Scales with Your Lifestyle* (Toronto: Page Two, 2020); and Lee LeFever, "About Us and Our Story," Common Craft, 2020, http://www.commoncraft.com/about.

Chapter 27: Save Someone Next Steps

271 ***I don't think necessity:*** Agatha Christie, *Agatha Christie: An Autobiography* (New York: HarperCollins, 2011).

Conclusion

281 ***The sight of any free animal:*** via Marie Winn, *Red-Tails in Love: A Wildlife Drama in Central Park* (New York: Pantheon Books, 1998); Arthur Shopenhauer, *Psychological Observations* (New York: A. L. Burt Company, 1851).

281 **the city Parks Department had counted:** John Leland, "He Wasn't a Bird Person. Then a Hawk Built a Nest on His Fire Escape," *New York Times,* May 7, 2021, http://www.nytimes.com/2021/05/07/nyregion/coronavirus-birdwatching-hawks-nyc.html.

On Work

285 ***On Work* by Khalil Gibran:** Kahlil Gibran, *The Collected Works* (New York: Knopf, 2021); and Kahlil Gibran and Rupi Kaur, *The Prophet.* 2nd ed., (London: Penguin Classics, 2019).

Acknowledgments

287 ***Alan Watts once asked me:*** Joseph Campbell, "On Becoming an Adult," YouTube video, Joseph Campbell Foundation, filmed in 1987, uploaded July 2, 2010, http://www.youtube.com/watch?v=aGx4IlppSgU.

Index

ABOUT THE AUTHOR

Jenny Blake helps forward-thinking organizations and individuals map what's next. She is an international keynote speaker and author of *Free Time: Lose the Busywork, Love Your Business* (2022), the award-winning *Pivot: The Only Move That Matters Is Your Next One* (26), and *Life After College* (2011). Jenny hosts two podcasts: *Free Time* for Heart-Based Business owners, and *Pivot with Jenny Blake* for navigating change. After two years as the first employee at a political polling start-up in Silicon Valley, followed by five years at Google in training and career development, Jenny moved to New York City in 2011 to launch her business. She graduated from UCLA magna cum laude with Phi Beta Kappa honors, with degrees in political science and communications. Jenny also studied interreligious engagement at Union Theological Seminary. She loves yoga and buys too many books. Jenny lives in Manhattan with her husband and their angel-in-fur-coat German shepherd.